THE JAPANESE
A Cultural Portrait

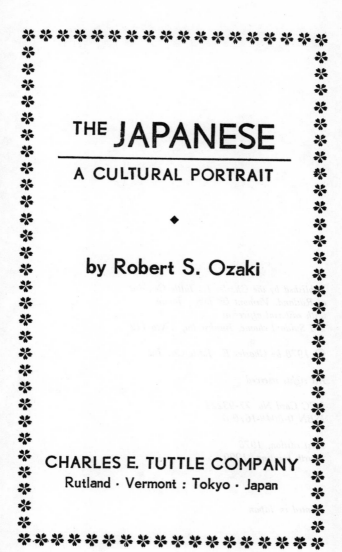

THE JAPANESE

A CULTURAL PORTRAIT

◆

by Robert S. Ozaki

CHARLES E. TUTTLE COMPANY
Rutland · Vermont : Tokyo · Japan

Published by the Charles E. Tuttle Co., Inc.
of Rutland, Vermont & Tokyo, Japan
with editorial offices at
2-6 Suido 1-chome, Bunkyo-ku, Tokyo 112

© *1978 by Charles E. Tuttle Co., Inc.*

LCC Card No. 77-93224
ISBN 0-8048-1670-0

First edition, 1978
Fourth printing, 1990

Printed in Japan

For Rebecca *and* Jennifer

who share two cultures

East is East, and West is West,
And never the twain shall meet.

[Kipling's verse as quoted by most people]

Oh, East is East, and West is West,
and never the twain shall meet,
Till Earth and Sky stand presently
at God's great Judgment Seat;
But there is neither East nor West, Border,
nor Breed, nor Birth,
When two strong men stand face to face,
though they come from the ends of the earth!

—RUDYARD KIPLING
in *The Ballad of East and West*

✦ Table of Contents

✦ Acknowledgments

For permission to quote from the works listed, the author wishes to make acknowledgment to the following: Houghton Mifflin Co. for Ruth Benedict, *The Chrysanthemum and the Sword* (1946); Iwanami Shoten for Takeo Kuwabara, ed., *Ichinichi Ichigen* (1971); Alfred A. Knopf, Inc. for Edwin O. Reischauer, *Japan: The Story of a Nation* (1970); Macmillan Publishing Co., Inc. for Robert Bellah, *Tokugawa Religion* (The Free Press, 1957); Praeger Publishers, Inc. for James Bailey, ed., *Listening to Japan* (1973); Prentice-Hall, Inc. for Herman Kahn, *The Emerging Japanese Superstate* (© Hudson Institute, 1970); the *San Francisco Chronicle* for Heuwell Tircuit, "Japanese Film Maker's Decorative Reality" (© Chronicle Publishing Co., 1973); Stanford University Press for Donald Keene, *The Japanese Discovery of Europe, 1720–1830* (1969); the Regents of the University of California for Michael Cooper, *They Came to Japan* (University of California Press, 1965).

✦ Prologue

*We pick our noses with our thumb or index fingers;
the Japanese use their little finger because their
nostrils are small.*

—LUIS FROIS, S.J.
(1532–1597)

*Even we are not sure of ourselves.
It really amazes me to see foreigners who come to
Japan to study and end up learning
to understand us. I don't.*

—SHINODA MASAHIRO

This book is an unofficial guide to Japan, containing un-
reliable and opinionated yet perhaps useful information
about her culture, its development and its characteristics.
It pretends to be neither a scientific treatise introducing
a seductive hypothesis on the social psychology of the
Japanese nor a recondite inquiry into some sublime
aspects of their history. It merely purports to draw in
broad strokes a representative landscape of Japan, to

compose an amplified free haiku that will reveal the distinguishing features of the Japanese character.

The reader of this book, having finished it, can go to Japan, meet people, and visit places, and he can experience and write his own story of the land. He will have learned more or less what to expect. Japan is at once beautiful and ugly, virtuous and vicious, strong and weak, consistent and contradictory. She can be ultra-modern or archaic, sophisticated or provincial, urban or pastoral, heartwarming or chilling, boisterous or serene, gay or tragic, rational or maniacal. Like objects in a kaleidoscope, what the traveler sees in Japan may change its shape, color, and meaning—depending upon the viewer's perspective and preconceptions. This book should provide enough clues, however, so that travel in Japan will result in an enlivening expansion of awareness rather than a premature and protracted cultural shock.

This book was difficult to write. Japan happens to be the country in which I was born, grew up, and have lived for many years. But that is hardly a sufficient condition for describing in a single volume some 100 million people whose history goes back at least 2,000 years. The relationship between an individual and his cultural heritage is like that between a child and his parent. In both cases, it is nearly impossible to sever the tie, and there are always hang-ups and an element of ambivalence. I had to guard against my own prejudices. I had to submerge myself in the culture I was depicting to unveil the intricacies of its inner workings and, at the same time, to keep my distance from it for the honesty of the portrait I was painting. Consulting numerous books and articles only added to the schizophrenic confusion of my mind. At one moment, noble theories advanced in scholarly journals seemed to contradict one another, or were less revealing of the truth than a few, casual passages in a Japanese novel. At another, they all seemed to be shifting shadows of the same tree. For a long time, until I finally wrote them out, my thoughts for this book were suspended in a state of turmoil and duress.

The Japanese are perhaps the most self-conscious people in the world. They not only talk about themselves incessantly but also have written thousands of books on Japan and the Japanese. Books on Japan, published in the West, are almost instantaneously and indiscriminately translated into Japanese; on the other hand, only a handful of their books have been made available to the West through translation. The language barrier is one obvious reason. Another is their peculiar obsession: the conviction that their culture is singular, that no outsider can possibly understand it, coupled with their masochistic delight in being misunderstood by foreigners. Only a few Japanese have bothered to write about themselves specifically for foreign readers; fewer have succeeded in reaching a wide audience abroad. The outstanding exception here is Nitobe Inazo,* a brilliant, multi-

---

* In citing Japanese names throughout the main text of this book I shall follow the Japanese convention of writing the family name first. Also following Japanese convention, a famous historical or cultural figure like Oda Nobunaga will be referred to by his personal name, Nobunaga in this case, following the full name's first appearance in the text. Please note, however, that in the notes and bibliography section Japanese authors are given personal name first to be consistent with the citations of Western authors' names there.

lingual scholar and statesman who, but for Japan's encounter with the West in the 19th century, would have ended up a sword-carrying samurai. His *Bushido: The Soul of Japan,* first published in 1905 and still in print, is a charming little book, a somewhat romanticized warrior account of the samurai code of ethics as the binding force beneath the surface of traditional Japan. Nitobe wrote his book in English, specifically for Westerners, out of exasperation with the ceaseless questioning of his American wife, Mary, about the mysteries of Japanese culture.

Books on Japan by Western authors abound. In 1853, when Commodore Matthew Calbraith Perry led his fleet of black warships to Japan to open her door to the West, there existed no more than forty books on Japan in New York or London libraries, and most of those were copies of the others or travelogues of questionable merit. Today one would easily find there forty thousand books, monographs, dissertations, and articles on Japan. While many of these are of excellent quality, most of them are quickly forgotten after publication or fail to reach the general reader because they tend to be too scholarly and esoteric, too topical to survive the test of time, or too grossly misinformed or biased to command serious attention.

The approach of this book is unabashedly eclectic. I have put together whatever I found was useful for my purpose. I have no ax to grind, no spite to vent, no course of action to propose, no grandiose thesis to prove, no plan to reduce the working of 100 million minds to a single-equation model. Japan of today is neither an Eastern nor a Western nation. Instead, she is a synthesis of the two that defies conventional classification. Yet a large element of the synthesis is of her own making, a distinctly Japanese pattern which can be baffling to the outsider. This book offers some hints for making sense of that pattern and tries to account for what makes the Japanese the way they are. Not infrequently, understanding—especially understanding of human subjects—is a delusion rather than an enlightened grasp of the ultimate truth. This book makes no guarantee of the accuracy of the information or interpretation contained within. My intent is simply to tell a story of the people whose culture I share.

—ROBERT S. OZAKI

PART ONE

✦ CONSTANTS AND VARIABLES

---

*They have rites and ceremonies so different from
those of all the other nations that it seems
they deliberately try to be unlike any other
people. The things which they do in this respect
are beyond imagining and it may truly be said
that Japan is a world the reverse of Europe.
So great is the difference in their food,
clothing, honours, language, management of the
household, curing of the wounded and sick,
teaching and bringing up children, and everything
else, that it can be neither described nor
understood.*

—ALESSANDRO VALIGNANO, S.J.
(1539–1606)

Of course, Japan is different. But not that different.
—PHILIP H. TREZISE
Former Assistant Secretary of State

1 ✦ How To Borrow Properly

> There is a sense of awkwardness and hesitancy among
> us, the Japanese, as we swallow the tidal waves of
> enlightenment engulfing the isles of Japan, for
> these waves are generated by the unfamiliar current
> of Western civilization. We are compelled to
> abandon the old waves of our own even before we
> have time to discern their truth and characteristics.
> Beneath the glare of enlightenment people cannot
> help but feel emptiness, discontent, and anxiety.
> Our enlightenment is not a movement from within; it
> is something superficial that reached us from without.
>
> —NATSUME SOSEKI
> (1867–1916)

Professor Erwin Balz, a German who came to Japan in
1876 to teach medicine at the University of Tokyo and
serve as family doctor for the Imperial Household, wrote
in his diary on October 25th in the year of his arrival:
"How wondrous! The present-day Japanese do not wish
to know anything about their past. Not only that . . .
the learned ones are ashamed of it. One of them said to
me, 'Indeed, everything in my country has been utterly

barbaric.' Another declared firmly, when I asked him
about Japanese history, 'We have no history. Our history
has just begun.' '' Professor Balz was not the only Westerner who was perplexed to observe the peculiar, self-
deprecatory attitude of the Japanese in the late 19th
century. Many another Westerner who came to Japan
was astonished to hear similar remarks everywhere he
went in the land that was then flooded by the tidal waves
of Western civilization. All the Japanese seemed to have
calmly resolved that their country, prior to the Meiji
Restoration* of 1868, had been mistaken for centuries.

In 1945, about eighty years later, the American conquerors marched into Japan. What they heard from the
Japanese was not much different from what Professor
Balz wrote in his diary. The Japanese, right after World
War II, apparently found masochistic pleasure in confessing that their country before the war had been all
wrong, unpardonably barbaric, and shamefully feudalistic. They sang a loud chorus, rejoicing that the true
Japan—a political democracy—had just been born.
What has happened twice is bound to happen a third
time. If Japan is beset again by a major political change,
no one should be surprised to hear her declare that postwar democracy without arms was total nonsense.

* For centuries prior to the Meiji Restoration the emperors of Japan were rulers in name only. Real power was held by a feudal
government (the Bakufu) led by a series of military strongmen (shogun). The Meiji Restoration, however, meant more than just the
collapse of the ruling Tokugawa Shogunate and the restoration of
the imperial throne in the person of the Emperor Meiji. It signified
the end of two and a half centuries of isolationism and the beginning
of Japan's modernization through absorption of Western knowledge
and science. The Meiji era (1868–1912) was a period of great turmoil as the Japanese faced the massive influx of things Western,
which to them represented a superior civilization.

The Japanese tend to show startling indifference to their own past whenever they experience an earthshaking event such as the Meiji Restoration in the 19th century or the total defeat in World War II. Their attitude of indifference goes hand in hand with a seemingly uncritical, wholesale acceptance of what is introduced from the outside. The Japanese have historically been vulnerable and susceptible to things foreign. While the country maintained a closed-door policy vis-à-vis the rest of the world before the mid-19th century, Europeans were "southern barbarians" (so called because they came from the south); but once the door was opened in 1868, the barbarians became conveyors of modern enlightenment. Before 1945 the Western powers were "beastly creatures"; yet, after Hiroshima and Nagasaki, the beasts quickly turned into messengers of peace, democracy, and advanced civilization. The Japanese seem capable of swiftly switching back and forth between fanatical ethnocentrism and blind worship of foreign ideas. When overwhelmed by a foreign influence, they abandon tradition, culture, and customs, and adopt foreign ways with the ease of people changing their wardrobes for a new season.

Japan's first direct contact with the Western world occurred in the mid-16th century with the coming of Portuguese missionaries and merchants. The very first ones arrived aboard a wrecked ship that barely made it to the island of Tanegashima off the southern tip of Kyushu. (That was in 1543, the same year in which Nicolaus Copernicus startled the world with his theory that the earth and the planets move about the sun.) Thereafter, the number of foreigners kept increasing. To accommodate the strange visitors from the south, the port of Nagasaki was opened in 1570. In twenty years its population grew to 5,000.

At first the Japanese formed the impression that Europeans were dirty-looking, poorly dressed creatures, interested only in trade. The first generation of Western missionaries was quick to sense how unfavorably the Japanese looked upon Europeans, and these missionaries tried to develop a new image of Westerners—as beautiful, elegant, respectable people. Perhaps the most successful of their public relations ventures took place in Kyoto, the capital, in 1591. Thirteen colorfully dressed Portuguese, led by the Italian priest Father Alessandro Valignano—together with the Japanese boys' mission that had just returned from an eight-year journey to Rome—paraded through the streets on their way to a visit with Lord Toyotomi Hideyoshi (1536–1598), then the most powerful military ruler in Japan. The foreign missionaries who had so carefully planned the procession were overwhelmed by the great stir that it caused in the city. The streets were filled with thousands of curious onlookers, men and women, young and old. Kyoto had never before seen such a massive assembly of spectators. Hideyoshi complained, ''As far as clothing goes, Japanese look like beggars in comparison with Europeans.'' Luis Frois, a Portuguese priest who participated in the parade, wrote with satisfaction: ''The native converts tell us that now all the people in Kyoto are talking about nothing but the elegance of Europeans, and are confessing to each other how wrong they were about their image of Europeans.'' The Portuguese customs became a raging fad among the Japanese, who wore Portuguese-style hats, clothes, shoes, beads, gold chains, and buttons as they walked the streets.

What the Portuguese ate also became a craze of the day. The Japanese tried beef and eggs with great enthusiasm, though these were foods to which they had traditionally shown aversion. Joao Rodriguez—another Portuguese priest, who arrived in 1577, mastered Japanese, and served Lord Hideyoshi as interpreter—wrote in 1593: "I am flabbergasted by the Japanese willingness to try and accept everything Portuguese." Even Lord Hideyoshi himself fondly tried on the Portuguese costumes; his retainers and vassals did the same. Many of them wore rosaries, hung little crosses from their hips, and carried white handkerchiefs. Some of them even recited Catholic prayers in broken Latin while walking in the street. They, nonconverts, were not ridiculing the Christians but were merely enjoying a new, elegant, exotic fashion that had arrived from the mysterious West. As fascinating as the quick spread of the "southern barbarian" fashion in the late 16th century was its rapid disappearance. It lasted for several years. Then it was gone with the wind, leaving behind no visible trace in the indigenous culture of the land.

In world history it has been an exception rather than a rule for a culture to spread over foreign territories slowly and in an atmosphere of peace and harmony. Typically, a sweeping assimilation of one culture into another is brought about and accompanied by military conquests, massacres, and political oppression. Almost always the conquerors impose their culture upon the conquered. But the Japanese, throughout their history, have been remarkably immune to this rule. Prior to 1945 their islands had never been extensively occupied by invading foreign troops, and during most of their premodern history they lived in isolation from the rest of the world.

The Manchurians tried to invade Japan in 1019, then the Mongolians in 1274 and 1284. These attempts turned out to be abortive for one reason or another. The Portuguese and Spaniards, who mercilessly destroyed native cultures on the new continents, failed to do likewise in Japan. The Western powers managed to colonize most of Asia during the 18th and 19th centuries, but Japan managed to stay independent while swallowing massive doses of Western civilization. The Japanese themselves take these events for granted and do not feel there is anything unique or extraordinary about their having absorbed over centuries, without the anguish of defeat or the shedding of their blood, the cultures of India, China, Korea, and the West.

To the Japanese, a "foreign culture" has always represented something elegant and superior to their own, a pleasant ornament to wear, a useful accessory to adopt. Since it was never forced on them by foreign invaders, they felt that they could choose to accept or reject as they pleased. As a result, they have developed a certain attitude toward things foreign, an attitude that gives varying impressions to outsiders. The ease with which they adopt foreign customs while abandoning their own, irrespective of whether what is abandoned is worth preserving, gives the impression that they are terribly naive and careless about their destiny. The rapidity with which they can give up what was recently adopted suggests their coolness in dealing with foreign cultures—a coolness that seems to hide beneath the exterior of change the constancy of their own culture.

The Europeans who came to Japan in the late 19th century were troubled as well as pleased to see the Japanese learn about and adopt Western culture with the defenselessness of a virgin and the eagerness of a beaver. The European teachers failed to realize that part of what they were teaching—modern arms and industry—was soon to be used against them by the Japanese.

The American conquerors who came to occupy Japan in 1945 received a similar impression. To their eyes, the Japanese who so earnestly and obediently learned American democracy and the American way of life looked docile and immature. The Americans could not help being magnanimous. Their occupation of Japan, as military occupations went, was just about the most humane, lenient, and civilized in the world's history. They generously poured in aid and technological assistance. The occupation lasted only five years. The Japanese were soon to begin flooding the American market with goods that embodied American technology.

The Japanese have historically managed to borrow foreign cultures not only painlessly but also on their own terms. In the 7th century A.D., Prince Shotoku (572–622) wrote a letter to the Chinese Emperor Yang Ti of the Sui dynasty that began with a famous line, "I, the Prince of the Land of the Rising Sun, address the Prince of the descending Sun." There is no way of telling if this was meant to be an insult. According to one interpretation, Prince Shotoku merely meant East versus West, the geographic positions of the two countries. The letter went on to express Japan's desire to import the fruits of Chinese civilization, its tone being that of one equal partner speaking to another. In the context of the time, this was extraordinary, for Japan then was a small, backward country, dwarfed by the vast, highly developed Chinese Empire. Somehow the Chinese emperor maintained his serenity and did not send his troops across the sea to slap down the arrogant inhabitants of the little islands. Instead, there began a steady flow of Chinese artifacts into Japan. Prince Shotoku initiated the periodic dispatch of Japanese missions to China as a means of systematically learning from the more prosperous, advanced neighbor. This mode of contact continued for a little over two centuries until 894, when the decline of the T'ang dynasty was visible. The missions were discontinued, for Japan had by then, presumably, borrowed from China all that was worth borrowing.

The 7th and 8th centuries witnessed a large influx of Chinese civilization into Japan, but the Japanese did not literally copy the legal codes and conventions of the T'ang dynasty. The official rank system that was actually put into practice in Japan was a simplified version of the original system. The Chinese all-male principle in farming was changed to a new rule under which both males and females, aged six or older, were to engage in cultivation.

In the 12th century, Japan's cultural intercourse with China grew again during the peak of the Sung dynasty and continued into the period of the Southern Sung dynasty. But the intercourse diminished once the Southern Sung started to disintegrate in the latter half of the 13th century. At the beginning of the 15th century, Shogun Ashikaga Yoshimitsu sent an envoy to the Ming emperor to open China trade. When Yoshimochi, Yoshimitsu's eldest son, assumed power, trade was abruptly stopped because Yoshimochi supposedly believed that it was against the will of God for Japan, the Divine Land, to trade with an impure nation. When Yoshinori, Yoshimitsu's fourth son, replaced Yoshimochi shortly afterward, he reestablished diplomatic relations with the

Ming dynasty, and China trade was once again resumed.

In the late 19th century, though French and Prussian legal codes were transplanted to Japan as part of the modernization of the country, they were adapted to local precedents. The final draft of the Meiji civil code, for example, carefully preserved the principle of primogeniture, for it was deemed consistent with the cultural milieu of the country.

In the present century, especially before World War II, Japan established a dubious reputation in the West as a quick copier of foreign designs and products. It must be noted that the forte of the Japanese has been quick borrowing and adaptation ever since the dawn of their history. After millennia, this practice became a national reflex which, like any other reflex, cannot be easily forgotten or relinquished.

*

The Japanese describe themselves as a people who are "quick to get hot, quick to cool down." Yesterday's ultranationalism and dogged ethnocentrism may turn into today's pacifism and fanatical advocacy of international cooperation. Arrogance and dogmatic nationalism may swiftly change to servile self-denial and worship of things foreign. On the surface, at least, it looks as though the Japanese cannot make up their minds about themselves. Their changeability however, is actually a survival technique—cultivated over centuries—akin to that of an opossum playing dead or a chameleon changing its colors to fool approaching enemies. Throughout their history, they have exhibited an awareness that incoming cultures were products of more developed, powerful kingdoms across the sea that might someday threaten their survival. The seas formed natural defense lines against foreign enemies, but apprehensions about the possibility of invasion persisted.

In this historical setting, the Japanese have cultivated an attitude of ambivalence toward foreigners. They welcome visitors from the outside world as long as these visitors serve merely as carriers of culture. Yet, like youngsters who have grown up behind the walls of a cozy house in which suffering was unknown, the Japanese become ill at ease with foreigners as people. They do not know what to make of these unfamiliar, unpredictable creatures, with their strange looks and peculiar manners, and they would rather receive the products of alien cultures than the aliens themselves.

The Japanese schizophrenia toward foreigners shows a certain pattern. In dealing with outsiders, they go their own way as long as that does not create a crisis. But when they reach a point where they know they cannot win the game, they are likely to make a sudden 180-degree turn in their attitude. When the Pacific War ended, in August, 1945, the American conquerors were astonished to observe that yesterday's ferocious enemies had become the friendliest and most cooperative pupils of Americanism. The Japanese—from politicians to ordinary people on the streets—bowed to young American GIs as though they were greeting their holy emperor. From the Japanese standpoint, what else could they do? They had lost the war; they were disarmed, totally defenseless. They had read tales of bloody military conquests in history books. Trapped in their four islands, there was no place they could escape to. The Americans could do anything they wanted, but the only thing the Japanese could do was minimize the risk to their lives by keeping their posture toward the victors as low as possible.

The sudden change of attitude in 1945 has many earlier counterparts. On May 11, 1891, a Japanese police officer named Tsuda Sanzo suddenly attacked and injured with his saber the visiting Russian Prince Nicholas II, instead of guarding, as he was supposed to, the Czarist procession through the streets of Otsu. Though this was in the days before radio and television, the news spread with lightning speed. The mood of the people suddenly changed, at a time when Westerners in Japan had been increasingly troubled by the arrogance and the rising anti-Western feeling of the local population. Hatred was quickly replaced by intense fear of retaliation from Russia—that vast, powerful, mysterious empire across the misty Japan Sea. The Japanese now began to show unbelievable timidity and obsequiousness toward the Russians. Countless organizations—from girls' middle schools to local medical associations—wrote letters of apology and sent delegations to the Russian headquarters in Kyoto to express their deepest regret and ask forgiveness. The Japanese emperor sent Viscount Enomoto and a member of the royal family directly to the Russian capital, and himself made a special trip to the port of Kobe, where the Russian flagship was staying, to convey his personal message of apology to the Russians.

On August 21, 1862, an English sailor was killed by a Japanese samurai for allegedly obstructing a procession of the local lord in the province of Satsuma in southern Kyushu. The English demanded execution of the samurai who committed the murder; the Japanese refused. In retaliation, seven English warships approached Kagoshima and began bombarding the city. The mood of the Satsuma warriors changed instantly. The theme

of "expel the barbarians" was no more. The Satsuma
delegates were brimming with friendship and cooperation at the peace conference held in Yokohama shortly
afterward, and issued a declaration that they had always
been interested in trade with England and had been
against the war from the beginning.

Besides Satsuma, the province of Choshu in northern
Kyushu was also noted for its die-hard nationalism and
anti-Western stance before the Meiji Restoration. The
Choshu leaders successfully pressured the imperial court
to issue a proclamation of war against the Western
powers. The fanaticism and determination of the
Choshu group impelled the central Bakufu (military
government) regime in Edo (pre-Meiji Tokyo) to produce a similar edict. On May 10, 1863, the Choshu
troops opened fire against the American, French, and
Dutch warships passing through the Shimonoseki strait.

The Western powers did not take this audacious act
lightly. On August 5 of the following year, 17 warships
(9 English, 3 French, 4 Dutch, 1 American) carrying
277 guns and 5,000 troops gathered off Shimonoseki
and attacked the city and its fortress for two days. Defenseless before the superior firepower of the Western
warships, Shimonoseki was destroyed far more extensively than Kagoshima had been two years earlier. The
allied Western troops who made a landing in the city
met little resistance.

The defeat of Choshu was thorough and complete.
On August 8, the Choshu government sent Takasugi
Shinsaku to the Western command to negotiate peace.
The letter he carried contained an apologia claiming
that the Choshu forces had been obliged to attack the
Western ships in the Shimonoseki strait in order to com-

ply with the imperial edict. On August 10, at the second peace negotiation, the Choshu delegation expressed its hope of establishing a friendly relationship with the Western countries and gaining superior knowledge from them. The identical Choshu government, only a short while before, had pressed the imperial court and the Bakufu regime to adopt a hostile policy toward the Western powers. Now, after the quick defeat, this same government was denying its responsibility for the belligerent act and was advocating peace and an amicable relationship. It was not only the attitude of the Choshu leaders but also the feeling of the populace that made a complete turn. On August 15, only a few days after the peace was negotiated, Western officers and sailors were walking freely through the streets of Shimonoseki. Ordinary people came out to welcome the Western barbarians. They offered dinner entertainment and sightseeing tours of the area. The Japanese officials brought water, food, and fuel to the Western ships.

Those Westerners who observed the raids of Kagoshima and Shimonoseki must have thought the Japanese were an easy people to handle. The only thing to do was to slap them down; then they would listen. The "easy-to-handle" image of the Japanese can also be confirmed in the first impressions, at least, of the Portuguese and Spanish missionaries who came to Japan in the 16th and 17th centuries. Many of them had previously served in India, but the work there tended to be an exercise in futility, an unending series of disappointments and frustrations. The natives were poor, ignorant, backward. They were too deeply enmeshed in their own ancient culture to be easily converted to Christianity. With mulelike stubbornness they refused to accept the truth of the Holy Bible. When the European missionaries came to Japan, they were astonished at the difference. The Japanese looked so clean, polite, orderly, disciplined, and eager to learn; it was as though they had patiently waited for centuries for the arrival of the missionaries. Japan appeared to be the ideal land for mass conversions.

Prior to his coming to Japan, Francis Xavier met in Malacca a certain Japanese named Anjiro whose diligence and intellectual curiosity profoundly impressed the Jesuit priest. Xavier wrote, "If other Japanese are as industrious as he, then they must be the most advanced people in the newly discovered world. I should be able to better serve God by converting Japanese than by dealing with those impossible natives of India."

*

In 1549 Francis Xavier came to Kagoshima aboard a Chinese ship. He arrived six years after European-made guns had been introduced to Japan by the Portuguese aboard a wrecked ship that sought refuge on the island of Tanegashima. The way the Japanese reacted to these events reveals much about their contrasting attitudes toward foreign persons and toward foreign things.

Within a short time after arriving in Japan, Xavier managed to win a surprisingly large number of converts. According to one historical account, in a matter of several weeks 150 Japanese were baptized in Kagoshima. But that was not the whole story. While it is true that many did become his followers, not all Japanese were enthusiastic about his presence. In fact Xavier's stay in Japan, which lasted for two years and three months, on the whole was an experience in discouragement and frustration. Native converts were far outnumbered by people who showed naked hostility, coldness, or indifference. Lord Shimazu Takahisa of Satsuma (the district in which Kagoshima is located), gave Xavier a seemingly warm welcome. He approved Xavier's mission, however, only as a means of encouraging Portuguese ships to come to the port of Kagoshima. Xavier later went to Kyoto, but his journey to the capital was miserable. Children threw stones at him. The natives he met on the way were anything but friendly and hospitable. Lord Ouchi Yoshitaka of Yamaguchi gave him the cold shoulder. In Kyoto he was denied an audience with the emperor, for the priest had no gifts to present. Xavier failed to see that the Japanese rulers then were interested in foreign products, not in foreigners or their strange teachings.

In marked contrast to the mixed reception accorded the missionaries was the Japanese reaction to the coming of Western guns, weapons far more accurate and powerful than the primitive Chinese versions that had been imported earlier. Lord Tokitaka of the island of Tanegashima immediately tried to determine whether the two guns brought to his island by the Portuguese could be duplicated by native craftsmen. In 1544, only a year after the arrival of the prototypes, a successful copy was produced. The gun fad spread like wildfire. Soon large numbers of the weapons were being manufactured in Negoro, Kunitomo, Sakai, and other places. In 1549, Oda Nobunaga (1534–1582), one of the military strong men of the day, ordered 500 pieces from Kunitomo. He was quick to see the strategic importance of the new weapon and swiftly extended his territorial control over those provinces which had major gun-manufacturing centers. Nobunaga organized, trained, and made effective use of special troops equipped with guns. In 1556,

Mendes Pinto, a Portuguese traveler, was flabbergasted to hear from Lord Otomo that there were 30,000 guns in his province alone, more than 300,000 in all of Japan, and 25,000 that had been exported to Ryukyu. Perhaps these figures were grossly exaggerated. What is astonishing, however, is that in thirteen years Japan had already become an exporter of guns.

Xavier learned a lesson from his abortive first trip to Kyoto. He changed his strategy to suit the wants of the Japanese rulers. From a newly arrived Portuguese ship he acquired as many material objects as possible. He threw away his dirty, worn-out robe, and replaced it with a most elegant, eye-catching one. When he went back to see Lord Ouchi Yoshitaka, who had previously been unreceptive, he made sure he brought numerous gifts— clocks, spectacles, wines, glassware, guns, and textiles. Predictably, the lord extended the warmest hospitality to Xavier, who began to realize that proselytism based solely upon spirituality would not work very well in Japan. This realization set the pattern of Catholic missions in Japan during subsequent years. Father Luis Frois, who came to Kyushu in 1563 after consulting with Xavier in Goa, wrote: "In order to open the road to God, we must first tempt them with objects that will satisfy their earthly desires." It is open to debate whether this was a case of hypocrisy on the part of the holy missionaries who let the end justify the means and who, consciously or otherwise, were serving as instruments of an aggressive European colonialism. In view of the material desires of the Japanese rulers, however, the European missionaries perhaps felt that such an approach, hypocritical or not, was just about the only feasible way to accomplish their task.

When the European missionaries began to arrive, Japan was not yet a unified country. The period was one of civil war; the political balance between provinces was precarious and shifting. The local lords, especially those in western Japan, were anxious to expand their power by accumulating wealth through trade and absorbing Western technology. They welcomed the Portuguese merchants as carriers of a superior civilization. Each lord tried to attract Portuguese ships to his port and to discourage them from entering ports controlled by his rivals. Many lords gave favors to the foreign priests and made contributions to their newly built churches. Not a few of the lords were even converted to Christianity, not necessarily for the salvation of their souls, but rather as a calculated means of winning the friendship of the priests. Lord Matsuura of Hirado, who once ordered closure of the churches in his province and expelled the priests, later changed his mind and withdrew the order upon hearing that a captain of a Portuguese ship, angered by Matsuura's act, had threatened to stop coming to the port of Hirado. Lord Omura, who stood in opposition to Matsuura, gave sizable donations to the churches in Yokoseura and Nagasaki and offered tax exemptions to merchants in his province who traded with the Portuguese.

In 1560 the troops of Nobunaga defeated those of Imagawa Yoshimoto in the battle of Okehazama. Nobunaga's victory made him a likely candidate for the position of national ruler. Many European missionaries flocked to his castle. He showed immense curiosity about Western knowledge and maintained friendly relations with the missionaries. Besides valuing them as useful agents for importing advanced knowledge and technology, Nobunaga considered the missionaries, as a religious group, a badly needed countervailing force against the Buddhist sects that were taking every opportunity to interfere with his struggle for power. This, however, was not the only reason for his cordiality to the missionaries. He remained cordial to them because he was ignorant of the alarming extent to which Christianity had spread in distant Kyushu and the western parts of Honshu. He was still on his way toward unifying the country. His immediate concern was with his enemies controlling the adjacent provinces. He was not aware of—nor was he much interested in—the political conditions in distant areas of the country. He did not realize that the strange religion being spread by the European missionaries was beginning to undermine the established cultural and social order.

By 1582, the year of Nobunaga's death, the number of converts throughout Japan had reached 150,000. Most of them were concentrated in western Japan, particularly in the provinces of Arima and Omura, which witnessed wholesale, mass conversions from the provincial chiefs on down. The number of converts under Nobunaga's rule in and around Kyoto, however, was no more than 10,000; the military strong man had been misled in thinking that the European missionaries were harmless as well as useful.

Hideyoshi, Nobunaga's contemporary and another contender for the central position of power, at first maintained a similar attitude. Under Hideyoshi were several Christian daimyo (lords), but he was not troubled by their new religion as long as they honored their absolute allegiance to his office. Hideyoshi welcomed the European missionaries as suppliers of exotic objects from the

West. On the night of July 24, 1587, however, his policy toward Christianity was suddenly reversed. In the town of Hakata, where he was staying during his Kyushu expedition, he issued a totally unexpected decree banning all missionary activities in his territory. This was a bewildering event, for on the afternoon of the very same day Hideyoshi had promised a Portuguese priest a parcel of land in Hakata as the site of a new church. Presumably, Hideyoshi sensed an encroaching crisis owing to the spread of Christianity, and was shocked to realize that the new religion's penetration in Kyushu and western Honshu was far deeper and more extensive than he had ever imagined while on his home grounds around Kyoto. On July 25, the day following the pronouncement of this decree, he told an assembly of his subordinates that he was now convinced that the missionaries, under the pretense of preaching the gospel, were actually plotting to overthrow the political order of the country by converting an increasing number of daimyo and persuading the masses to rebel against the authorities.

Tokugawa Ieyasu (1542–1616), whose decisive victory at the battle of Sekigahara in 1600 set the course toward unification of the entire country under his powerful dictatorship as first shogun of the Tokugawa regime, also had a deep, pragmatic interest in Western products and technology, combined with a basic distrust of the motives of the European priests. He was particularly interested in trading with the Spaniards, who then operated a large trading depot in Manila. In 1605, he wrote in a letter to the Spanish governor-general of Manila: "Since time immemorial, gods of Japan have been revered by countless generations of my people and this fact I alone cannot revoke. Therefore, I am unable to welcome prop-agation in any manner of your religion in my country." There is, however, no record of Ieyasu's systematic sup-pression of Christian missionary work during the early phase of his reign. He was anxious to acquire Western technology and goods, if not Christianity. He tried to learn techniques of shipbuilding from the Spaniards and the method of silver mining they had developed in Mexi-co. He repeatedly persuaded Spanish ships to stop at the port of Uraga, in Honshu, on their way from Manila to Acapulco.

A strong man inside Japan, Ieyasu kept a low posture toward the Spaniards. In 1602, he wrote a note of apology when Spanish sailors were molested by local Japanese at the port of Shimizu. After the incident he issued as many as eight decrees ordering that a cordial welcome be given to all Spanish ships arriving at any port in Japan. In 1611, he even permitted a Spanish ship to conduct an oceanographic survey of the Japanese coast.

In 1600 an English sea captain, William Adams, had come to Japan aboard a Dutch ship. He met Ieyasu in Osaka about a half year before the Battle of Sekigahara and later became Ieyasu's confidant. In 1609 two Dutch ships arrived at Hirado. Before the end of that year, the Bakufu issued a trading permit to the Dutch. Soon an office of trade was established in Hirado, and an increas-ing number of Dutch merchants began to arrive. These Protestant Europeans—to whom the Spaniards and the Portuguese were commercial rivals—took every occasion to tell the Bakufu officials that the real intent of the Catholic mission was to prepare for the eventual military conquest of Japan. They cited specific examples—how

Mexico, Peru, and the Philippines fell under Spanish colonial rule. William Adams warned Ieyasu that the Spanish oceanographic survey along the coast of Japan in 1611 was but preparation for a contemplated attack.

In 1612, Okamoto Daihachi, a vassal of a close attendant of Ieyasu, was sentenced to death for the crime of bribery. During the course of investigation, Okamoto was found to be a Christian. Alarmed by the discovery that a convert was among those closest to him, Ieyasu ordered a further investigation only to learn that there were more than ten converts among his immediate retainers, ladies' maids, and others directly below him. This episode marked a turning point in the history of persecution of Christians in Japan. On August 6th of the same year, the Bakufu regime in Edo promulgated its first formal ordinance prohibiting the practice of Christianity. The oppression was first aimed at the converts among provincial lords, samurai, and other members of the ruling class, then later at those among the masses. By the time Hidetada succeeded Ieyasu and became the second shogun of the Tokugawa regime, it had become clear that the mere internal ban alone was not sufficient to stop the spread of Christianity. More and more restrictive rules on trade and overseas transportation were introduced. The trend reached a climax in 1639 when the policy of isolation was proclaimed with a total ban on the entry of Portuguese ships into Japanese ports.

The period from the mid-16th century through the early decades of the 17th century had been one in which European culture as well as Europeans poured into Japan. Compared with foreigners in past centuries, the European missionaries of this period were neither a passive foreign minority to be absorbed into Japanese society nor meek carriers of a different culture to be remoulded by the Japanese to their taste. They were the active, confident, persuasive ones, seemingly capable of converting the very fabric of Japanese society into their own. Rulers like Hideyoshi and Ieyasu tried to separate trade (beneficial) from religion (harmful). Sooner or later, they learned that such a separation was impossible. The European missionaries were expelled, the native converts punished.

Yet the Japanese rulers were too curious to shut their minds off completely from the rest of the world. They remained attentive—keenly attentive—to outside developments even during the period of isolation. The method used was in line with the tradition of Japanese cultural history. A tiny island called Dejima, off Nagasaki, was chosen as the only place to which foreign ships (but not Portuguese ships) were allowed to come, under severe restrictions. Foreigners were not allowed to leave the island, though Western goods and books continued to enter Japan. In this way, the country successfully kept the foreigners out while managing to absorb their culture. Through the little window of Dejima, the Japanese perceived and absorbed foreign culture as a highly abstract matter detached from the men who created it. In the context of the time, this was the only feasible way for Japan to preserve her cultural autonomy.

Historians have suggested many explanations for the Tokugawa regime's adoption of isolationism in 1639. Some have argued that it was a means of tightening internal political control. Others have held that it was a way to monopolize foreign trade. It has been argued that the decree of 1639 actually prohibited only the overseas travel of Japanese and the entry of Portuguese ships, that the regime did not mean literally to isolate the country from the outside world. While all these may be plausible partial explanations, the more direct reason was the Tokugawa regime's fear—almost an instinctive sort of fear—of the growth of Catholicism in Japan. Shortly after proclamation of the isolationist policy, an English ship of the East India Company arrived and requested the opening of trade. The Bakufu at first gave a favorable response since it was a ship from a Protestant country . . . only to expel the ship soon afterward upon discovering that the king of England was married to a former Portuguese princess. If nothing else, this event reveals the pathological anxiety the Japanese rulers must have suffered about the venomous influence of the Catholic religion.

Historical evidence does not indicate that Portugal and Spain were then actually contemplating military aggression against Japan or that their missionaries in Japan were deliberately serving as advance agents for their imperialistic ambitions. The Portuguese stationed in Macao hardly possessed enough arms and manpower for the invasion. Their colonies in Macao and Goa were maintained primarily as bases for their trading in Southeast Asia. The Spaniards in Manila had some armed troops, but they were scarcely sufficient to effect an extended military conquest of Japan. They were realistic enough to know that the conquest of China or Japan, unlike that of Peru and Mexico, was out of the question. In fact, generations of Spanish governors-general in Manila were careful not to provoke Japan. Arai Hakuseki, an able theoretician and an important advisor-official of the Bakufu in the early 18th century, said at one point, "I now have come to conclude that Christianity is not a plot to take over our country." There is no record that the Bakufu officials anticipated the coming of a Spanish-Portuguese armada to their shores.

In the early years of the Catholic mission in Japan, the Japanese rulers were tolerant or only mildly hostile. Hideyoshi's initial anti-Christian edict said, in effect, that it was permissible for ordinary people autonomously to choose and practice the new religion but it was not admissible for the converted daimyo and samurai to force their subjects to follow suit. Similarly, Ieyasu at first was concerned only with the spread of Christianity among the ranks of samurai. Subsequently, the anti-Christian policy became more oppressive, thorough, and far-reaching. Christianity was no longer viewed as merely another faith that might coexist in peace with the native religions; it became an evil belief—dangerous, lurid, poisonous. The Japanese rulers came to realize that the conversion of the masses could be far more frightening than that of the ruling class.

The adoption of Christianity, for many daimyo, was actually a "conversion of convenience." There were, of course, exceptions but, by and large, they accepted Christianity as a means of promoting their trade with the Portuguese and the Spaniards. Without torment, they abandoned their new faith the moment they were told to do so by the higher authorities. The converted masses were different, though. Often they stubbornly resisted the Bakufu's oppressive measures. They chose happiness in heaven over glory on earth. In October, 1613, three samurai converts and their families were executed near Nagasaki under Ieyasu's anti-Christian edict of the year before. The night before the execution, 20,000 native Christians spontaneously gathered around the jail to pray for the martyrs. The guards' attempts to disperse them had no effect. They preferred to die by bullets and arrows rather than obey the guards' order. Torches were burning all over town; the Christians prayed with rosaries in their hands. On the morning of October 7th, the prisoners were transferred to the site of execution. They showed no sign of suffering or fear of the dreadful moment that awaited them. On the contrary, they looked calm and relaxed, as though they were on their way to a happy banquet. Thousands and thousands of Christians marched after the holy criminals. The streets were packed with people—not only the marching Christians but also others who came and waited all night to have a glimpse of the martyrs, to bid farewell to the courageous.

The event naturally shocked Ieyasu and his young prince, Hidetada. Those Christians listened to foreign padres rather than the Japanese sovereign. They honored as holy martyrs those who were found guilty of violating the national law. To Ieyasu, whose ambition it was to control the entire land, the massive resistance of the Christians was totally unpardonable.

Of course, it was not the first time that Japanese rulers had faced resistance movements from below. Since much earlier times, peasant rebellions had erupted to resist high taxes and excessively stringent political rules. Many were small in scale, sporadic, brief; a few were large, well-organized, relatively long-lasting. All the peasant revolts, however, had one thing in common. They were economic in origin and were not intended to undermine the fundamental political structure of the country. They were not backed by an alien ideology incompatible with the principles of internal polity. The political rulers found them fairly easy to handle. The solution to the

problem was a matter of a few more bowls of rice for the
peasants, a slight loosening of the political grips that
regulated their lives. In contrast, the Christian resistance
movements were qualitatively different. They held a
clear purpose and a firm ideology. While the peasant
rebellions tended to disintegrate quickly, the revolts of
Christians were like an epidemic spreading without end.

In 1613, the Bakufu destroyed all the churches and
arrested the Christians in Edo and Kyoto, who were
told to abandon their alien faith or suffer expulsion from
the country. Those who refused to apostatize were sent
to Nagasaki. While they were waiting for ships to take
them abroad, the magistrate of Nagasaki threatened to
torture them to death unless they changed their minds.
Instead of being intimidated, the Christians took it as
a matter of honor. They tightly organized themselves in
small groups, signed their names, and made a firm pledge
that no matter what suffering they might experience
they would never be coerced into giving up their faith.
All the men and women—and even small children—
made the same pledge. Then they proceeded to march,
night and day, through the streets of Nagasaki, per-
forming penance in the open and praying to God for
strength and courage. The first march of atonement,
consisting of more than 300 men and women, took place
on Friday, May 9, 1614. The next day, a large number
of local Christians came out and joined the march; the
following Monday there were as many as 3,000 Christians. Some carried heavy crosses. Others dragged big
stones and sacks filled with gravel. Many were bleeding
as they beat one another with bamboo sticks. Their
necks, hands, and feet were tied with ropes and chains.
The tied hands held images of Christ to which the others

knelt and prayed. The procession of atonement continued for seven days.

The Christians as a group transcended the fear of religious persecution. Their belief enabled them to accept as a reflection of their own sin the political oppression they suffered. Perhaps never before in Japanese history had anyone encountered such a spiritual attitude. The idea that each man is ultimately responsible for his sin and that, in this sense, all men are equal under God must have had a tremendous appeal to those who lived under the oppressive policy of the feudal regime. Of course, many native converts did not understand the subtle aspects of Christian doctrine. Yet, from the doctrine they grasped—intuitively perhaps—the meaning of liberation. From the standpoint of the political rulers, the converts were most troublesome beings who apparently could withstand any amount of physical and spiritual suffering on account of, and for the sake of, their faith.

In their previous history, the Japanese masses had never been exposed to the direct and immediate influence of such an alien philosophy. The whole development was new and different. Unlike Buddhism, in its early phases in Japan, the Christian culture that penetrated Japanese soil was hardly abstract and was scarcely meant for aristocrats only. The Europeans, the very creators of the culture, marched into the country. Their culture embodied specific, spiritual principles to guide one's life and death, and it began to move the masses in a direction that was incompatible with the political and social order of the day. Underlying the Christian philosophy was a universalistic view of men and the world too advanced to be readily swallowed by the Japanese rulers, whose reactions were, therefore, intuitive and instinctive. They grasped the encroachment of Christianity as an evil spirit on its way to desecrate their holy land. This was the limit of their thought processes. For their own survival, they were willing to employ cruel methods to efface from their territory Christianity and those who represented it.

*

Some two hundred years later, a wave of Western culture again approached Japan. But it was a wave of a different sort. The Westerners who came were not Christian missionaries determined to save the souls of the Japanese. Rather, they were merchants of a new Western capitalism, interested in trading with Japan. Changing the cultural fabric of the country was not their concern. They were content as long as they could sell their products and find native goods that might be sold at a profit back home.

This new wave of Western culture did have a powerful impact on Japan, and the latter half of the 19th century was a period of great turbulence in which the country struggled to lay the foundations for a modern state. The crisis of the 19th century after the collapse of the Tokugawa regime, however, was qualitatively different from those in the 16th and 17th centuries. For Japan's new political leaders in the late 19th century the main question was how fast they could catch up with the West through absorption of Western science and technology—all on their terms—and not whether their cultural hegemony was being undermined. In other words, they were back in the traditional pattern of accepting a foreign culture and not those who created it. Practically all the Westerners—technicians, engineers, scientists, doctors, legal experts, educators—who came to Japan in the late 19th century did so at the invitation of the Japanese. They were there not to take over Japan, but rather to assist the Japanese who were deciding—in line with their own tastes and preferences—what sort of changes should be instituted so as to modernize their country.

2 + The Taste of Forbidden Fruits

> *Comparatively few people in eighteenth-century Japan
> ever saw a foreigner. Those who lived in Nagasaki
> might occasionally have come across Chinese merchants
> and sailors, and those who lived along the road to
> Edo might even have caught a glimpse of a Dutchman
> in his palanquin being hurried off on the annual
> mission to the capital, but most Japanese regarded
> foreigners (and particularly Europeans) as a
> special variety of goblin that bore only a superficial
> resemblance to a normal human being.*
>
> —DONALD KEENE

In the middle of the 19th century, the Western powers,
the United States among them, were intensifying their
efforts to penetrate China, a promising new market.
The United States had signed a commercial treaty with
China in 1844. The next logical step was to sign a
similar treaty with Japan, since that nation was con-
veniently located near the Chinese mainland. The
first bid was made in 1846. Commodore James Biddle
attempted to enter with his East India fleet of two
warships into the port of Edo. He was told that foreign

commerce was banned in Japan and all diplomatic affairs were dealt with only in Nagasaki. Biddle, apparently a courteous and compliant man, turned his fleet around and went back to Canton.

Since Biddle's peaceable approach had no effect, President Millard Fillmore fired him and appointed Commodore Matthew Perry as the new commander of the East India fleet. Perry was ordered to accomplish three objectives: to have the Japanese assure the rescue of American seamen and the protection of their lives and property when their ships were in distress near the Japanese coasts; to open trade between the United States and Japan; and to build coal depots along the Japanese shores for American steamships.

Perry was aware that, to a large extent, the Europeans were to blame for Japan's prolonged isolation. As far as Western powers went, America's hands were still clean. His country had not meddled with feudal Japan before. He was hopeful that with a fresh approach his mission would succeed. As a precautionary measure, he shut out from his fleet all the European scholars and amateur adventurers who wanted to accompany him. On November 8, 1852, President Fillmore paid a personal visit to the flagship *Mississippi* to wish Perry good luck. Eight months later, Perry's fleet of warships, all painted black, passed the Izu Peninsula and entered Uraga Bay. Japan would never be the same again.

*

In many respects, Japan around the 17th and 18th centuries was no more underdeveloped than European countries. Major cities such as Edo, Osaka, and Kyoto were on a par with their European counterparts in size, volume of commerce, administration, and facilities. If the Europeans traced their philosophy to ancient Greece, the Japanese traced theirs to Buddhism and Confucianism. There existed in Japan highly developed literature, arts, crafts, and music—even though their forms differed considerably from those of the West. So, with respect to these subjects, the opening of Japan to the West did not shock the Japanese. They could compare the new forms of literature, art, and music from the West with their own, and through comparison they were able to understand, appreciate, and absorb those fruits of Western culture with relative ease. The same, however, was not quite true for science and technology. The Japanese had their indigenous mathematics called *wasan,* which was more in the nature of advanced arithmetic and intuitive geometry, as well as highly developed skills and techniques in the hands of native craftsmen. But these were utterly ineffectual when compared with Western science and technology.

Japanese who read naturalistic Western novels in the 19th century were reminded of their 17th-century literary figure, Ihara Saikaku (1642–1693), who wrote in a similar genre. The realism and beauty of Western oil paintings were impressive, but they were not necessarily superior to the qualities of traditional Japanese paintings. In contrast, however, electricity, steam engines, and other products of Western material civilization found no counterparts in Japan. As the Japanese quickly learned, one element of Western civilization had made possible the building of powerful guns and formidable warships, and had placed the West militarily ahead of the Orient in a relatively short span of time. That crucial element was Western scientific technology.

Japan had no choice, then, but to borrow science and

technology from the West in order to join the ranks of powerful, civilized states. How could this be done? The only way was to learn Western languages, to read Western books, and to go to Western countries for study. After the opening of Japan, learning Western languages (especially English) and going overseas to study became a great craze for a while, a phenomenon to be repeated after World War II. Before 1868, 93 Japanese had already left their country to study in the West. In 1870, the government established new rules concerning studies abroad. One rule required each student to visit a local shrine before departure and pray that his study abroad might be successful and might contribute to the building of their new nation; the rule also required the student to pledge with a cup of sacred wine never to engage in shameful acts while abroad; and upon return he was to report his accomplishment to his ancestral gods by revisiting the shrine. By 1910, the number of students who had gone overseas on scholarships granted by the Ministry of Education alone reached 444, a large number in view of the costs involved at a time when the country was still poor. Many others paid their own way.

The task of those students would have been far more difficult a few generations later. In the 19th century, however, science was still primitive and approachable to beginners. Research was conducted by small groups or individuals rather than by teams consisting of large numbers of highly trained technicians and scientists. Experimentation was still very much in the nature of a handicraft, compared with today's sophisticated laboratory projects requiring staggering sums of money. By sending a modest number of students to the West, Japan could absorb Western science at a manageable cost.

Much the same was true of 19th-century technology—which could be learned by any minimally intelligent and motivated individual. Yamabe Tadao, who founded the Osaka Textile Mill in 1883, first went to England to study the insurance business; later, he switched to textiles in response to a suggestion from his entrepreneur friend, Shibusawa Eiichi. Even in the West technology was not much more than an extension of artisanship, and it could be copied without excessive difficulty by Japanese craftsmen. In 1874, the first jacquard, a then-advanced weaving machine named after its French inventor, was imported to Japan. Araki Kohei, a man of noted eccentricity and a skilled carpenter specializing in manufacturing weaving machines, immediately proceeded to copy the French product. In 1877, more than ten units for the manufacture of jacquard cloth were already operating in the city of Kyoto.

In the 19th century, too, science still retained a human flavor. There were neither atomic bombs nor napalm. Progress in bacteriology produced modern methods of vaccination and sanitation, freeing civilized men from the horror of epidemics. New agricultural technology brought about a greater abundance of better foods. Electricity purged darkness from the night; the inconvenience of gas and oil lamps was no more. Steam engines and new machines raised labor productivity. The wealth of the Western nations kept rising, and the future of Western civilization looked bright and promising.

Into the world of Western civilization, then, a strange-looking group of Asians called Japanese—about whom the Westerners had known so little—began to arrive. They came to the Western countries with childlike eagerness to study science and technology. Somehow they did not fit the image of Asians which the Westerners had built up through their colonial experiences. The Japanese studied English, German, and French with dogged diligence. Once assigned to laboratories, they worked like maniacs and produced fairly good results.

Nagai Nagayoshi, to cite a typical example, went to Germany as the first Japanese to study pharmacology in the 19th century. His German landlord in Berlin was extremely kind to him. The landlord went overboard in taking care of this short young man from the East, and patiently taught him German manners and etiquette . . . then persuaded him to become a Christian. Katsu Taro and Shinagawa Yajiro, Nagai's roommates, received the same warm treatment. At the university, they were touched by the generosity of their German professors. Japanese students were similarly welcomed in many other countries.

To the Westerners who firmly believed that the whole world rotated around them, these students who came all the way from the Far East were lovable creatures, kneeling at the feet of masters whose teaching they humbly requested. The Westerners could not help but feel magnanimous and extend help with benevolent smiles.

*

Strangely, the very first Japanese who came to the United States to study had not been a bright young samurai or a promising son of a noble family but an obscure fisherman from Tosa who, were it not for his extreme luck, would have died at sea at the age of fifteen.

On Sunday, June 27, 1841, an American whaler, the *John Holland*—while cruising near the island of Hachijojima, 480 kilometers south of Tokyo—spotted an uninhabited island. The ship's skipper, a Captain Whitfield, sent two boats to the island in the hope of finding some sea turtles. The sailors who went ashore found no turtles; instead, they met five starving survivors of a shipwreck. They spoke a language no American aboard the whaler could understand. It was only after the survivors were taken to Honolulu that they could be identified as Japanese. One of the five was a fifteen-year-old boy named Nakahama Manjiro, whom the captain grew fond of. The boy worked aboard the whaler for a while. Later the captain arranged to send him to school in New Bedford, Massachusetts. Manjiro was the first Japanese who had ever enrolled in an American school. Thanks to his youth, his English improved rapidly. After leaving school he stayed on in the United States for nearly a decade, traveling at one point to California to join the gold rush. When he returned to Japan at the age of twenty-five, he could speak English as fluently as a native American.

In 1853, one year after Manjiro came home, Commodore Perry brought his fleet to the Japanese coast, demanding the opening of the country. The Tokugawa regime, still in control, badly needed someone with a sufficient knowledge of the English language. Manjiro appeared to be the logical choice to serve as interpreter, but his choice was at first opposed by the elder statesmen, who suspected that Manjiro possibly was an American spy. Their suspicion was not totally irrational. They could not see why Americans had singled out this young man and given him an education, except perhaps for a conspiratorial motive. Even if this were untrue, Manjiro's sense of indebtedness to the Americans, who had not only saved his life but had also treated him well, might undermine his loyalty to Japan. His superb command of

English, however, was too precious to be wasted. Faced with mounting problems of diplomacy, the Tokugawa regime eventually decided to hire him as its official interpreter. In 1860, Manjiro sailed across the Pacific aboard the *Kanrin Maru* with the first Japanese diplomatic mission to the United States. In 1869, he was made a professor, second-class, at Kaisei Academy, the predecessor of the Imperial University of Tokyo. It was an epoch-making event for a humble fisherman's son from Tosa to become a government official and then a professor, at a time when those who aspired to be educated and to serve as high-ranking bureaucrats of the feudal regime came exclusively from the ruling samurai class.

The American whaler that saved Manjiro's life was one of some three hundred vessels operating from the port of New Bedford, south of Boston. They were modest-sized wooden ships with three masts, weighing barely four hundred tons. Whaling was a booming industry in mid-19th-century America. From the small port in New England, the whaling boats sailed to all corners of the globe to catch the sea mammals whose oil was used in manufacturing soap and as an illuminant. The whaling boom in America actually lasted only three decades— approximately from 1830 to 1860. Prior to this period, there was little demand for whale oil. Later, demand suddenly dropped, mainly because whale oil was replaced by petroleum. After 1860, then, there were no more American whalers around the Japanese islands. Were it not for his shipwreck that fortunately took place during the American whaling boom, Manjiro would have perished at sea instead of living to play an important role in the opening days of a new Japan.

Manjiro's rescue from the sea was a mere accident, but his rise to eminence symbolized the decisive change that had occurred since the arrival of the first Westerners in his country. While Japan had been sleeping in peace and quiet behind the curtain of isolationism for more than two hundred years, the West had managed to develop science and technology, double-edged swords that could be used for betterment as well as destruction. Then the Westerners had returned—this time on warships equipped with powerful guns. And the foreigners, this time, did not go home when told to do so. The Japanese were forced to realize that science now dictated world politics. Their rich cultural heritage weighed nothing against the power of the weapons built by modern technology. The only choice open to Japan was to swallow as quickly as possible the effects of Western science in order to build her own strong arms and modern industry, or face the humiliation of being colonized by Western powers. She did begin to swallow them, with the frenzy of someone tasting forbidden fruit. Some results of that early frenzy are outlined in the rest of this chapter.

The Calendar. The modernization of Japan did not mean simply the copying of Western knowledge. It also dictated changes in customs and life-style. For 2,000 years, the Japanese had been using a calendar based upon both solar and lunar movements. Originating in China, it set the length of one year by the sun and of one month by the moon. It was adjusted to the four seasons of the year and hence to the associated cycles of agricultural production. Under the traditional calendar, the new year signified not only the abstract beginning of spring but also the start of a real spring season. There was always a full moon during the ageless *bon* festival each summer when the spirits of the deceased ancestors returned. The calendar had been carefully studied and improved over centuries. It could accurately forecast solar as well as lunar eclipses.

In 1868, the new Meiji government commenced the gigantic task of modernizing Japan after the Western model. Already, in 1870, the government decided to move toward adoption of the Western calendar. Uchida Yasushi and Tsukamoto Akitaka, two mathematicians commissioned to examine the matter, submitted a proposal in 1872 recommending the complete replacement of the traditional calendar with the Western solar one.

Just before the proposal was submitted, the government had approved a new rule to pay the bureaucrats' salaries on a monthly basis, and 1873, according to the old calendar, was a leap year with thirteen months. Switching to the Western calendar meant that one whole month of salaries could be saved. Given the critical shortage of public funds then, this was reason enough for the government to welcome the proposal.

Money saving, however, was not the only motive behind the government's approval. By this time, the Japanese had experienced a good deal of inconvenience in diplomacy and commerce, since the Westerners used a different calendar. Not only days and months but sometimes even years had to be adjusted before an agreement could be reached and a contract signed. Since it was absurd to ask the advanced Westerners to learn to use the Japanese calendar, it would be simpler and more practical for the Japanese to accept the Western one.

Adoption of the new calendar was carried out with

ease and rapidity. An imperial edict, issued in November, 1872, changed the third day of December, 1872, to the first day of January, 1873. The first and second days of December, 1872, became the thirtieth and thirty-first days of November, 1872. Thereafter, the days were to be counted in accordance with the Western calendar. With the stroke of a pen, the month of December vanished for good from the year 1872 in Japanese history.

Habits and customs, however, do not change easily. Introduction of the Western calendar caused much confusion. Dates of annual holidays, Shinto festivals, Buddhist ceremonies—all had to be changed. For a long while, the government was obliged to use both calendars in citing dates of important events. Many rural districts continued to celebrate New Year's day under the traditional calendar. Odd expressions such as "New New Year" and "Old New Year" became part of the language during the Meiji era. Confusion and inconvenience were the price the nation had to pay for becoming a member of the community of modern states.

Weights and Measures. The calendar was not the only problem the Meiji government had to contend with. In traditional Japan, there was no nationwide standard for measuring distance and weight. *Ken* was a common unit of distance; but one *ken* (about six feet) could be several inches shorter or longer, depending upon the particular province in which one happened to be measuring. The Tokugawa regime permitted the use of only those measures and scales which had been officially validated, but, in practice, the law was not always followed. The need for adopting a standard measurement for the whole country was recognized by the Meiji government.

As early as 1868, the first year of the Meiji era, Lord Matsudaira of Fukui Province recommended to the government introduction of a unified measurement system which he himself had developed. In 1870 a new section was established in the Ministry of Finance to study the problem. The government scientists came up with a proposal to define one *shaku* as 1/120,000,000 of the meridian in the manner the French had perfected— basing a metric system on the distance around the earth. The idea was too revolutionary for most people. Nobody had ever heard of "meridian." People were more used to thinking of distance in terms of the length of one's arm or finger. Besides, to define the unit of distance for the sacred land of Japan in terms of the size of the barbarous globe at large seemed offensive, sacrilegious, and incompatible with the spirit of national polity. Scientists were of the opinion that science knows no borders and that, in the age of enlightenment, all civilized nations should accept a common unit of distance based upon a universal standard. But the scientists' opinion received scant notice. The legislators immediately voted down the proposal, 235 to 10.

The spirit of national polity notwithstanding, the government was badly in need of a uniform measurement system—particularly for collecting taxes, which were still paid largely in rice. In 1891 the first session of the Imperial Diet managed to pass a compromise plan that allowed the use of traditional units, *shaku* (for distance) and *kan* (for weight), while these units were determined by the metric system. Though Japan signed the international metric treaty in 1885, only in 1921 did she finally adopt the complete metric system as the official standard of measurement for the nation.

Medicine. Thanks to modern preventive medicine, acute epidemic diseases such as cholera have been removed from the daily lives of contemporary Japanese. This was not so in the 19th century. There is no record of the spread of cholera—originally a local disease along the Ganges in India—inside Japan prior to the beginning of the 19th century. Its first entry into Japan occurred in 1822; the germs presumably traveled through Korea. The second outbreak was in 1858; this time the deadly germs were brought in through the port of Nagasaki by sailors aboard the U.S. warship *Mississippi,* none other than the flagship of Commodore Perry's fleet that had come to Uraga to force the opening of Japan to the West in 1853. The disease spread with frightening speed. In major cities such as Edo, Osaka, and Kyoto, the number of those infected increased rapidly and, as a document of the period recorded, "funeral processions continued night and day." In Edo alone, 260,000 died.

This was at a time when there was no knowledge of the disease and no effective method of prevention or cure. All people could do was wait for the arrival of cool weather, when the epidemic would recede naturally. In Nagasaki there was a medical school built by the Tokugawa government. The chief instructor was a Dutch military doctor named Jonkee Johannes Lydius Catharinus Pompe van Meerdervoort—popularly known as Dr. Pompe. His only recommendation to the authorities was: "Do not eat cucumbers, watermelon, plums, apricots, peaches. Do not drink too much alcohol. Do not overwork in the daytime under the hot sun." This was the extent of preventive medicine, East or West, against cholera. Bacteriology and vaccination were still unknown even in the West. Dr. Pompe noted the stoicism of the Japanese about the disease. In 1833, when cholera spread widely through Europe, people in cities had become panic-stricken and had rushed through the streets in mass hysteria. A Russian doctor in St. Petersburg was thrown into the river by excited crowds. Mobs in Paris tossed three French doctors into the Seine. Terror was widespread in Western countries, but not in Japan. Dr. Pompe wrote, ''The Japanese face the epidemic far more calmly than the Europeans, who call themselves civilized.''

Japan was stricken by cholera for the third time in 1862. In fifty-six days, between June 16th and August 11th, 560,000 were infected. Deaths numbered 73,000 in Edo alone. In 1877, a British warship entered the port of Nagasaki; so did the cholera bacillus. This being the end of a civil war fought in Kyushu, returning soldiers brought germs to the rest of the country. Soon 8,000 people were dead. The disease continued to be a major threat during the early period of Japan's modernization: 100,000 died in 1879; 110,000 in 1886; 40,000 in 1895; 7,000 in 1916; and 3,500 in 1920. The country has been free of the scourge of cholera since 1920, except for a brief outburst that claimed 560 victims in 1946, shortly after World War II.

Because of prolonged peace during the country's isolation, Japanese doctors were totally inexperienced in the art of military medicine. When civil wars broke out between those for and against the opening of the country, in the closing years of the Tokugawa regime, both sides used guns, causing a large number of casualties that indigenous medicine could not effectively cope with. In Tokyo and Yokohama, emergency military hospitals were set up. A team of Western doctors led by William

Willis of the British Consulate took charge of surgery. Soldiers suffering from heavy wounds inflicted by swords as well as bullets were brought in. As the Western doctors performed amputations and other surgical operations, the Japanese doctors watched in awe. In Kyushu, the wounded soldiers on the die-hard conservative side were treated by Matsumoto Ryojun and other Japanese doctors who had studied Dutch medicine under Dr. Pompe.

Actually, this was not the first time Western-style operations were performed in Japan. In October, 1858, a Presbyterian medical missionary named James Curtis Hepburn came to Japan. Born in Pennsylvania in 1815, this American minister was a man of vitality and of many talents. In 1861, he opened an infirmary in Kanagawa, where he operated a free clinic for eighteen years. In 1867, he published the first English-Japanese and Japanese-English dictionaries. There were as yet no well-developed printing facilities in Japan. Copies of the dictionaries had to be printed in Shanghai at a shop managed by an American missionary group. He also devised a phonetic system for writing Japanese words with roman letters.

Hepburn was a full-fledged doctor, trained in Pennsylvania. Within five months after the opening of his infirmary, as many as 3,500 patients had consulted him. A versatile surgeon, he was particularly skilled at eye operations. His office was often packed, not only with patients but also with Japanese doctors and medical students who had traveled long distances to see him. He once treated Sawamura Tanosuke, a famous Kabuki actor, who had been attacked by gangrene. Hepburn successfully amputated the actor's whole right leg and replaced it with an artificial leg shipped all the way from the United States. Sawamura's stage comeback was the big news of the day. Not a few Japanese became convinced of the superiority of Western medicine.

In 1877, the Seinan War broke out between troops of the new Meiji government and the last remaining opposition forces. Guns were the main weapons on both sides. The number of seriously injured multiplied. The battle provided a test case for the medical corps of the government troops. When sporadic fighting had taken place toward the end of the feudal period, medical services for war casualties had been mainly rendered by Willis and other Western doctors who happened to be in Japan. Now, about a decade later, the army doctors were all Japanese. Practically every Japanese doctor who had received training in Western medicine was mobilized. Field stations to give first aid were built near the battle-grounds. Serious cases were sent to the emergency army hospital in Osaka. Surgical operations and sterilization were all performed in the Western manner. There was as yet no modern pharmaceutical industry in Japan, and an imported supply of carbolic acid, used for disinfection, ran short toward the end of the war. Still, the Japanese army doctors did well. With no help at all from their Western colleagues, they treated 6,000 wounded soldiers and performed 357 major operations.

It was not surprising that the Meiji government, determined to pattern the country's modernization on Western models, moved to have Western methods replace the Chinese medicine that had been practiced for centuries in Japan. Iwasa Jun and Aira Tomoyasu were commissioned in 1869 to study medical reforms for the government. Both had studied Dutch medicine, and their appointments were indicative of what was about to happen to the overwhelming majority of doctors who practiced Chinese healing arts.

In February, 1875, the government instituted a new medical examination system which was first put into effect in Tokyo, Osaka, and Kyoto. Those who wished to be licensed as physicians were now required to pass tests in physics, chemistry, anatomy, physiology, pathology, internal medicine, surgery, and pharmacology. The system was almost exclusively based upon the German model. This was a serious blow to the practitioners of Chinese medicine, who still outnumbered Western-style physicians. The intent of the government, however, was clear and forthright. Japan had to be modernized as quickly as possible. For this objective the medicine of the advanced West was to be adopted and the short-run pains and commotions to be ignored. The country could not afford to wait for the old system to give way slowly to the new. Once the new system was built, people's understanding and adjustment would follow.

Noble intentions aside, the government was faced with a critical shortage of doctors, and it had to make accommodations. Those who were already practicing Western medicine when the new medical examination system was introduced were granted a license without passing the tests. Over a period of transition the Chinese-style practitioners, too, were allowed to continue their profession, which the government hoped would approach extinction under the new system in two or three decades.

While in theory Western medicine became the only officially approved medicine, in practice Chinese medicine remained popular among the masses. In general, people tend to be conservative about the treatment they are willing to receive. A large number of high-ranking

officials of the government quietly continued to support
the traditional medicine, and their faith, at times, seemed
justified by events.

There was a physician of the Chinese school in Tokyo,
named Enda Toan. For many years he had been a well-
known specialist in curing beriberi, a disease which is
seldom observed in present-day Japan but was widespread in those years. Any doctor who could cure it was
bound to assure his reputation. A chamberlain in the
Ministry of the Imperial Household suffered an attack
of beriberi. He was treated by Dr. Enda, and soon recovered. When the Emperor Meiji himself was attacked
by the same disease, the chamberlain and Okubo To-
shimitsu, a famous and influential politician of the period,
tried to appoint Dr. Enda as physician to the Imperial
Household so the doctor could treat the emperor. This
was a great opportunity for physicians of the Chinese
school to roll back the trend. If one of them could be the
emperor's doctor, people would certainly regain faith
in their art. Indeed, practically all the old-fashioned
ladies-in-waiting and other aides in the royal court still
firmly supported the traditional medicine.

This development was embarrassing to those in the
government who were promoting Western medicine. As
a countermeasure, they built a beriberi research hospital. The alleged reason for opening the hospital was to
study the effectiveness of medicines prescribed by Dr.
Enda. Physicians of both Western and Chinese schools
were appointed to the hospital. People called the arrangement the "East-West beriberi wrestling match."
The trouble was, at this moment in medical history,
nobody in the world knew what caused the disease, so
one school was no better or worse than the other. With-

out knowledge of the cause neither could offer a cure. The contest ended anticlimactically, with neither school emerging as the winner or loser. The hospital was simply closed down, without fanfare, in June, 1880.

Research into the cause and cure of beriberi continued, however, under other auspices. The disease was a major problem not only for the rice-eating public but also for the Imperial Army and Navy. Every summer as much as 20 per cent of the army suffered its symptoms. The problem was worse in the navy. Every long cruise produced a large number of casualties. The warship *Ryujyo* set out on ocean navigation to Latin America and New Zealand in December, 1882. During the nine-month cruise, 169 men out of 371 aboard suffered from beriberi; 25 died. Takagi Kanehiro, a medical officer of the navy, noticed that essentially the same kinds of cruise produced different numbers of patients. If the type of cruise was not the differentiating factor, then the difference in foods served aboard the ships might offer an explanation. He proceeded to take and examine food samples whenever there were major outbreaks of the disease. Discovering that a high frequency of beriberi correlated with an unbalanced diet containing too much carbohydrate and too little animal protein, he designed a menu that left out the traditional staple, rice, and substituted bread and foods rich in animal protein. In 1885 the warship *Tsukiba* made the same long-distance cruise to Latin America and New Zealand that the *Ryujyo* had made in 1880. All members of the crew were served foods based upon Takagi's menu. This time only 15 were attacked by the disease and no one died. Takagi's experiment thus demonstrated that beriberi was a result of malnutrition.

The army ignored Takagi's discovery. Rice continued to be the main item on its menu. During the Sino-Japanese War, as many as 47,000 soldiers suffered from beriberi. Still the army did not change its dietary rules. This puzzling inaction manifested the rivalry that had already come into existence between the two branches of the Japanese armed forces. Takagi of the navy at the time was just about the only military doctor who had studied medicine in England, whereas the mainstream of Japanese medicine was of the German school. Having studied in Germany, the army doctors tended to look down on Takagi. They were of the opinion that beriberi was due to caloric deficiency. Rice contained more calories than the wheat bread served in the navy, and that was reason enough for the army doctors to stick to rice.

Beriberi was rampant among criminals held in the Kobe prison. The warden tried barley in place of rice and, lo and behold, the number of patients decreased considerably. Upon hearing the news, the army commander in charge of the district ordered a switch to barley. The number of patients among his troops also diminished. In 1885, however, when the commander made his recommendation to the central office of the army, that branch of the military turned it down on the ground of insufficient evidence.

The Russo-Japanese War broke out in 1905. The army meals still consisted mainly of rice. During the war 43,000 were killed and 167,000 wounded. Of 220,000 who became sick, half of them were victims of beriberi. These facts were hard to ignore. The army finally conceded that there was something to Takagi's theory. In 1908 the army and the medical faculty of the University of Tokyo launched a joint, full-scale research study on the causes of beriberi. The pathbreaking discovery leading to the development of a definitive treatment for the illness, however, was to be brought forth much later, not by the joint research team, but by a lone individual, Professor Suzuki Umetaro, in the agricultural department of the same university. The final proof by Suzuki that deficiency in vitamin B is the cause of beriberi was not available until 1919, and nobody in the world knew the method of manufacturing pure vitamin B before 1927.

Theories of Man and Society. On the evening of June 17th, 1877, a passenger ship entered the port of Yokohama. An American disembarked and went directly to an adjacent hotel. A night view of the city from his room, the smell of the air, the strange sounds of the language coming from the streets, the unfamiliar songs of the fishermen as they rowed their small boats home after the day's work—all these reminded the American traveler that he had come a long way from his homeland. His name was Edward Sylvester Morse, and the day of his arrival in Japan happened to be his 39th birthday. A Harvard graduate, he was a biologist with a special interest in lamp shells. In the United States he had found very few specimens of that rare species, and had decided to go to Japan upon hearing that this newly opened little country in the Far East was a paradise for shell collectors. With a Japanese assistant, he proceeded to take samples at Enoshima, on the outskirts of Tokyo. Then, on July 30th, he was visited by Professor Sotoyama Masaichi of the University of Tokyo, who had once heard a public lecture by Morse at the University of Michigan. Sotoyama asked the American to teach biology at his school. Knowing little Japanese, Morse declined the offer, but Sotoyama would not give up, assuring the foreign scientist that all the students had studied enough English to follow a lecture in that language. Morse changed his mind and accepted.

The young Japanese students who gathered in a large lecture hall of the University of Tokyo wore native trousers called *hakama,* which, to the American professor, looked more like skirts. He wrote in his diary, "I felt I was lecturing to a group of first-year coeds." His lectures were well received. Afterward the university formally asked him to become a professor of biology. Accepting the invitation, he went back to the United States and five months later returned to Japan with his family. Apparently he was good at collecting things. He brought back with him 25,000 books on biology and numerous animal samples which he had gathered during this brief stay in the United States.

As a biologist, Morse was keenly interested in Charles Darwin's theory of evolution. This was at a time when few Japanese had heard of Darwin, though his theories were stirring up fierce opposition in Western religious circles. Devastating enough from the standpoint of Christian belief had been Copernicus's idea, advanced three centuries before, that the earth moved about the sun. The Copernican cosmology had removed man's home from its favored position at the center of the universe. Now, by theorizing that men and beasts shared a common origin, Darwin and his followers seemed to be advancing the blasphemous thought that man, created in the image of God, was on a par with the monkey. The shocked religious authorities attacked Darwin and Thomas Huxley, a great follower and popularizer of the evolutionary theory, but the book-buying public reacted differently.

When Darwin's *Origin of Species* was published in England in November, 1859, a printing of 1,250 copies sold out the first day. The second printing of 3,000 copies also quickly disappeared. During the next twenty years, 16,000 copies were sold. In a short while the book was translated into numerous languages. The Japanese version, translated by Tachibana Tetsusaburo, was published in 1896.

A friend of Huxley's, Morse was a strong supporter of Darwinian ideas. At the University of Tokyo he freely incorporated the theory of evolution into his lectures on biology. During his last year of tenure at the university, he delivered a weekly series of special lectures on the theory of evolution. These lectures were transcribed into Japanese by Ishikawa Chiyomatsu and were published as a 133-page monograph in 1883.

Morse would repeatedly emphasize the importance of establishing the truth on the basis of scientifically observable facts. He openly criticized churchmen who laxly attributed to the work and will of God what was hard for men to understand in the universe. Following Huxley's example, he urged Japanese students not to listen to the voice of religion as a way of discovering the truth. Without hesitation, he told them that they and monkeys shared a common ancestry. In those days, many of the Westerners teaching at the University of Tokyo were Christian missionaries. Some of them preached to their students that the theory of evolution was total nonsense, a foolish idea worthy of no one's attention. This had the opposite of the intended effect. The Japanese students were not Christians. They did not possess a built-in prejudice against the theory. The idea that they and monkeys were relatives did not necessarily cause them spiritual anguish. The missionaries' arguments only intensified their curiosity about Darwin's earthshaking theory. When Morse delivered the first special lecture on the theory of evolution on Saturday, October 6th, 1877, the huge lecture hall was filled. The audience of 600 included students, professors, and their wives. Most of them were taking notes. Morse observed that nobody in the audience was offended, as some had been in the United States, with his sacrilegious ideas. At the end of the lecture there was a sudden outburst of enthusiastic applause. He wrote that night: "I felt heat on my cheeks."

In 1889 a big reception was held in Fujimi-cho in Tokyo, under the auspices of the Tokyo Zoological Association and the Tokyo Botanical Association, to commemorate the thirtieth anniversary of publication of *The Origin of Species*. In the front room was a portrait in oils of Charles Darwin by Harada Naojiro, one of the earliest artists to adopt the Western style of painting in Meiji Japan. On display were works by Darwin, biological samples, archeological finds, and charts and pictures illustrating the process of evolution and the principles of survival of the fittest. There was a model of the *Beagle,* the ship on which Darwin served as official naturalist for five years. Whoever made the ship model had a feeling for puns as well as a good knowledge of English. An anchor was held by a "bee" and the body of the ship was in the shape of an "eagle." The reception was attended by a hundred first-rate scholars—practically all the leading figures in all disciplines then existing in Japan.

While Morse was introducing Darwinism to the Japanese intellectual community, Ernest Francisco Fenollosa, an American philosopher and a great student of Japanese art, was teaching Herbert Spencer's theory of social evolution at the University of Tokyo. Spencer had applied Darwin's vision to the analysis of human society in general. He considered the development of human society to follow much the same pattern of natural selection as the development of species in Darwin's biological kingdom—from simple and primitive forms to complex and advanced ones. Primitive societies, like primitive organisms, "learn" to organize themselves against foreign enemies. Organization allows a concentration of power, which in turn induces industrial growth. As society becomes more industrialized and affluent, the constraints of status and class distinction begin to erode. Individuals gain greater liberty; they become more productive and capable of playing more diversified roles. As a result society moves onto a higher stage of social, economic, and political development. This neatly complements Darwin's theory that the winner of the race for biological survival moves only in an upward direction.

Spencer's theory of social evolution and Darwin's theory of biological evolution were, of course, a reflection of 19th-century English society. At that time, English science and technology were producing the fruits of material wealth, and the expansion of the British Empire seemed undeniable proof of English political supremacy. Both theories shed optimistic light on the future of the English, if not the rest of mankind. From the viewpoint of the Meiji leaders, they seemed particularly relevant to 19th-century Japan. Japan had just come out of the cocoon of feudalism. The rigid social structure had been dissolved. An age of new enlightenment had begun. It is no wonder that the Meiji leaders and the Japanese intellectuals responded to the Western theories with such enthusiasm. Between 1877 and 1897 there appeared thirty-two Japanese translations of Spencer's major works.

Darwin and Spencer suited the Meiji intellectuals in search of a new image of Japan. Even Kato Hiroyuki, the first president of the University of Tokyo and dean of Japanese academic circles at the time, became a convert. There was a peculiar twist to Kato's interpretation. He had previously been influenced by the works of Jean Jacques Rousseau, and he had once contended that all men were born with equal rights. Having read Darwin and Spencer, Kato switched to a new philosophy which leaned more toward Darwin than Spencer. Now he argued that the presence of a class system, even in a progressing society, was in accord with a certain natural law, and that some men are born more equal—stronger and fitter to survive—than others. Progressive thought and social reforms are legitimate if we assume that all men have equal rights. If we begin with the premise, however, that all men differ in their abilities, then the concept of equal rights is bound to be more illusory than real. Thus did the advanced thought that emerged in mid-19th-century England make a conservative of a scholar in a land halfway around the globe.

Kato was not the only Japanese intellectual of the time who was influenced by Darwinism to the point of accepting it not simply as a new biological theory but as the basis for a vision of contemporary social problems. Ishikawa Chiyomatsu was another example. While studying zoology at the University of Tokyo, he was profoundly moved by Morse's lectures on Darwin. Later, besides teaching biology at his alma mater, he wrote numerous popular articles on science, civilization, and social issues for the general audience. He was fond of discussing men and their society in biological terms. Cells that compose a human body correspond to individuals who make up a society. A set of cells forms an organ that serves a certain function different from those of other organs, and yet all organs of the body are interdependent. The principles of division of labor and mutual dependence, Ishikawa held, are what characterize a nation-state. In each nation there are politicians, capitalists, workers. There are those who lead an easy, affluent life as well as those who must work hard, day in and day out. The different tasks performed by all these people are all necessary for the making and maintenance of a nation. Each individual should dutifully carry out his work no matter what it is. Since people differ in ability and talent, the existence of social classes is a natural consequence of that human truth. Throughout the animal kingdom, male and female are given different roles. In the human world, men have men's roles, women, women's; it is the human way for men to live like men, for women to live like women.

One is not sure if Darwin would have agreed with Ishikawa's interpretation of his theory of evolution. Ishikawa died in Taiwan in 1935. In the latter part of his life, his writings became rather anachronistic. They always began with a tacit acceptance of the status quo and predictably ended with an apologia for it. While Ishikawa was writing, however, the winds of change were beginning to blow over the Japanese islands. The ghost of Karl Marx was already haunting Japanese capitalists. An increasing number of authors wrote in favor of equal rights for women and the underprivileged. But Ishikawa did not change his mind. Though he never read much of Marx, he was staunchly against Marxism. "From the biological standpoint," he wrote, "the idea of a classless society is sheer nonsense, a fantasy."

Still another Japanese biologist, Oka Asajiro, was sufficiently influenced by Darwin's evolutionary theory to use it as a tool of his social commentary. A prolific author, Oka wrote many texts and popular books on biology as well as numerous essays on a wide range of subjects. His popularized version of the theory of evolution, published in 1904, became a best seller.

In contrast to Ishikawa's simplistic affirmation of the status quo, Oka's interpretation of Darwinism led to a highly pessimistic conclusion. He upheld the idea of survival of the fittest. But he looked at the other side of the coin—at the loser rather than the winner in the survival race. If the fittest are to persist and prosper, the unfit are destined to suffer and perish. The theory of evolution, then, is also the theory of the expiration of the weaker. While Ishikawa drew an analogy between human society and the animal kingdom, Oka focused on the differences between men and lesser animals. In the human world, property may be inherited. This is not so among lesser animals. The bloody contest for survival is held anew for each generation of animals. Only the stronger of each generation survive, but they cannot pass their strength on to their own offspring except through the endowment of their bodily constitution. In contrast with the lesser animals, some human chil-

dren inherit huge assets from their parents, and others
none. At the starting point of the survival race, some
children are already more handicapped than others.
One wins, not necessarily because he is truly powerful,
but because of the power of his inherited wealth. Unlike lesser animals, men make things with machines and
tools, as well as with their hands and feet. Those with
machines and property can lend them and collect interest from those without. The rich get richer, the poor
poorer.

According to Oka, the fundamental causes of injustice in the human world are man's egoism and the
irrationality of the social system. He did not propose a
revolution as the cure, for man's egoism stems from human instinct, which cannot be altered by a political
revolution. Mammoths became extinct because of the
abnormal and unbalanced growth of their organs. The
widening income gaps between the rich and the poor
will eventually destroy man. This is the fate of the
human species, and there is really nothing one can do
about it. Let us abandon our hope and learn, instead,
to accept cheerfully our doom.

Unlike the days when Morse was introducing Darwinism to Japan, the turn of the century was a rather
anxious period for that country. Her fragile capitalism
was beset by periodic recessions. Farmers were plagued
by falling prices. Industries grew; so did urban poverty.
Socialism and the labor movement had already gained
a foothold. Oka's pessimism reflected the feelings of
tension and misgiving prevailing in Japan during the
early 1900s.

Mathematics. During the Edo period (1603–1868),

preceding the Meiji Restoration, members of the samurai class and motivated commoners were expected to know how to read, write, and count. Children went to temple schools privately managed by Buddhist monks, village doctors, and lordless (that is, unemployed) samurai. Instruction in the use of the abacus became common in the 18th century. During the Edo period's extended internal peace and political stability, the warriors had little to do. Swordsmanship had ceased to be the way to build their reputations. Now, talents in finance, management, and politics claimed higher priorities. Each provincial lord competed against others—not through military conflicts but by strengthening the economic position of his domain. Many samurai became merchants *de facto*. Money mattered, not the sword. Ihara Saikaku, a great novelist of the day, wrote numerous stories on his favorite theme—"In the final analysis, a man can depend only on his money."

While merchants and samurai were learning to use the abacus, Japanese mathematicians were improving their art, known as *wasan*. It originally came from China. Many texts and treatises on the subject were imported from China during the 16th century. The Edo period produced a large number of talented mathematicians who expanded the original Chinese mathematics into new fields of analysis that corresponded to algebra and geometry. *Wasan,* however, always remained a technique and art of solving particular problems. Japanese mathematicians composed for themselves problems involving a large number of shapes and objects and derived deep and leisurely pleasure from solving them. Applying their art to practical matters, such as developing an efficient method of counting in commerce, did not interest them. They were above such mundane, mercantile dealings. The abacus would suffice to do the counting. They concentrated on impractical uses of their art, finding delight in celestial numbers and abstract shapes. Answers to difficult questions were humbly presented and displayed, along with challenging problems yet unsolved, at shrines and temples that served as galleries for mathematical contests. Some mathematicians composed more problems than they could solve in their lifetimes. Before death, they published books of unsolved questions, challenging future generations to tackle them.

Japanese mathematicians did solve difficult equations and complicated problems in geometry, but they were mainly interested in finding particular techniques for answering particular questions. Unlike their counterparts in the West, they somehow paid little attention to the discovery of axioms and theorems. From the 18th century to the mid-19th century, however, mathematicians like Yasujima Chokuen, Aida Yasuaki, and Uchida Kyo began to work on common techniques to solve different problems, bringing Japanese mathematics to the point of vaguely resembling Western mathematics—though differing in notations and numerical systems—at the time of the Meiji Restoration.

Western mathematics entered Japan with Western military science in the middle of the 19th century, when the encroachments of foreign warships impelled the Tokugawa regime to build its own navy. A naval academy to train Western-style officers was founded in Nagasaki in 1855. The first generation of instructors at the academy was recruited from Holland. The Dutch naval officers gave no-nonsense instruction in Dutch on mathematics as well as navigation, oceanic surveying, and shipbuilding. They taught algebra, trigonometry, and even calculus. In 1866, the Tokugawa regime established an army academy where the first generation of officers of the modern Japanese army was trained by the French. The curriculum at the academy included Western mathematics. The Western texts were written in notations and numerical systems that were too different from those of Japanese mathematics; modification of the Japanese rules to fit the system of Western mathematics would be too cumbersome and difficult. In order to catch up with the advanced West by absorbing its military science and technology, the fruits of Japan's native mathematical studies had to be given up in their entirety.

The study of *wasan* began to diminish with the coming of Western mathematics. In 1877, when the Tokyo Mathematical Association was founded, 82 of its 114 members were of the traditional school. Western mathematics, as a basic tool of modern science and technology, was quickly gaining in popularity. The traditionalists were frowned upon for wasting their time on a useless art. One by one, the *wasan* schools in the country had to close their doors. Western mathematics was the only kind taught at the universities. When in 1884 the first class of mathematics majors was graduated from the University of Tokyo, only a handful of traditional mathematicians retained membership in the Tokyo Mathematical Association.

Despite its decline, the study of *wasan* contributed to the relative ease with which the Japanese managed to master Western scientific technology, which was invading her civilian industries as well as her military science. The Nagasaki Steel Mill, predecessor of the present Nagasaki shipbuilding complex of Mitsubishi Heavy Industries, was completed in 1861. The first shipment of 15-horsepower steam engines arrived from Holland about the same time. A modern shipyard was built in Yokohama under a French plan. The number of factories using Western machines and equipment increased rapidly, and a minimal knowledge of Western science was required for their operation and maintenance. Those employed in industry were obliged to learn Western mathematics; but because the machines built in those days were crude and simply structured, the mathematics needed to operate them was correspondingly simple. Operators trained in *wasan* discovered that the so-called Western mathematics was not totally alien to their minds. To their disappointment, Western mathematics was anticlimactically easy.

Education. In 1872, the Meiji government introduced a nationwide, unified system of compulsory education. Like the study of mathematics, the idea of public education was not unfamiliar to them. Even during the premodern period, commoners went to temple schools to learn reading, writing, and the use of the abacus. Samurai studied, as part of their expected education, Confucian ethics, political philosophy, and history at provincial schools sponsored by the local lords. The Japanese were used to education as a human activity. They were acquainted with the meaning of books, that they contained many kinds of knowledge. This may sound self-evident, but consider another cultural environment. In the premodern Islamic world, for ordinary people, ''the book'' meant the Koran—and nothing else. To the less sophisticated Moslems, the Koran represented the text of religious faith and prayer. All the truth was there. It was hard for them to conceive that there could be other books containing other sorts of knowledge.

During some three centuries of peace under the Tokugawa rulers, there was a great diffusion of printed knowledge in Japan. It is impossible to estimate how many books were printed during that time. Books were published by the Tokugawa regime, by the offices of local lords, and by private individuals as well. Catalogues, then prepared by bookstores, classified publications by subject—looking not much different from the catalogues in use today. They listed dictionaries, Chinese texts, scholarly monographs, essays, history books, novels, collections of poems, textbooks on flower arrangement and tea ceremony, manuals on the care of miniature plants (*bonsai*), handbooks on raising goldfish, and much more. The Japanese were familiar with books and what books represented. They knew that to open a book meant to open a door to new knowledge. When Dutch books came in, they experienced no critical psychological resistance to reading them. On the contrary, those strange-looking pages only aroused their curiosity about subjects they had never heard of before. After the Meiji Restoration in 1868, English, German, and French books began to arrive en masse. Those books did not overwhelm Japanese intellectuals. Rather, educated people were overwhelmed by the discovery that they had been deprived of the advanced knowledge of the West for so long.

The network of public education, instituted in 1872, was patterned after the French system. A grade school was built for every 600 people, and a middle school for a population of 130,000. The nation was divided into 8 university districts, 256 middle-school districts, and 53,760 grade-school districts. While the system itself was mainly French, the curricula were developed with the help of American advisors. Despite the long native tradition of learning, this sudden emergence of a modern system of public education caused a good deal of confusion. Counting by abacus was removed from the school curriculum; addition and subtraction were now done by paper, pencil, and memory. Japanese numerals were replaced by Arabic numbers. While maintaining the appearance of modernity, the system gravely suffered from a shortage of qualified teachers and good texts. At first, all the textbooks were either direct translations or adaptations. Of these, a physics textbook, written by Katayama Junkichi and published by the Ministry of Education, became a best seller. In 1874 alone, 95,000 copies were sold.

*

Japan was lucky to commence her modernization in the middle of the 19th century, when the European powers were rapidly expanding their colonial interests in India and Southeast Asia. (As for the United States, the vastness of the Pacific Ocean presented a formidable problem of transportation, and the western regions of the country still remained underdeveloped). From the standpoint of the European colonialists, Japan was situated too far east. Before reaching Japan, there was China, a huge untapped market. Once the outcome of the Sino-Japanese War revealed the vulnerability of China, the Western powers poured into that region, searching for opportunities to squeeze every drop of profit from it. A nation can colonize only so much at a time. China served as something of a breakwater. While the Western powers busied themselves on the Asian continent, Japan could concentrate on her own modernization and progress.

3 ✦ Date with a Virgin

*The Japanese were the most alien enemy the United
States had ever fought in an all-out struggle. In no
other war with a major foe had it been necessary to
take into account such exceedingly different habits of
acting and thinking. Like Czarist Russia before
us in 1905, we were fighting a nation fully
armed and trained which did not belong to the
Western cultural tradition. Conventions of war which
Western nations had come to accept as facts of
human nature obviously did not exist for the Japanese.
It made the war in the Pacific more than a series
of landings on island beaches, more than an
unsurpassed problem of logistics. It made it a major
problem in the nature of the enemy. We had to
understand their behavior in order to cope with it.*

—RUTH BENEDICT

There is no nation in the world which fears death less.

—FRANCESCO CARLETTI
(came to Japan in 1597)

According to one historian, during the period of 461 years from 1480 to 1941, Britain fought seventy-eight wars, France seventy-one, Germany twenty-six, and Japan nine. These figures may vary somewhat, depending upon one's definition of war, but the point is clear. Prior to the opening of the country to the West in the mid-19th century, Japan had remained remarkably pacific, relative to the European nations. Compared with the history of Europe, which is one of innumerable battles and conquests, Japanese history is like the story of a delicate flower growing in a greenhouse.

This fact—which places Japan in a unique position in world history—tends to be obscured by the more colorful and explosive events of recent decades, as Japan and the West have played adversary roles against each other. Yet Japan's performance in world power politics since the late 19th century has been amateurish in the extreme. Starting with their war with China in 1895, the Japanese began acquiring new territories from foreign states; but their expansionist dream was short-lived. In a matter of fifty years the country was rolled back to its original four islands. It was as if a pale, sheltered young man, in a fit of hysteria, had suddenly jumped into the ring to confront a giant-sized professional boxer—only to be mercilessly pounded to the floor within seconds. In other words, what is symbolized by Pearl Harbor is terribly misleading in assessing the political personality of the Japanese, a personality that has been moulded over many a century in the context of their particular history.

Even before the 15th century, Japanese pacifism was evident. Japanese rulers, many of whom were noted for their culture and learning rather than their brilliance as war strategists, built capitals in Nara as early as the 7th century, while in Europe at that time the Frankish kings kept migrating from one area to another in the course of their military conquests, rather than settling down to establish the capital of their empire. From the end of the 11th century to the latter half of the 13th century, the Europeans mobilized their resources to carry out seven rounds of crusades against heathens in the Orient and Africa. The crusaders included not only kings, feudal lords, and professional warriors, but also peasants and their young sons. Nothing of this scope has ever been attempted by the Japanese, and even when the Mongolians tried to take over their islands in the 13th century, the invasion was stopped not so much by the gallantry of the Japanese defenders as by the timely storms which destroyed most of the enemy ships.

Western civilization and culture have grown in an environment of unceasing belligerence. Living in a more or less chronic state of war over long centuries, however, did not necessarily make European minds barbarous. On the contrary, since early times, efforts were made to minimize the human cost of war. Means were devised to reduce the number of casualties, if not to abolish the wars themselves, which seemed to recur as though in compliance with some divine law. It became common practice to return prisoners of war at a price, since wars then, as now, were fought to the extent that each party believed them to be profitable. King Richard I of England was captured by an Austrian prince on his way home from a crusade. The prince handed the royal prisoner to a German king. After a year of captivity in Germany, Richard I was returned to England alive and unharmed in exchange for an exorbitant sum of money.

This was not an exceptional, isolated event in medieval Europe. Those captured enemies who could be used as hostages to collect money later from the other side were allowed to live. In 1415, during the Hundred Years War between England and France, the victorious English troops, alarmed by a false report that massive waves of French reinforcements were coming, suddenly massacred a large number of French prisoners of war. For a long time, this incident remained an object of criticism in England. The people there kept grumbling, not over the atrocity committed by their troops, but rather over the missed opportunity to collect a handsome sum from the French, which would have greatly helped deflate the cost of the protracted war.

Europeans became experienced and professional about warfare. They developed a set of rules and conventions of war that were practical and almost businesslike. War was waged to realize a net gain. Killing enemies was not an end in itself; it was a means of enhancing the profitability of war. No war was to be fought if there was little chance of winning it. In a losing battle it was sensible to surrender rather than keep fighting till no one was left.

These fundamentals in the European philosophy of war have survived through the modern period. For example, though the convention of paying for the return of the captured is extinct, the ethos of the convention persists. Each modern war produces a large number of prisoners on both sides. The captors do not butcher the captives unnecessarily or purposelessly. After the war, the captives are routinely sent back to their homelands.

This is certainly not the sort of attitude that the Japanese have developed in the course of their history.

Particularly with respect to wars against foreign states, they long remained almost totally inexperienced. No foreign barbarians had marched in en masse and ransacked their country, nor had the Japanese gone out en masse to occupy vast overseas territories. For nearly three hundred years prior to the mid-19th century, peace had prevailed inside Japan. There was a series of civil wars in earlier periods, especially from the 11th through the 13th century, but they were child's play compared with the wars that were being chronically fought on the European continent. In premodern Japanese history, peace—not war—was the norm. There developed in the Japanese mind a consciousness that a full-fledged war is something extraordinary and abnormal, something that suggests desperation, utmost gravity, and inevitable death.

The difference between Europeans and Japanese appears in their attitudes toward weapons. Surviving under circumstances of inveterate belligerence, the Europeans came to take for granted the private use and possession of weapons—especially during the premodern era when war, more often than not, meant civil war of one kind or another. To them, each individual's right to bear arms for self-defense was almost self-evident. In medieval Europe, private citizens took arms and revolted against their tyrannical lords. In Japan, it was more common for ordinary citizens to hire masterless warriors to do the job. Modern states everywhere, as they achieve a greater concentration of power, are bound to tighten control over the use of arms by private citizens. In Europe at large, however, what was banned was not the possession of arms but rather the carrying of arms in public. Commoners as well as aristocrats continued to have relatively easy access to arms. (To a large extent, the success of the French Revolution was conditioned by the fact that peasants and merchants were acquainted with weapons.)

The tradition survives to this day in the West. In France a man may own a pistol with a permit. In the United States practically anyone can casually walk into a local shop and purchase a gun, or even order one by mail. In Japan, on the other hand, it seems strange for ordinary people to carry arms around. This notion goes back at least as far as the 16th century, when the military dictator Hideyoshi successfully conducted a series of nationwide sword hunts, removing weapons from the hands of peasants and all others who were not members of the samurai class. The norm set by Hideyoshi in the late 16th century holds true for the present. In the minds of contemporary Japanese, a civilian who possessed a weapon would probably be a criminal or an underworld figure. Japanese visitors to the United States find it incomprehensible as well as frightening that in America almost anyone can acquire, without much difficulty, a pistol, an instrument specifically designed to murder another human being. The visitor's fright will be heightened when the friendly American host proudly displays his private gun collection right in the living room of his house. This is a scene one never encounters in Japan.

The Westerner's attitude toward the right to bear arms for self-defense has, of course, been closely interwoven with the Western conception of individualism and of the individual's right to resist authorities.

Even in the middle ages, the thought was not uncommon in Europe that it was perfectly legitimate and just to assassinate a tyrannical ruler. No equivalence is found in Japanese history. Japan never had a Magna Carta or a Declaration of Independence. The postwar Constitution of Japan plays up the theme of human rights for the first time in a two-thousand-year history. Yet that constitution was imposed upon the Japanese by the United States occupation authorities.

Thus, if war and the sight of weapons represented an abnormality of the human condition in the context of Japanese history, more abnormal was the idea that common people may take up arms and try to overthrow their rulers. To be sure, there were numerous revolts of all kinds. But they were, with the exception of the Christian resistance movements of the 17th century, impulsive, brief, and *ad hoc*—acts of abnormal psychology induced by starvation, the desire for revenge, and the like, rather than a way of manifesting fundamental belief in the inalienable right of individuals to resist corrupt authorities. The Japanese mind was endowed with too strong a philosophy of nonresistance and blind conformism to initiate a French Revolution.

The European continent has always been an open world. No seas have separated one kingdom from another; walls could not be built long enough to seal off threats of invasion from hostile empires. This physical setting has inevitably conditioned the geopolitics of the area and the character of Western civilization. Kings and emperors could not solve their problems unilaterally; they were impelled to calculate and act bilaterally, trilaterally, and multilaterally. Before making a move, a French king had to calculate the countermoves of an English king and a German emperor as well as the implications of his move on the position of the Church. Daughters of royal families were freely wedded to princes of other sovereign states as a means of political maneuvering. Political problems, including domestic ones, were settled on an international scale. Isolationism was not a practicable alternative by which a king could build up his power within his own land.

In contrast, Japan prior to the mid-19th century had consistently been a closed world. Practically all the major problems faced by its rulers were purely domestic in scope and nature. The presence of Chinese and Korean emperors was but dimly felt across the dense fog hanging over the Japan Sea. The only other authority the Bakufu regime had to deal with in the 17th, 18th, and 19th centuries was the politically powerless imperial court, situated in Kyoto, and it was the isolation of the country that sustained the court's longevity. If there had been, in the past, cycles of occupation by foreign powers, the court would have perished long ago.

Since early times the openness of Europe encouraged the cultivation of a European consciousness of "world" and "nation-state." In medieval Europe, popes demanded their rights as spiritual rulers of all mankind. Emperors and kings tried to claim their rights of political control over all peoples. The crusades were an expression of the ideology of global order. In the modern period, there arose the consciousness of "nation" as a reaction to the conception of world order. As early as the 17th century, attempts were made, on the basis of principles of equal rights among sovereign states, to develop the idea of international law as a way of reconciling and synthesizing the concepts of "nation" versus "world."

To the Japanese, on the other hand, "global order," "national sovereignty," and "international law" were totally unfamiliar ideas. In the political sphere everything was blurred, like a Japanese landscape covered with a gentle spring mist. The whole domain of political relations was encompassed by the catch-all term *tenka* (literally "under heaven"), which could mean universe, world, nation, empire, kingdom, province, town, district . . . or anything else "under heaven." It was with this sort of political mentality that the Bakufu officials received the representatives of Western powers in the early 19th century. The ease with which the Bakufu officials signed unequal treaties astonished the Westerners. This was to be expected, however. Those Japanese officials had no idea what they were doing.

If *tenka* was the all-inclusive sphere of political relations, what then was the ideology by which the Japanese managed to develop a sense of social cohesion, a fundamental conception of themselves as a nation? In old Japan, especially following the medieval period, allusions to "family" became frequent in explanations of the logic of political organization. Many theorists argued that the relationship between the lord and his subjects is like that between parent and child. In both cases, the two are irrevocably tied together by reciprocity. The lord treats his subjects as parents treat their children. The subjects revere the lord as children revere their parents. Loyalty to the lord is but an extension of filial piety. The two constitute one entity of a nation-family. They are stuck to each other like Siamese twins and rise or fall together. What is good for the lord is also good for the people. Moreover, since a well-to-do child would never allow his aging parents to go hungry, the welfare of the subjects determines the welfare of the lord.

All these arguments are based on an interesting analogy, but analogy should not be confused with theory or a rational explanation of human truth. The idea of "family" was brought into the sphere of political organization, and the resulting concept of "nation-family," illogical and unsatisfactory as it was, was just about the only quasi-ideological basis upon which the Japanese developed their self-image as members of one nation. Their history had not provided much room for the nourishing of social and civic consciousness. Their culture was not conducive to the delineation of things in life with precision and consistency. While Westerners long ago came to cultivate a clear conception concerning the distinct relationships between "individual," "citizen," "nation," and "world," all these ideas, in traditional Japan, were thrown into one pot and mingled in an indistinguishable mould called "family."

Japanese family consciousness has always been integrated with the cult of ancestor worship. The "we" feeling extends not only to present family members living together under the same roof, but also to generations of long-dead ancestors. In Japan as well as in Europe, ancestor worship was a form of ancient folk religion. In the West, it began to wane with the coming of Christianity. In Japan, on the other hand, all the Buddhist sects, except Shinshu, incorporated ancestor worship into their dogmas and conventions. It became a firmly established ritual. Souls of the deceased stayed on in this world, protecting present members of the family. Each household maintained a family memorial tablet from which the long dead continued to watch their living descendants, night and day.

The agrarian economy of the country helped to sustain the cult of ancestor worship. In traditional Japan, commerce never became a predominant form of industry, relative to agriculture. (For a long time, the only coins circulating in Japan had been those imported from China. Only toward the end of the 16th century did Japanese-made coins begin to circulate for the first time.) Agriculture encourages a conservative mode of living. It is safe to follow the old way, tested over many centuries. Acts of adventure and innovation are prone to fail, though steady, hard work does not necessarily bring fortune. Conspicuous consumption is a cardinal sin, and parsimony becomes not so much a virtue as the only means of survival. Agrarian society thus nurtures a passive, tradition-oriented personality receptive to the idea of ancestor worship.

In contrast, the openness of the European continent led to the rise and expansion of trade in the West much sooner than in Japan. Commerce demands boldness. Especially in the age of primitive technology, trading, to a large extent, was a matter of speculation and adventure. There was little chance of success for those who could not take risks. The traders had to make daring decisions—though there was no assurance that fortune would smile on them. In order to succeed, they were required to think for themselves and to do what no one had done before. The cult of ancestor worship, which did flourish in Europe in the distant past, began to wane, for it ceased to be compatible with the emerging individualism of entrepreneurs who had learned to think rationally, independently, and logically, and to analyze and explain things with clarity.

The development of Western philosophy has been strongly conditioned by Aristotelian logic. According to the Western mode of thinking, things must be classified, understood, and judged in terms of premises and principles. Analysis is made within the framework of dichotomy: water is either hot or cold; an act is either right or wrong; a proposition is either relevant or irrelevant; an interpretation is either correct or incorrect; a convention is either good or bad; a dogma is either acceptable or unacceptable. This dichotomous way of seeing things has implanted in the Western mind an attitude of confrontation that demands a clear-cut solution to each and every problem in life, an attitude that expects nothing to be left ambiguous and without a logical explanation. The intensity of the Europeans' religious controversies—to say nothing of the bloodiness of their religious wars—is not encountered in Japanese history. The attitude of confrontation also breeds an intellectual stance that is aggressive, harsh, and intolerant of other viewpoints. You confront because you know you are right and superior to your opponent. You insist that the right and the superior will triumph, and the wrong and the inferior will be vanquished. Without such an intellectual stance, the crusades or the more recent expansion of Western civilization into the non-Western world would not have occurred.

The Japanese mode of thinking has been of a different variety. Buddhism, which originated in India and reached Japan via China and Korea, continued absorbing elements of native cults instead of rejecting and replacing them. Buddhism and the indigenous Shinto religion have always coexisted in Japan. A doctrinal synthesis of the two has often been made. Between them there has been no fundamental confrontation analogous to the conflicts between the Catholic Church and Protestantism in European history. Such a tradition of peaceful coexistence has survived into the present age.

In contemporary Japan you see the same people celebrating the birth of a child at a Shinto shrine and attending a Buddhist funeral for a dead parent. They are not manifesting any remarkable spirit of religious tolerance that might finally have been achieved after long, hard controversy. They attend both the Shinto shrine and the Buddhist temple because that is the way it has always been. The Japanese have preferred the intuitive, the emotional, the all-inclusive to the rational, the logical, the dichotomous. If it is not strange for a man to have two eyes instead of one, then—they might say— there is nothing strange about his following two religions.

Rice has been a staple in the diet of the Japanese since the early Yayoi period (200 B.C.–A.D. 250), and this fact has much bearing on the formation of their character. Unlike wheat, rice production requires hard, steady, meticulous care. Historically, Japanese farming has been more like gardening. Farmers were driven to work around-the-clock—from seeding, planting, and irrigation to weeding, drying of the land, and harvesting. Rice growing was peculiarly suited to family farming; family members tended the rice paddies together and in close cooperation with one another. Thanks to the intensive method of cultivation, rice yield per acre of land was much greater than that of wheat in European agriculture. The rich yield helped sustain a high population density within a relatively small mass of land—which in turn enabled the Japanese rulers to hold effective political control over their subjects. The island economy remained more or less self-sufficient. The Japanese became inward-looking, and their economic self-sufficiency made it unnecessary for them to invade foreign lands in search of new food supplies.

The Japanese diet had been basically vegetarian until the Westerners came in the 19th century. In the early years of encounter with them, the Japanese were frightened to death at the sight of the bottles of red wine carried by the Westerners. They thought that the newly arrived barbarians were drinking the blood of some animal, or possibly even human blood. Sukiyaki (thinly sliced beef and vegetables cooked with soy sauce and sugar), which every foreigner would think of as a traditional Japanese dish, cannot really be described as such. In traditional Japan, eating beef was a taboo.

The development of European agriculture followed a different path. Wheat became a popular staple but its yield per unit of land was small. To sustain a given population, a much larger area had to be cultivated than in Japan. People tended to be dispersed over greater distances—which made it difficult for European rulers to control their territories. Periodically, critical shortages of food drove one group to invade another.

Since early times the Europeans had supplemented their wheat-based diet with meat. They readily slaughtered their cows. There was no contradiction in loving animals that helped them in farming, and then killing the same animals to consume their meat. Nowhere in the Christian doctrine was it suggested that a cow a man was about to butcher might possibly be an incarnation of his ancestor. On the contrary, the Church's teachings made everything perfectly clear. Only human beings were the children of God; all other animals on earth existed to serve the needs of men. The sight of blood became an integral part of life. The meat-eating Europeans developed a certain toughness that the vegetarian Japanese lacked. In traditional Japan, the people's reaction to blood was qualitatively different. It represented something abnormal and terrifying. When animals had to be killed for skinning, the task was usually left to outcasts. In Europe, the first autopsy was performed in the 16th century. Two centuries later the first autopsy was *observed* in Japan by Yamawaki Toyo and Sugita Gempaku. The body was cut open by a specially hired outcast because the two men were too scared to do it for themselves.

The personality of the Japanese, nurtured through centuries, is essentially more feminine than masculine. It leans toward passivity, conformism, intuition, pacifism, collective welfare. In contrast, the European mind is more masculine and forthright; it demands autonomy and distinctiveness of thought, and it embodies the spirit of resistance, the will to win and conquer.

It takes the masculine personality to view and approach women as a group apart from men. In Europe, there has been a lingering theme that womanhood symbolizes what is beautiful, mysterious, and sacred in life. At one point in history, it took the form of deification of womankind, in the figure of the Virgin Mary, and led to the worship of women by medieval knights. No comparable examples are found in Japanese history. The things the Japanese have loved and understood most deeply were neither feminine nor masculine; rather, they were neutral objects. The sight of the moon, the shape of a mountain, the color of a rock, the design of pebbles, the sound of crickets touch the Japanese heart. The notion of "opposite sex" in the Western sense has always been vague, and coeducational public bathing used to be common—till 19th-century Westerners reminded the islanders that the practice was a sign of barbarism. In Japan, homosexuality has been viewed merely as an oddity, if not fully accepted as an honorable tradition.

The confrontation of Western powers with Japan in the 19th century was like a date between a tall, aggressive, mature man and a small, fragile, inexperienced virgin who has hardly stepped out of her parents' home all her tender years. The analogy was made by a magistrate of Shimoda city when Townsend Harris, first United States consul in Japan, was pressuring local officials on matters of treaty agreements. In the name of international conventions, Harris bombarded them with technical questions and demanded immediate straight answers. In desperation, Inoue Shinanokami, first magistrate of Shimoda, told him: "Please go easy on us. Japan is an innocent maiden who has led a quiet, cloistered life. She means well but it'll take her some time to learn to act like a professional geisha."

If the subject of international jurisprudence was esoteric in 19th-century Japan, so was just about everything else the Westerners brought with them. The Japanese showed keen interest in the material aspects of Western civilization but failed to see that Western science and technology, as well as the political, economic, and social systems of the West, had a common origin in a rationalistic spirit traceable to ancient Greece. They noted the supreme importance of Christianity as a foundation for the spiritual unification of the Western world; yet they were unable to see that the tenacity of Western rationalism was strengthened by centuries of bloody struggle against the authoritarianism of the Church. Nor did they quite understand that from the standpoint of the Western conception of man's existence there was no contradiction between rationalism as embodied in science and social institutions, on the one hand, and Christian irrationalism as it was concerned with the problems of man's soul, on the other.

The Japanese did not know what to make of the complex of Western influences flooding their country. Sakuma Shozan, one of the most brilliant minds of the day, managed to go only so far as to suggest a vague synthesis of "Eastern philosophy" and "Western science." In the early years of modernization, the writings of Jeremy Bentham and John Stuart Mill gained wide popularity among educated Japanese. The moderate philosophy of these Western thinkers, however, defined the limits of the liberal movement in Japan. Even Jean Jacques Rousseau was too radical and controversial to suit Japanese tastes. Rousseau's idea that all men have equal rights and that the state is based on a social contract between the authorities and the people sounded subversive to the political leaders of the Meiji era. Despite their admiration for things Western, they were not quite ready to swallow such a dangerous thought. The Meiji Constitution of Imperial Japan, promulgated in 1889, contained little trace of liberal philosophy concerning the rights of the people.

Rejection of Rousseau's philosophy did not mean advocacy of a return to isolationism. On the contrary, Japanese intellectuals showed insatiable curiosity about all aspects of Western civilization. They noted particularly that Christianity not only coexisted in peace with Western rationalism but also continued to exert a great, stabilizing influence over the soul of Western man. In their attempt to make sense out of the mystery of the West, some Japanese hypothesized that the Christian religion itself contributed to the strength of Western rationalism. Not a few theoreticians urged that Japan be Christianized, not necessarily to bring the gospel truth to the people but, instead, to help with the country's modernization—which in the context of the time was indistinguishable from its Westernization.

The idea of Christianization, however, was a little too far-fetched. The Japanese—who felt uncomfortable enough with Rousseau—were still more ill at ease with Jesus Christ. Still, they could not rid themselves of the notion that the expansion of Western civilization had something to do with Christianity. If it was not feasible to transplant Christianity to the alien soil of Japan as an instrument of modernization, they wondered whether they should perhaps look for a substitute. Nishimura Shigeki was among those who advocated the substitution of the imperial court of Japan for Christianity. He felt that Confucianism, once a standard of morality in Japan, was no longer powerful enough to be counted on for that purpose, and contended that, since European countries upheld Christianity as a way of unifying people's hearts, the Japanese could forgo the necessity of finding a religion to serve the purpose by letting the people concentrate their minds on the emperor and the imperial court, objects of awe and reverence from time immemorial. A student of Western civilization and a high official in the Ministry of Education, Nishimura was anything but a reactionary.

Having rejected Rousseau and Christ, the Japanese leaders moved on to build up the cult of the emperor. To do so at that time was not so easy as it might seem today. Shinto as an organized national religion hardly existed when Japan's feudal era ended in the mid-19th century. Both Shinto and Buddhism, while coexisting in peace, lacked dynamism and vitality. It was only in the remote past that the emperor had been a god as well as a political ruler in fact. Ever since, he had remained no more than a symbolic figure. There was no ready-made basis upon which the cult of the emperor could be promoted.

In search of an effective ideological foundation for the cult, Japanese leaders turned to the traditional family consciousness of the people. The doctrine of nation-family was expanded and strengthened. Filial piety was identified with loyalty to the emperor. All Japanese became children of the emperor, and the cult of ancestor worship was integrated with that of emperor worship. The people were told that in the beginning of their history their ancestors all came from the imperial family that founded the nation, and, therefore, the emperor's family was the family of all families in Japan. Shinto, the native religion that had always incorporated ancestor worship in its doctrine, was uplifted to the status of a new national religion. The emperor was resurrected as *arahitogami* (man-god), a god in the figure of a man. The nation was said to be something of an organism. The emperor represented the mind, the people the arms and legs. Unless the arms and legs followed the dictates of the mind, the nation, like a human body, would be paralyzed. Therefore, went the argument, it was imperative for the people to obey the orders of the emperor.

Interestingly, many of those Japanese intellectuals who argued in favor of emperor worship as a medium of national unification also insisted that it was not to be confused with a religion. Nishimura Shigeki and Ito Hirobumi, the two outspoken members of this group, knew what freedom of religion meant and how it had come about in the West. It was too awkward for them to maintain that, while Japan was adopting Western principles of rationalism in modernizing the country, such an irrational practice as emperor worship should be made into a new state religion. They pointed out that Japan was trying to establish a new political system in accordance with the Western model, which provided no room for a fusion of politics with religion, and that the government had no authority to designate an official religion. But there were others who found this view too Western to be acceptable, and the issue was dissolved in a peculiar manner by mixing the two schools of thought. The Meiji Constitution avoided the question of state religion, whereas the Imperial Edict on Education (1890), which set the course of education in the decades to follow, installed the cult of emperor worship at the newly defined center of spiritual unity of the Japanese people.

There was a Japanese twist even in the system of public schools that the Meiji government built. The idea was imported from the West. On the surface, primary schools were even more democratic than their Western counterparts. Children from all backgrounds sat at similar desks in similar classrooms. No child who wanted to go to high school was discriminated against on the basis of his family's class. They were all equal children of the emperor. What they were taught, however, had little to do with democracy. They received a thorough and intensive indoctrination in the new nationalism of Imperial Japan. They bowed to the holy picture of the emperor hanging on the wall. They were taught to revere their parents, ancestors, and, most of all, the divine emperor. They recited the Imperial Edict on

Education, written in archaic Japanese which few of them comprehended. They celebrated the newly instituted Empire Day, the Emperor's Birthday, and other such holidays. They learned that they were going to be privileged citizens of the only divine country in the world. In the official history of the divine Japan that they studied, mythology was indistinguishable from fact. They traveled in groups to the Imperial Palace and the Ise Shrine, where the souls of past emperors lay. In short, they were brainwashed to become homogenized members of one nation indivisible under the imperial throne.

All the teachers at public schools were products of public teachers' colleges where students received intensive instruction in the ideology of the new nationalism. Those who did not go to a public teachers' college— including graduates of imperial universities—could qualify only as substitute teachers. Curricula at high schools and universities were relatively free of ideological biases; everyone reaching these higher levels of education, however, had already gone through several rounds of brainwashing.

While public schools were turned into hotbeds of the new nationalism, the army and navy were destined to become bastions of the cult of emperor worship. In the early years of the Meiji period, however, the government's attempt to build a modern military system had encountered many difficulties. After all, the country had seldom faced major battles with foreign states. Most Japanese were alarmed at the idea of establishing national armed forces that every man was required to join. The first conscription decree, issued in 1873, was full of loopholes and exemption clauses. Still, it stirred up

massive opposition from all corners. Many former samurai, still clinging to the notion that theirs was the
only class authorized to bear arms, considered it humiliating and degrading to fight alongside members of the
lesser classes. Farmers preferred ploughshares to guns.
Throughout the country there were numerous riots by
peasants who disapproved of the decree.

The Meiji government met the protests with a hard-
line response. It mobilized the loyal former samurai
and sent them to suppress anticonscription groups by
force. It eliminated escape clauses one by one from the
original decree. By 1889, the principles of universal
conscription had been firmly established. Army and
navy officers were trained at academies that were totally segregated from the mainstream of higher education. Besides training in war technology, cadets were
given massive doses of indoctrination in the cult of
emperor worship and the ideology of Japanese imperialism. In all cases, the sense of duty and subordination
was emphasized. At all times, criticism and independent
thought were cardinal sins.

Consciously or otherwise, the government made the
military establishment into an insulated world, in which
little room was provided for intellectualism or rationalism. University students were given draft exemptions
until graduation. After graduation, there was little
chance of being drafted in peacetime. Those with higher
education had to serve for only one year instead of the
regular two years. Slowly but surely, the military
establishment was turning into a monster with a small
brain and powerful reflexes. The creators of the establishment failed to foresee that the monster would eventually go berserk and bring the whole nation to ruin.

By 1930 the trend toward militarism in Japan had become seemingly irreversible. After winning the Sino-Japanese War in 1895 and the Russo-Japanese War in 1905, Japan was deceived into thinking that war always pays. This false vision was only fortified by the windfall profits reaped from World War I. Not a few Japanese began to believe that they really were the chosen people, under divine protection. Arrogance drove the militarists to launch an armed aggression into Manchuria in 1931, allegedly to solve the problems of overpopulation and economic stagnation in the homeland. The League of Nations almost unanimously voted to denounce Japan, which withdrew from the league in 1933. A deepening sense of isolation in the world encouraged irrational thought patterns. Like a stepchild rejected by everyone, Japan was led to believe that the rest of the world was out to get her, and she had only herself to count on. An atmosphere of crisis was mounting.

Nationalism was gathering more and more elements of fanaticism, and irrationalism was becoming the norm of the day. In 1936 a group of young ultranationalist officers in the army instigated an abortive coup d'etat, assassinating a large number of high-ranking officials in government and business. By overthrowing the corrupt government, they would presumably save the country from stagnation and social disorder. What if the young army officers' plot had succeeded? The only blueprint for a new Japan was a sketch of vague slogans such as ''establishment of a military regime,'' ''abolition of the Diet,'' ''negation of capitalism,'' ''return of all industrial rights to the emperor,'' ''emphasis on agriculture,'' and ''more military expansion in Manchuria and the rest of Asia.'' In 1935, a school principal in Yamaguchi prefecture had been burned to death while trying to rescue a photo of the emperor and a copy of the Imperial Edict on Education from the burning school building. Instead of ridiculing his folly, the nation had enthusiastically honored the dead principal for his heroism. In that year, too, Professor Minobe Tatsukichi, a prominent scholar of the Meiji Constitution who held that the rights of governance belonged to the state rather than to the emperor, was purged from his office for being too reactionary. Communists and socialists were everywhere arrested by the secret police. What happened after the arrests illustrates the strength of traditional family consciousness, compared with imported leftist ideology: many of the prisoners easily changed ideologies after a brief, face-to-face appeal from a family member.

Ancestor worship—once a primitive folk religion, later synthesized into the emperor cult by the Meiji political leaders—began to transform itself into something of a world religion. The fanatical believers in the divine destiny of Japan were no longer satisfied with the idea that their emperor was a god of their nation alone. Since there could not be more than one true god in the world, their true god might as well be the god of all mankind. The ambition of imperialism became inseparable from the motive of saving the souls of less-fortunate peoples by spreading the veritable teaching of Japan's national religion.

The Japanese invasion of the Chinese mainland, euphemistically described then as the ''China Incident,'' started in 1937. The ''spiritual mobilization of all people of Japan'' was the slogan of the day. In 1938 the government pronounced the "Declaration for Establishing a New Order in Asia"—demanding that Manchuria and China be included within the sphere of Japanese influence. Two years later, the government came up with a more ambitious plan for a "Greater East-Asia Co-Prosperity Sphere" that included all of Southeast Asia as well.

Manchuria was made into a sister state subordinate to the divine state of Japan. The Emperor Fugi of the puppet regime was forced to practice Shinto as the official religion of the newly born Manchurian empire. A branch of the Ise Shrine was built in Shinkyo, the capital. It was not easy to define the status of the Emperor Fugi. There was considerable controversy as to whether he was a god, a semigod, a man-god, or merely a man with the imperial title. Kume Masao, a noted author who was sent to report on the tenth anniversary of the founding of the Manchurian Empire, outraged the Japanese fanatics because he used the expression *arahitogami* (man-god) in describing Fugi, whereas this expression was supposed to be employed only in reference to the Japanese emperor. Kume learned his lesson: there might be numerous emperors on earth, but divinity was embodied only in the Japanese emperor. When Japan had engaged in wars with China and Russia around the turn of the century, her declaration of war in both cases carefully stipulated that war was to be fought "within the bounds of international law." Such a clause was conspicuously missing from her Declaration of the Pacific War in 1941. International law presupposes equal rights for all sovereign states, but according to the theory of the divine mission of the Japanese Empire, all other states were less equal than

Japan; hence, insertion of the clause was presumably neither necessary nor relevant.

War is fought with guns and tanks. Ideology and faith may help but they are not sufficient. By 1940 the Imperial Army and Navy of Japan had grown to monstrous size, relative to the size of her economy. They comprised thoroughly conditioned and well-trained soldiers; yet the overall mentality of their leaders was fanatic and extremely irrational. The rifles Japanese soldiers carried during the Pacific War were Model–38s, designed in the 38th year of the Meiji era, or 1905. For a period of forty years there had been no model change whatsoever. Although their weapons were generally inferior to those of the Western powers, the Japanese militarists contended that the spiritualism of the East would win over the materialism of the West. In other words, defects in their armaments could be more than offset by the valor of their fighting men. Of course, there were some among the top military strategists—especially within the Imperial Navy—who were aware of the limits of Japan's war capability on the basis of rational analyses of the information then available. But so stridently hysterical was the mood of the country that they could not, and did not, voice their opinions openly. General Tojo Hideki, the wartime prime minister, used to say, ''There are moments in life when a man has to close his eyes and jump from the stage of Kiyomizu Temple.'' The stage of the temple, located in Kyoto, is forty-three feet above ground. There is no record indicating whether the general really jumped from the stage to test the wisdom of his aphorism. He did push the whole nation into a great war, in the total absence of a rational calculus of the prospect of victory.

The war, of course, was a disaster. Thanks to the unpreparedness of the other side, Japan made rapid progress at first. Once the United States recovered from the shock of Pearl Harbor and readied herself for the real fight, however, the two were no match at all. During the war, the Imperial Army and Navy mobilized 10 million men. By the end of the war, 2 million were dead or missing. In contrast, the United States lost only 300,000 men. Many of the Japanese casualties were not war dead in the strict sense of the term. In Burma, of 30,000 soldiers, only 10,000 came back alive; most of the remaining 20,000 died not in fighting but of starvation or illnesses in the Burmese jungle.

While thousands of young Japanese were being slaughtered in the Pacific, ultranationalism in the homeland was increasing in intensity. Even after B-29 air raids had become a daily routine, the myth of Japanese invincibility continued to be intoned as an article of faith. The logic of illogicality was reaching its zenith. People used to say, "To lose a war means to surrender. Since we are never going to surrender, there will be no defeat." Predictable was the commencement of the Kamikaze (Divine Wind) strategy, suicide dives by pilots who flew to enemy ships with bombs but no fuel for a return trip. At first, 27 per cent of the Kamikaze planes managed to hit their targets. In the Okinawa theater of war, the rate was 15 per cent. When hostilities ended in August, 1945, a young Japanese girl wrote in her diary: "I did not know that war is something that can be stopped."

The Pacific War was a nightmare. Its human and material costs were horrendous. It was also a perplexing event in the light of Japanese history. A harmless folk religion for centuries, ancestor worship metamorphosed itself into the cult of emperor worship in reaction to the influx of Western civilization in the 19th century. The cult quickly developed the characteristics of an aggressive monotheistic religion. In a short time, it not only became powerful enough to silence all the voices of reason within Japan but also became fanatical enough to contemplate bringing the rest of the world under its hegemony. If anything, this was a strange replica of the past aggressiveness of Christianity—almost a grotesque Westernization of the native cult. And the ultranationalists who advanced the idea of Japanizing the world were those who hated the West.

Modern rationalism—which Japan tried to learn from the West in the 19th century—originally sprang from Europe's continuing confrontations with the dogmatism of the Church. Unlike the devotees of the Emperor cult, who quickly picked up the aggressiveness of the West, however, rationalists in Japan somehow did not cultivate sufficient fortitude to confront and overcome the cult's growing dogmatism. On the contrary, in the era of collective insanity, rationalism and irrationalism blended together. Hashida Kunihiko, for example, a first-rate biologist and minister of education in the wartime Tojo cabinet, proposed a Japanistic science that would synthesize science, religion, and morality. The Pacific War, as it were, was the delayed explosive conclusion of the profound cultural shock Japan experienced as a result of the confrontation with Western civilization in the 19th century. For better or worse, Japan attempted to modernize herself by copying the West. The historical personalities of the two, however, were not necessarily compatible, and the incompatibility caused tension, which eventually led to mass hysteria. It was as if the body of a frail woman had rejected violently the alien protein incautiously injected into her bloodstream.

Japan has experienced two reforms of major proportions during the past century. The first one, the Meiji reform which began in 1868, was an engagement between feminine, passive Japan and the masculine, aggressive West. The reform occurred as a reaction to pressure from the Western powers. Japan was compelled to strip off her old familiar attire of feudalism and switch to a new, unfamiliar robe of Western design with uncomfortable edges. The second major reform took place during the occupation of Japan, following the Pacific War. It was her second date with the West in her modern century. The victorious Americans marching into Japan were struck by the total personality change of the Japanese. Yesterday's fanatical warriors had suddenly fallen into sheeplike passivity and were ready to subjugate themselves to the will of the foreign conquerors.

Most Americans failed to see that what had happened was not so much a case of personality change as the resumption of an earlier historical personality now that the days of mass hysteria were over. Amidst the unprecedented national crisis, the Japanese themselves were too bewildered to understand what was happening. The huge mythological tower of divine Japan had crumbled. The cult of the emperor had suffered a mortal blow. In September, 1945, Emperor Hirohito paid a personal visit to General MacArthur, the supreme commander of the allied forces, and the next day's newspapers carried a photo of the two men standing next to each other. It gave a profound shock to the Japanese.

What they saw bore little resemblance to the godlike emperor they had imagined. Hirohito the divine stood there—looking small, awkward, apprehensive, and even provincial—beside the towering figure of the American general. In January, 1946, Hirohito went on the air to make a declaration of his humanness; he told his people that the idea that he was a god destined to rule not only Japan but also the whole world was empty and misguided.

The emperor cult perished along with the Japanese Empire in 1945. Yet the emperor system survived. Most of the occupying allied powers were in favor of abolishing the system altogether, and General MacArthur, as the supreme commander of all the occupation forces, could easily have abrogated it if he had so desired. He did not—because he believed that the emperor was worth twenty divisions of security troops; without him the whole country would be thrown into chaos. General MacArthur's belief was based upon a sound assessment of the Japanese mind. Despite the nightmare from which they had just awakened, practically all Japanese favored the preservation of the emperor system. The Communist party was just about the only group that openly advocated its termination. While deification of the emperor was futile as a means by which the Japanese militarists could realize their fanatical dreams, the fact remains that the emperor did let himself personify a cult which drove the entire nation down a suicidal course. If it takes an extraordinary circumstance to carry out an extraordinary transformation of major institutions in a country, the end of the Pacific War provided just such an opportune moment. The Japanese had a chance then to destroy the emperor system (if not the emperor himself) as an institution which had caused them untold misery. But nothing of the sort occurred. Unlike the French, the Japanese lacked the firmness to overthrow an established regime by bloody revolution. They had lived with the emperor system, in one form or another, since the very beginning of their history. Without it, they could not quite imagine themselves.

A vivid sign of Japan's return to her original historical personality has been her attitude toward war and peace since the shock of the Pacific War. She fought a full-fledged total war for the first time in her 2,000-year history, and suffered a full-fledged total defeat, also for the first time. That was enough to revive her traditional sentiment that war is deadly and abnormal. The wartime hysteria was followed by militant and emotional pacifism. Since then, categorical denial of war has been mixed with obsessive advocacy of peace. Few people ask if prayer and slogans suffice to achieve eternal peace. All wars have become evil and immoral, any peace good and desirable. The postwar Constitution of Japan, promulgated in 1946, made a declaration of a sort unheard of in the history of nations. Article 9 of the constitution states: ''Aspiring sincerely to an international peace based on justice and order, the Japanese people forever renounce war as a sovereign right of the nation and the threat or use of force as means of settling international disputes. In order to accomplish (this) aim, . . . land, sea, and air forces, as well as other war potential, will never be maintained. The right of belligerency of the state will not be recognized.''

The truth of the matter is, the Japanese government, under pressure from the United States, began rearmament during the occupation period, and Japanese ''land, sea, and air forces'' have been steadily growing ever since. The people have been torn between the ultra-idealism of Article 9, which suits their traditional sentiment, and the dictates of political reality. The pull of war-phobia, if not pure pacifism, has been strong. The ''land, sea, and air forces'' of postwar Japan are still called ''defense forces.'' Article 9 has been a taboo: no politician dares to suggest revision of the article, whereas everyone more or less agrees that Japan's ''defense forces'' are unconstitutional.

4 ✦ Law and Order

Always respect the Constitution and observe the laws; should emergency arise, offer yourselves courageously to the State; and thus guard and maintain the prosperity of Our Imperial Throne coeval with heaven and earth. So shall ye not only be Our good and faithful subjects, but render illustrious the best traditions of your forefathers.

—EMPEROR MEIJI
October 30, 1890

In Japan very few things can be done which escape the minute vigilance exercised by the authorities of their cities.

—FRANCESCO CARLETTI
(came to Japan in 1597)

Except for the constitution and the criminal code, the basic structure of the Japanese legal system as it exists today is approximately a hundred years old. The modern legal codes were drafted and brought into force during the last decade of the 19th century. This was not quite so simple as it might sound. In the late 19th century, the Meiji government was determined to introduce modern laws as quickly as possible as part of the building of a new Japan. In the context of the time, "modern" meant "Western." Those laws which had operated under the Tokugawa regime were too feudal, arbitrary, and illogical to be accepted. It was natural for the Japanese government to borrow the cumulated technical knowledge from the West. Doing so, however, was far from easy. Japanese college students of today can casually walk into any bookstore in Japan and easily acquire all sorts of dictionaries—English, French, German, Italian, Russian, general or technical. In the mid-19th century, there hardly existed definitive dictionaries that Japanese legal scholars could use for translating European languages into Japanese. They had to start from scratch, understanding and digesting not only the technical legal language of the West, but associated concepts reflecting an alien philosophy and tradition. A large number of new words had to be invented simply because the traditional Japanese language offered no equivalents.

By any standard, the legal scholars charged with the drafting of the modern legal codes were a brilliant lot. The Meiji Constitution was introduced in 1889. The five major codes came into being within a span of less than a decade (1890–1898). These codes were not abridged, haphazardly written patchworks. Copied and adapted mainly from the German and French laws, the codes that the Japanese experts completed were voluminous, systematic, comprehensive, and meticulously detailed. The Meiji Constitution contained 76 articles; the Civil Code 1,046; the Commercial Code 689; the Criminal Code 264; the Civil Procedure Code

805; and the Criminal Procedure Code 334. Even with the aid of foreign legal experts, it was a herculean task.

If the speed at which these codes were written was astounding, no less astounding was the motive behind the achievement. They were drafted and promulgated with amazing rapidity, not so much because the Japanese, autonomously and spontaneously, came to believe in the legal system that had grown out of the European tradition, but because it was a matter of political necessity in the face of the encroaching Western powers, a political means of saving the nation's "face."

In June, 1858, Japan had signed the Ansei commercial treaty with the United States, Holland, Russia, Great Britain, and France. The treaty opened the ports of Kanagawa, Nagasaki, Niigata, and Hyogo. It was a very explicitly unequal treaty in favor of the Western signatories. Under its provisions, all the Western parties maintained extraterritorial jurisdictions in Japan. Great Britain and France claimed the right to station their armed troops in Japan, and the treaty did not give Japan the right to determine her own rates of import duty. The Western argument was a familiar one. Japan then was a backward country, and equal treaty rights could be exchanged only when both parties were equal. The Western powers were not suggesting that Japan was permanently incapable of building a modern state or was forever doomed to an inferior status. When Japan fulfilled the necessary requirements, the elements of inequality would be removed.

To the Japanese, this was a humiliating experience. Their sense of pride and national heritage was badly hurt. They were labelled backward because their traditional systems were not Western. They wanted to kick out the foreign barbarians, but the Western powers had powerful guns for which Japanese firearms were no match. It became a national obsession to accelerate the framing of a modern legal, political, and economic system—minimal requirements of a modern state. This had to be done quickly to wipe from the face of the country the disgrace of being a *de facto* colony. Throughout the Meiji era (1868–1912), repealing the Western powers' extraterritorial rights remained one of the country's deepest concerns. In 1894, Great Britain gave in. By 1911, the last year of the Meiji era, all the extraterritorial jurisdictions claimed by the Western powers had been eradicated from the books.

The modern statutes of Japan were thus created as stepchildren of 19th-century Western imperialism. When one reads the Meiji legal codes alone, they give the impression that Japan in the late 19th century was a highly advanced capitalistic society. Of course, nothing was farther from the truth. The Meiji codes were a façade, a surface ornament affected in a poignant pretense at advanced modernity in Western terms. The language, ideas, philosophy, and logic of the codes were distinctly European. There were fundamental discontinuities between the contents of the codes and the substance of Japanese life, which, the Meiji lawmakers vaguely assumed, eventually would change to become more consistent with the spirit of the codes. For many years, especially in rural Japan, it was not the sparkling new light of enlightenment from the West but centuries-old customs and mores that regulated people's daily lives. Their philosophies and attitudes toward the law continued to be tradition-bound.

*

It is no surprise, then, that the Japanese word *kenri,* for "right," had to be invented by the Meiji legal experts drafting the modern codes. Such a word did not exist in traditional Japan. The absence of the word indicates that the concepts concerning human rights were lacking or suppressed in old Japanese thought. Instead, the emphasis was on duties and obligations. The majority of people were subjects of landowners, feudal lords, the emperor. Above each average man's head was a myriad of authorities. To think of one's rights, at least at the conscious level, was improper and unpardonable. In old Japan, individuals did "own" houses, lands, and other properties; money was lent and borrowed. Such economic transactions necessarily involved the concept of rights. But such modern capitalistic ideas as title of property ownership, legitimate deed, financial claims, assets, and liabilities were somehow blurred in the mist of the feudal system. Toward the end of the Edo period, it became increasingly risky for wealthy merchants to lend money to local *daimyo* in financial stress. In case of default, the merchants would not dare to appeal to the courts that represented not the people, but the authorities. If property was damaged, what was emphasized was not the right of the injured party but rather the obligation of the offender to pay.

In a modern Western society, the idea of rights is like the air one breathes. It is always there, taken for granted in the back of one's mind. In traditional Japan, however, a man did not question his obligations, while society did not permit him to think of his rights. What mattered was who had power. One with power could enforce his rights, but the rights of those without power were nominal and, at times, nonexistent. The traditional employment relations assumed the characteristics of a patriarchy. Each enterprise was like a family. The owner no more thought of his right to hire labor than a father thought of his right to ask his son to do household tasks. The employees did not think of their rights to ask for wages. The compensation they received was an expression of the master's benevolence, affection, and generosity. Wages were a reward to be accepted with a deep bow. One prototype of this quasi-familial employment pattern was found in the relationship between a landowner and tenant farmers in old Japan. In bad years, the landowner would reduce or exempt rent from the hard-pressed tenants, and he would provide aid of one sort or another in the event of illness, death, or marriage in the tenant's family. In reciprocity, the tenant was expected to repay the master's generosity by offering, on occasion, free, extra labor for the benefactor's household.

This traditional mode of thinking, after centuries of conditioning, could change only slowly. It was much easier to write and install new statutes than to change people's minds. The exterior of Japan's legal system was hastily modernized in the 1890s. On the other hand, the substance of Japanese legal thought—not what was written in the lawbooks but what people thought and felt about the law—resisted rapid transformation. A second wave of modernization followed World War II. Japanese labor was given the right to organize and bargain collectively, and even to strike against employers. But for ordinary workers, especially those in small firms, many years were needed to correct the discrepancy between their newly acquired rights and their deeper feelings about the employer-employee relationship. They continued to feel that a strike against management was unnatural, disagreeable, and shameful. The management side, too, showed the persisting influence of traditional thought. Japanese firms spent lavishly on fringe benefits of all sorts: subsidized cafeterias, company vacation houses, company-sponsored trips, athletic facilities for men, company-paid lessons on flower arrangement and tea ceremony for women. It is true that these benefits, in the context of Japanese culture, helped to raise the morale of employees. It is also true that, at least in part, these benefits were for tax purposes. The more fundamental reason, however, was management's sense of its obligation and responsibility to provide private welfare benefits for its employees.

Even during the postwar period, the persistence of the traditional emphasis on duties rather than rights is revealed in the manner in which the law is interpreted and applied by the courts. Driving along streets in the United States, one frequently comes across signs saying Yield—which, of course, stands for "yield the right-of-way." The concept of right-of-way is incorporated in the Japanese land transportation law, but the law also stresses the importance of defensive driving and caution by those with the right-of-way. The spirit of the law is that every driver, irrespective of who has the right, is obliged to refrain from endangering traffic; a driver is expected to yield even when he has the right. Exemplifying this spirit was a decision made by a Tokyo local court on March 24, 1959, in a case which involved a collision between a small car and a truck. The small car, which clearly had the right-of-way, was driving on a main street. The driver of the truck, without bothering to check the approach of the other car, steered into the main street from a narrow sidestreet, and hit the small car. In the United States the court ruling on this case would have been straightforward and predictable. The Tokyo court's decision, however, showed a Japanese twist. The truck driver was let off with a minimal fine, for the court found the driver of the small car had erred because he neglected to slow down and be prepared for a complete stop, even though, as he testified, he had seen the truck moving into the main street.

*

The major concern of the constitution of a democratic state is to guarantee and protect basic human rights. If left without a legal check, the state is bound to be too powerful and overbearing, and the rights of people will predictably be suppressed and abused. The constitution tries to set limits to what government can do to its people. In this respect, the postwar Constitution of Japan, initially drafted by General MacArthur's legal staff, is extremely democratic. It is for only a brief time after World War II, however, that the Japanese have lived with constitutional enlightenment. The Meiji Constitution, which had stayed in force for half a century from the end of the 19th century until the end of World War II, was anything but democratic. It was a powerful instrument of the state, by the state, and for the state. It superficially mentioned freedom of religion, assembly, speech, the right of people to maintain private residence, to exchange private communications, and the like, but these rights were carefully and extensively qualified by numerous escape clauses such as "as long as they do not violate the existing laws," "unless otherwise stipulated by special laws," or "insofar as they do not subvert the national security and/or internal social order."

What the Meiji Constitution established was not the

legal relation between the state and its people but the power relation between the two—the state assuming the overwhelming amount of power and rights. People were subjects of the state. There was little legal guarantee of their rights vis-à-vis the government. All people could do to protect themselves was to hope for government "restraint." Often their hopes were not fulfilled. From the prewar period one can draw numerous examples to illustrate that the Meiji Constitution at times became a *de facto* instrument of tyranny. There was a clear line of demarcation between public and private laws. The public laws protected the activities of the state and exempted most of its conduct from allegations under the private statutes. Individuals' deeds against the state were punishable, but the converse was not true. A private person could bring suit against the government only to a special "administrative" court which was not bound by the existing laws—hardly a court. To the government officials, the law was something like a memorandum concerning their behavior. A bureaucrat violating a law might be scolded and sanctioned in some mild manner by a higher official—and that was all.

Under the Meiji Constitution, what would sound incredible today could and did happen. On August 31, 1935, the Japanese Supreme Court dismissed a personal injury case involving a man who was severely crippled by a recklessly driven fire engine. The sense of the argument was that the fire engine was exercising the state's authority, and there was no law under which the charge of reckless driving and personal injury against the state could be made. Thus, every fire engine in Japan had a legitimate right to run over pedestrians.

On March 2, 1910, the Supreme Court told the Oji

Paper Company, whose property was extensively damaged by an explosion of a nearby arsenal in the Itabashi ward of Tokyo, that the government was not responsible for the damage. The court's argument was that the manufacturing of gunpowder was an act of national defense, intended to promote public good; no charge of damage to private properties could be brought against the arsenal, which was under the domain of public laws.

A professor of neurosurgery at the Kyoto Medical College, a state-financed school, made one of his patients a permanent invalid through negligence. The patient sued the doctor in the Osaka Appeals Court, which declared, on December 19, 1905, that the doctor was innocent of malpractice. According to the court, he was technically an agent of the state authority, whose activities were protected under the public laws; no allegation of malpractice could therefore be made against a private physician acting in the public interest.

One can keep on citing similar examples. On January 10, 1916, the Tokyo Local Court issued a verdict which said in effect that a judge who deliberately misused the law and sent an innocent person to jail was not responsible for his deed. Article 195 of the prewar criminal code banned the use of torture by police. It was an open secret, however, that in prewar Japan a number of people were cruelly treated by the police. Not a few innocent persons were forced to make false confessions through torture, hastily declared guilty, and sent to prison. The extent of injury—financial as well as psychological—to them and their families was unspeakable. Even the state acknowledged the need for giving them some compensation when, with their innocence established, they came out of jail. However, the opinion of many legal "experts" who insisted on the infinite, unconditional power of the state was strong and influential. Only in 1931 was a criminal compensation law finally passed to provide for innocent victims of the law. In prewar Japan, a publications law permitted the government to forbid the sale and distribution of any publication deemed detrimental to the cause of public morality, national security, and social stability. The Ministry of Home Affairs was the sole judge authorized to decide which books or magazines should be banned, and the law contained no provision for appeals.

*

The Meiji civil code of 1896 systematically incorporated the Western concept of private property ownership. In language few people really understood, the code stipulated that, in principle, the rights of private property ownership were absolute, exclusive, and independent of whoever actually controlled or managed the properties. Use and ownership were conceptually separated, and the private owner had the right to use, sell, give away, or even destroy his property.

This was like grafting a branch of one tree to the trunk of another. There was a basic discontinuity between the spirit of the new code and the traditional stream of Japanese consciousness about property ownership. The Japanese language then did not even have a word for "private." The common, colloquial expression used today is "puraibēto," which is a transmuted form of the English equivalent.

Each piece of property in a human community—anywhere, anytime—is "owned" by someone in the sense that the person in question is entitled to use it. This is true even in socialist countries. The Western world has historically put strong emphasis on the privateness of owned property. Especially in the United States, the word ''private'' carries a keen, biting connotation. Nobody would ask a well-to-do Texas rancher, the private owner of thousands of acres of land, if there are moments he feels un-Christian in claiming so much of God's land. Traditional Japan, before the Meiji Restoration, did not leave much room for growth of the idea of private ownership, for it was incompatible with the workings of a highly collective society, which Japan was. A merchant lived in his modest home, which was neither private nor public; he just used it as his place of residence. The principle preferred was factual rather than conceptual. What mattered was who actually used the property rather than who held abstract rights of private ownership.

The traditional notions of property were strong and widespread at the time the Meiji civil code was being established. In one form or another, they linger on. Even in contemporary Japan, a person who doggedly pursues his rights of private property ownership is considered selfish and avaricious—a foe of society. One afternoon in 1969, I was talking with an American banker in Berkeley, California, about ''hippies.'' As we talked, he grew angrier and angrier about those troublemaking, dirty, parasitic people. Suddenly, he pulled out a ballpoint pen from the chestpocket of his dark, conservative suit. ''Look,'' the man said, his face getting red, ''this pen costs only 19 cents, but it is my private property. You understand? It is my private property. No one can ever take it away from me.'' In America, this banker might be described as up-tight or hard-headed. In Japan, he would be declared insane.

Who has what rights concerning property ownership?

What is the precise meaning of "rights"? What principles should be adopted in determining "ownership"? What is meant by "private"? Traditional Japanese culture had no interest in answering these questions. The traditional attitude can be illustrated by the experience of urban families compelled by air raids to evacuate to rural areas during World War II. Not every family was fortunate enough to have relatives or close friends in the countryside. Personal property in many cases had to be stored in the homes of mere acquaintances or total strangers, and it was not uncommon for city families to discover later that rural folks had opened the packages without permission and used clothes, clocks, precious pots, rare supplies of soap, and what not. This should not be attributed solely to the wartime scarcity. Wartime or not, the rural families could have asked for permission. Apparently, their consciousness of "private" property was so weak that they felt quite innocent about what they were doing.

Similar events can still occur in Japan. Someone who has borrowed a book from you may not bother to return it for the next several years. Of course, the same sort of thing can happen elsewhere. The difference is that, while an American would ask the borrower to return the book in a businesslike manner, the Japanese lender would underplay his right of private ownership and make a request in an apologetic tone—often giving an excuse such as "Could you please return it because another friend of mine wants it?"

In 1965, a private detective was shot to death in Honolulu while secretly trying to take a picture of a man who was, at the time, at home in his own house. Through a window, the man happened to see the detective intruding into the backyard. The man took out his gun and shot the intruder. The following day, a local paper ran an editorial which deplored the conduct of the detective more than the excess of the man's reaction. This editorial would never have appeared in Japan. The Japanese do not see how the idea of privacy can be deified to such an extent.

In Japan, members of a road gang may suddenly march into your yard and eat their lunch on the lawn without your permission. Ishihara Shintaro, an author-politician, was once flabbergasted to see three young men, total strangers, climb over the wall of his house, disrobe, and begin swimming in his private pool—with no sign of embarrassment or guilt. Japanese travelers in the United States find forbidding the big signs saying "Private Property" or "No Trespassing" in the middle of a vast no-man's-land. The unsophisticated Japanese would wonder what is so wrong about walking across those grassy acres where no one is in sight. They wish the American landowners would forgive their trespasses as the Japanese forgive those who trespass against them.

*

To an American businessman, a contract is strictly a business deal. It is a formalized promise that spells out his rights and obligations relative to another contracting party. When endorsed by both parties, it becomes legally binding. He must honor it, or else he may be sued in court. He understands its working principles and underlying assumptions. This is the way business always has been done and continues to be done in the West. He wants the contract terms to be as clear, specific, detailed, and definitive as possible. He wants them to cover even Acts of God; he wants no element of ambiguity;

he wishes to minimize subsequent troubles. The more detailed the contract is, the less likely are disputes later. There is much disparity between this straightforward American approach and the traditional Japanese one. In the present statutes of Japan, there is no shortage of provision for the modern contract system. However, the Japanese mentality continues to be influenced by the pull of the past.

An American would not find it difficult to separate a promise from a friendship. To him, a promise is a promise—whether the other party is a mere acquaintance or a close friend. An old friendship may come to an end because of a broken promise, but he will not hesitate to remind his friend of his unkept word. The Japanese feeling about this is qualitatively different. To them, a promise is a deal that is more emotional than business-like. It represents a human connection. The specific content of a promise is important, but more important is what surrounds it: another person's kindness, favor, consideration. A Japanese would not willfully make a habit of breaking it. If he does not return a book to his friend by a specified date, it is not because he is deliberately trying to antagonize his friend, but because his culture makes him inattentive to the terms of the promise, to such an impersonal aspect of the promise like a deadline. The borrower is so intoxicated by the warmth of the friend's heart that he forgets about the date the object was borrowed as well as the ownership of the book itself.

Awareness of this psychology provides at least a clue to understanding how business contracts are made in Japan, if not what Japanese contract law says. In many instances, Japanese businessmen will proceed to make a deal without drafting a formal contract, while in the United States, under similar circumstances, the signing of a written contract would be taken for granted. A contract in Japan, if drafted and signed, tends to be brief and general; it merely gives a broad outline of the terms of agreement. An American businessman would not like such a contract. It makes him feel insecure. He prefers elaborate, even microscopic detailing to allow for all possible contingencies. An American in Tokyo may experience a mild shock on learning that a Japanese business partner's reaction is the exact opposite. It is the detailed contract that gives the Japanese a sense of insecurity and apprehension. A contract with lengthy specifications makes him feel constrained. He feels his hands are tied. He knows that things will not proceed exactly as perceived in the beginning. Such a contract will keep him forever worried that he may unintentionally violate some minute clause hidden somewhere in the bulky document every time he makes a move or redesigns his business strategy. If the American continues to insist on the details, the Japanese will take it as a sign of the American's distrust.

Preference for a simple contract, however, is not universal in the Japanese business world. Contracts drafted in banking, trust, and insurance are American-style, filled with lengthy details. But in most other industries—even among major corporations—a typical contract is much briefer than its American counterpart, indicating that the Japanese system not only is preferred but also apparently works well. A major business contract in the United States almost always includes an arbitration clause stipulating how a dispute, if it arises, will be settled. Such a clause is usually not found in a Japanese contract. Instead, the Japanese version typically includes a "sincere negotiation clause" or "harmonious settlement clause." These clauses state that, in case of a dispute, two parties shall come together, face-to-face, and settle it in an atmosphere of harmony and sincere cooperation. The popularity of these clauses shows that this way of dissolving a problem is preferred to going to court.

An American's reaction to this approach is predictable. He will ask: "What assurance is there that the negotiation will be sincere?" "What if one or both parties turn out to be insincere?" "What is to be done if the negotiations, harmonious or not, break down and produce no mutually acceptable solution?" These are logical and legitimate questions. The point is, however, the Japanese system may not work in the United States or in Europe, nor is it likely to work in U.S.–Japan business relations; yet, somehow, it does work in Japan.

The culture of old Japan gave preference to the personal and emotional approach in dealing with human problems. Before World War II, a Japanese building contractor would typically start working on a new house without a written contract. Only a rough estimate might be made at the outset. The contractor would keep adding costs for tiles, lumber, cement, wallpaper, and so on, as he went along. The buyer of the house was expected to know that the final bill would be much higher than the initial estimate. This principle of vagueness was not confined to small business dealings. Though the prewar code required a written contract to be signed by the government and the construction firms commissioned to work on public buildings, in practice the written contract, filled with ambiguities and escape clauses, was seldom followed literally. Instead, problems were settled through a series of *ad hoc,* face-to-face negotiations between the bureaucrats in charge and the president or executives of the construction firm. The bureaucrats spoke from a position of superiority. More often than not, the company representatives, in a subservient role, had to accept a smaller sum even though it meant a technical violation of the contract. The session would end with an emotive code language. The chief bureaucrat would say, "I want you to cry" (meaning, "I want you to reduce your price"). The company president was expected to reply, "Yes, your honor, I shall cry for you" (meaning, "Yes, I shall reduce my charge").

A majority of contemporary Japanese firms—including major corporations—require each newly hired worker to submit a "personal reference contract" signed by another person. This should not be confused with the standard references requested of a job applicant in the United States. The reference contract in Japan is short and simple; it says in effect that a person who signs it becomes a total guardian and assumes unlimited responsibility for the deeds of the new employee. This is a carry-over from the old days, when a similar guarantee had to be made before a person could get a job outside his household. If literally interpreted, the reference contract obliges the present-day guardian to pay for property damage caused by the employee, to search for and locate him if he disappears, and to look after him when he falls ill. In reality, such an interpretation is seldom made. When a problem does arise, the company and the guardian negotiate in an atmosphere of harmony and sincere cooperation, and simply work out a mutually agreeable compromise.

The Japanese are not fond of solving their disputes in court. They do everything possible to dissolve their conflicts extralegally. This does not mean, of course, that they are, by inclination, anarchists or a nation of lawbreakers. In principle, they respect law and order. Deep in their hearts, however, they feel that the modern court system represents a fiction . . . a delusion about human relations. A popular Japanese proverb holds, "In a quarrel both parties are to blame." They believe that this proverb is an honest and accurate description of most (if not all) disputes. Yet this sentiment is inconsistent with the assumptions of the modern court, which must decide in each and every case if the law has been violated, if a defendant is guilty or not guilty. Such an "all or nothing" approach leaves them cold and uneasy. They know this is not the truth; the truth of human relations is more complex and elusive. They feel it is not possible to spell out one's rights and obligations in precise legal language and let the court evaluate and judge every case with surgical accuracy. In their eyes, the rights and duties of men are all blurred. To say that each human dispute can be decided in a "black or white" manner is to indulge in considerable distortion of the facts of life.

The dislike of going to court may be motivated in part by the associated high costs—not just the financial cost of hiring a lawyer but also the opportunity cost of so much time that must be expended. In many instances, it would be more rational not to go to court. What is the use of spending 10 million yen on an attorney plus ten months in court in order to get back 5 million yen from another fellow, unless you believe in going to court as a matter of principle? The costs involved provide only a partial explanation, for the dislike of court trials is not restricted to ordinary people with modest incomes. Large corporations, which can certainly afford legal expenses, also follow the same pattern. Even the government, entrusted to manage public properties for the people, seldom initiates a prosecution. The same government, however, when sued rather than suing, quickly becomes a staunch supporter of the court. In losing court battles, it will obstinately keep on fighting to the very end to save face and preserve its image of superiority and power.

Judges anywhere in the world are human and cannot ignore the values and mores of the people. Each law has to be interpreted rather than mechanically applied. Consciously or otherwise, judges make allowances for the unwritten moral code of society. If the law is always applied literally, the legal system is prone to break down. The English Common Law acknowledges the necessity and desirability of this spirit of accommodation so that the courts can remain viable. It comes as no surprise, then, to note that Japanese judges show a similar inclination toward the mores of their society.

This inclination toward local mores is shown in a case involving the death of an assistant driver of a truck that belonged to the Toyo Kogyo Company. The truck, in a clear violation of the traffic code, was trailing behind another car in the dark. The driver of the truck failed to see another truck parked ahead. He hit the parked truck, and his assistant sitting next to him was killed. The mother of the victim brought a lawsuit against the company to claim financial and psychological damages of 320,000 yen (about $1,300). In its final verdict delivered on September 29, 1954, the Osaka District Court reduced the claim to 280,000 yen (about $1,120). The reason: The assistant driver was asleep at the time of the accident and, had he been awake, he could have helped avert the collision by warning the regular driver about the parked truck or taking some necessary action himself. In other words, the victim, too, was partially responsible for the accident.

Many litigations under the Japanese civil procedure code evaporate before they reach the trial stage through the method called *wakai* or "harmonious dissolution." This means that a defendant and a complainant agree, on their own or at the suggestion of the court, to sign a pledge that obliges them to get together, make honorable concessions, and work out a mutually satisfactory solution of the dispute outside the court. The *wakai* method works effectively in Japan, for it suits the temper and sentiment of the people, many of whom change their minds after filing a litigation procedure. A pecuniary reason is there, too—the cost of court proceedings may run to an astronomical sum. A plaintiff might be aware that the defendant is already bankrupt and there is little hope for collecting what is legally claimable. More importantly, both sides never believed in going to court in the first place. The complainant decides to yield because he does not wish to engage in an open confrontation with another individual, which sounds so dissonant in the chamber of Japanese culture. A lawsuit is an ultimatum, a declaration of personal war. Even if the man wins the court battle, he has to pay a high price. He will be labeled contentious, bellicose, stonehearted, a bloody Shylock. In the tightly knit society of Japan, he may have to spend the rest of his life in fear of suffering revenge.

The theme of harmony runs deep in Japanese history. In A.D. 604, Prince Shotoku wrote in Article 1 of his famous Seventeen-Article Constitution, "Harmony is to be valued, and an avoidance of wanton opposition to be honored." In the tales of old Japan, heroes are often those constables and judges who ingeniously twist or subtly violate the law to arrive at a peaceful, amicable settlement of a dispute. In contemporary Japan, campaign speeches, company presidents' addresses to the boards of directors, principals' commencement messages, and diplomats' prepared texts for foreign consumption are packed with the word harmony. The company anthem of Matsushita Electric ends with a bravado "Harmony and sincerity! Matsushita Electric!" It borders on a national obsession. One becomes suspicious that things, in reality, have not been very harmonious.

In 1937, the heyday of Japanese ultranationalism, the Ministry of Education circulated 2 million copies of a booklet entitled *Fundamentals of Our National Polity,* which contained a pompous message on the nation's ideals or what the Japanese people were supposed to be like. One of the ideals was, of course, harmony. The booklet had this to say: "When we trace the founding of our country and the progress of our history, what we always find there is the spirit of harmony. Harmony is a product of the great achievements of the nation and is the power behind our growth. It is also a humanitarian Way inseparable from our daily lives."

The theme of harmony underlies the mediation system in Japan. In the West, mediation usually means that two parties in conflict, being unable to solve their problem by themselves, let a third person act as mediator and agree to accept the mediator's decision. In Japan, too, mediation involves a third person. But the role expected of him is not so much that of a quasi judge presiding over the case, as that of a sage, a fatherly figure who serves as a catalyst for successful settlement of the issue. The accent is not on legal technicalities but on moral suasion and the warmth of human understanding. The mediator is supposed to steer the course of controversy in such a way that before long all parties concerned begin to feel, their hearts being enveloped by the intoxicating charm of the man, that the problem is not worth fussing about.

In old Japan, it was punishable for two persons to bring their grievance to a feudal court without evidence that they had duly tried but failed to dissolve it with a village headman or a man of influence in their town acting as arbiter. After the Meiji Restoration, mediation procedures were provided for by the prefectural courts established in 1875. The public peace courts later took over the mediation service in 1881. Under a new rule set up in 1884, each public peace court appointed two mediators, one of whom was to be a man of wide knowledge and long experience in local customs and tradition. The mediation was very popular as well as effective; some courts had to handle close to ten thousand cases a year. Each mediator was instructed to rely on moral suasion and to pay due attention to all sides of the argument. Japan then was a tightly hierarchical society where one's social status carried heavy weight. A word or two said by the local boss, in the role of arbiter, usually settled the issue. It was next to impossible for an average complainant to object to the holy word descending from the man of influence. Fair or unfair, the complainant would bear the verdict in silence for the sake of communal harmony.

The Civil Procedure Code of 1890 tried to do away with mediation and to put more emphasis on trials in court. The trend, however, did not last long. After the turn of the century—especially after World War I—Japan began to experience the growing pains of industrialization. Signs of social unrest became more visible. Labor was beginning to organize itself. Tenant farmers were forming their associations to counteract the landowners. In cities, apartment-dwellers were establishing tenants' unions to cope with the exploitative landlords. The government was alarmed. Little people were no longer quiet. As a way of siphoning off the rising bubbles of discontent, the government passed a series of new mediation laws between 1922 and 1926 to cover disputes concerning tenant farming, home leasing, and labor-management problems. A nationwide system of mediation committees was established at the lower courts, one member of each committee being a judge to provide, if needed, legal information for the rest of the members. In practice, his expert knowledge was seldom relied upon. In a typical proceeding, the working principle was one of common sense, well-rounded settlement, peaceful and amicable agreement. This was when the emperor was still a god, the ruler of all Japan. To the less sophisticated, a court trial and mediation were more or less the same thing. It was not uncommon that a sticky point of disagreement would quickly disappear when the mediator raised his voice and told a trembling complainant, "Look, this hearing is in the name of our emperor. I know you are an honorable and reasonable man. Why don't you make a concession?" This was not too outlandish a move for the mediator to make, for Article 57 of the Meiji Constitution, then in force, did state that justice in the land was administered in the name of the emperor.

The theme of harmony persists even in the period after World War II. *A Handbook of Mediation,* published in 1954 by the Japan Association of Mediators, includes many aphoristic passages like: "Cultivate the art of avoiding a 'black or white' solution to the problem," "refrain from showing off half-digested knowledge of technical rules," "one's duties and rights should not be viewed as something impeccably distinguishable or clearly definable," and "love and mercy, not logic and reason."

In 1953, a well-known professor emeritus of jurisprudence at the University of Tokyo went to a mediation hearing on behalf of his relative who was threatened with eviction from his apartment, not because he had failed to pay his rent, but because the landlord was trying to replace him with a prostitute from whom a higher rent could be collected. The professor thought it would be useful for everyone in the room if basic and pertinent facts of the law were clarified. He proceeded to mention Article 1, Section 2 of the House Lease Law that required the landlord to have "justifiable reasons" to evict a tenant. He could not finish his lecture. He was abruptly stopped by a mediator who became visibly angry. Not knowing who the lecturer was, the mediator told the professor emeritus in a shaking voice, "Don't meddle with the law. This is not a court. Stop being argumentative, and keep your mouth shut." This gave the professor a profound cultural shock. Never had he realized before that such a gap existed between the practice of the law in Japan and the theory of the modern legal system on which he was an authority.

Despite the tradition of extralegalism, Japanese society has not collapsed in total chaos because it has obeyed, along with the modern network of jurisprudence, an invisible code of social behavior. The difficulty with this code is that it defies coherent, comprehensible explanation. It is just there, without shape or color—an elusive entity which, like an amoeba, elastically adjusts itself to the changing constraints of society. It is a vague mixture of a sense of justice, understanding of human frailty, an attitude of tolerance, and a touch of fatalism. The ethos of extralegalism does not provide, however, a totally satisfactory solution to the problems of an advanced society. Behind its façade of love, harmony, and benevolence, thousands of offenders have gotten by and thousands more innocent people have had to swallow doses of injustice. It breeds a certain intellectual laziness not compatible with the requirements of a modern society. Too much is left undecided, too much decided arbitrarily. The proverb "In a quarrel both parties are to blame" is reasonable enough. But another saying of equal popularity in Japan, "Despise the crime but not the criminal," amounts to a sophism. It is anybody's guess how it is possible, without cheating and self-deception, to punish the crime but not the person who committed it.

5 ✦ The Case of Formidable Servants

> *The three-power relationship between the administrative bureaucracy, the ruling party, and organized business is analogous to that of the three-sided "tossing game" called "janken," in which paper, stone, and scissors are featured. Paper is stronger than stone, which it can wrap; stone is stronger than scissors, which it can break; and scissors win out over paper, which they can cut.*
>
> —YANAGA CHITOSHI

Politics in any nation is inseparable from bureaucracy. Every government must depend upon its bureaucrats to carry out the objectives of the state. They are intermediaries between the ruler and the ruled. To govern, the government needs tax collectors, constables, compilers of official documents, legal experts, and many others who engage in public administration. Without them the whole process of governing will break down.

General MacArthur, when he was the ruler of occupied Japan after World War II, once described the Japanese as 12-year-old children. Ironically, he, the mature ruler, had to depend upon the Japanese bureaucrats in administering the military occupation of the conquered land. All the political and military leaders of prewar Japan had vanished from the scene. Even major business executives and financiers had been purged from their posts. Yet the basic structure of the Japanese civil service remained intact. The French Revolution could not destroy the French bureaucracy, nor could Japan's total defeat in World War II dissolve the Japanese bureaucracy. On the contrary, without it the Allied occupation of Japan could not have been carried out.

As a rule, bureaucrats in any country are not objects of affection. They tend to be disliked or even hated. The attitude of ordinary Japanese toward their public officials is ambivalent: the bureaucrats are respected and disliked at the same time. As for the officials' attitude toward the common people, it reflects considerable psychic distance. Often the former refer to the latter as civilians.

The system of bureaucracy has existed since the dawn of Japanese history. But it has played a particularly significant role during Japan's modern century. It served as a powerful arm of the Meiji government in spreading modernization in the late 19th century. By providing a potent apparatus of public administration, it contributed to the transformation of the country from an agrarian society to a superstate in less than one hundred years. The phenomenal economic growth of Japan after World War II may, in the main, be attributed to the hard work of the Japanese; but their hard work would not have borne fruit in the absence of sufficient political stability, which in turn depended upon the effective functioning of the bureaucracy.

Japanese bureaucracy constitutes a huge establishment with tremendous political power and includes a large number of the nation's brains. Japanese politics cannot be separated from it. Most of the prime ministers of postwar Japan—Yoshida Shigeru, Ikeda Hayato, Kishi Nobusuke, Sato Eisaku—were former bureaucrats. About 30 per cent of the Diet members who belong to the conservative Liberal-Democratic party are also former bureaucrats. The establishment, consisting of brains and power, commands deference; yet people dislike their bureaucrats immensely. They say that the bureaucrats form a special group whose language, manners, ways of doing things, and even faces are different from those of other people. They contend that the bureaucrats may be passable as private individuals but that, once inside the system, they become arrogant, overconfident, inflexible, and disagreeable. In fact, Japanese bureaucrats are always criticized by the "civilian" Japanese as conservative, inefficient, self-protective, promotion-conscious, faction-minded, and unkind and contemptuous to those below them, while being remarkably accommodating and pathetically self-abasing to their superiors.

There is, however, one thing on which everybody agrees: Whether you like it or not, the bureaucracy is here to stay. Like the Rock of Gibraltar, it has always been there; so shall it always be. Besides being powerful and huge, the system consists of administrative experts with extensive knowledge of the law. Without these technocrats, Japan, as a modern state, cannot function. The Japanese bureaucracy is an unconquerable fortress for outsiders. It is an Invincible Armada that moves with its own will, logic, and pathology.

Who are the rulers of contemporary Japan? "Those

who control big business and the top-level political leaders'' seems to be the obvious answer. If you interview a Japanese business executive and ask him the question, he may reply: ''Of course, it is those politicians. We must supply them with large sums of campaign funds. They control the Diet, and our life hinges on the laws they make. We are in a thankless position. We contribute an astronomical amount of money each year, while they as individuals do little for us.''

So you proceed to question a Cabinet member or an influential member of the conservative Liberal-Democratic party. With a smile, the man points his finger to the top echelon of the administrative bureaucracy. ''It is those bureaucrats who really run the show,'' he says with an air of magnanimity. ''I realize it is very difficult for a foreigner to understand the inner mechanism of politics in this country. You see, we are mere clowns on the stage. The bureaucrats are the directors hidden behind the curtain. They write the laws. They plan, design, and regulate the national budget. They are the only experts who know the technical details of the political process. They not only know but also manipulate the process to their liking.''

You now turn around and look up a high-level bureaucrat, perhaps a bureau chief in the prestigious Ministry of Finance. The chief replies: ''What the politician told you about us might have been true before the war, but not any more. We no longer have the imperial privileges we once had as direct servants of the emperor. We are deprived of the confidential operations funds we once held in abundance. Our pay is low. Our retirement comes early. We must beg politicians or businessmen for our post-retirement jobs.

Compared with the situation in the prewar years, the present prestige of our profession has diminished considerably. Nowadays, the author-intellectuals are more influential than we in guiding the course of the nation. The author-intellectuals are a peculiar group in this country—consisting of scholars, writers, and free-lance critics who keep pouring out voluminous books and articles on social, economic, and political problems. The Japanese are a literate people, and their intellectual climate is decisively conditioned by this group. If you don't believe me, why don't you interview them?''

You follow the chief's advice, and visit the University of Tokyo to see a professor of political science noted for his prolific authorship of social commentary. The scholar answers: ''The bureaucrats in this country habitually indulge themselves in mock humility. Of course, what the chief told you is nonsense. We are a vocal minority. We make a lot of noise through the mass media, but we have no power. What we write has little influence on actual political decision-making. 'Loud barking of a feeble dog,' as we say in Japanese. Besides, our opinions are conditioned by those who control the mass media—magazines, books, television, radio. Without their approval, we have no chance of expressing our views. The true opinion leaders in this country are journalists . . . the first-line reporters and editors of the major newspapers. They are known as 'kings without crowns.' They have a tradition of opposing and criticizing the government. Public opinion in Japan is largely determined by what they write. They have tremendous power to influence politics. I suggest that you interview a leading journalist.''

You continue your frustrating inquiry. A leading

journalist responds to your query: "The professor's assessment of our power to influence public opinion is rather misleading and exaggerated. There is a catch. The life of newspapers depends upon the sponsors of our advertisements. We cannot always write what we want to. We must adjust our views to those of our sponsors who are all, directly or indirectly, controlled by big business. In the final analysis, those who control big business are the ultimate rulers of Japan."

Thus, a circle is complete. Japan is found to be a nation without a ruler. No group claims for itself the leadership of and ultimate responsibility for the affairs of the country. They all respond in tones of dubious modesty. All that is revealed in their statements for external consumption is that the ruling of Japan seems to rest upon a mechanism of mutual dependence in which each points his finger at another and the title of rulership is acknowledged by no one.

A nation is like a tree. Blossoms and fruits on the tree are politicians and business leaders. Their splendid appearance and brilliant colors are the focus of attention. Numerous roots, buried under the ground, are the masses. They quietly gather and supply water and nutrition from the soil to sustain the life of the tree. Their functioning is inconspicuous, their presence unnoticed. The trunk and branches of the tree are the bureaucrats. They connect the bottom with the top. They support the tree by pumping up nutrition from the ground to the blossoms and fruits. The trunk is hard and strong. It remains upright after the flowers and fruits decay and fall to the ground each winter. It stands there, unaffected by the coming and going of the seasons.

Social Darwinism prevails in the human world. The strong rule the weak. The doctrine of survival of the fittest applies to nations as well as to individuals in society. The superior tend to persist, the inferior to vanish. Darwinism may be a grand tautology; nevertheless, it is a fact of life. To become a successful politician or a top business executive requires many qualities: talent, drive, looks, psychic and physical stamina, wealth, cunning, family background, capacity to adapt to changing circumstances, power of persuasion, quickness in making a correct decision, ability to manage people, and so on. How does one become a successful bureaucrat? In Japan the formula is well defined. One makes top grades at all levels of schooling, passes an entrance examination to the University of Tokyo (or to a handful of other prestigious national universities), majors in law, and then passes the civil service examination with top grades. Up to this point the bureaucrat must be a master technician in passing all sorts of examinations. After the civil service examination, he is assigned to one of the ministries of the central government. Then he must thoroughly learn all the laws and regulations that are relevant to his post, maintain an absolutely noncontroversial personality, avoid getting involved in jurisdictional disputes with other bureaucrats inside or outside his ministry, and develop the right connections with men of influence. If all these requirements are duly met, the man will more or less automatically climb the ladder to the top.

Bureaucratic control of a modern state requires professional skills. A bureaucrat is expected to be a seasoned administrator whose work is always accurate and speedy. Japanese bureaucrats know their laws, regulations, decrees, ordinances. They are walking encyclopedias who can instantly recall which matters come under the jurisdiction of which section of what ministry. On the surface, they maintain an image of the ideal public administrator—cool, selfless, objective—who can get his job done quickly and impersonally. A closer look would reveal a certain duality in their personalities. When a problem reaches their desks from outsiders or those below them, they are prone to apply laws and regulations with objectivity and precision. Yet, if precisely the same problem is transmitted from a peer or superior, they suddenly become flexible and subjective in interpreting the existing rules. Adept use of this dual personality is a political skill that they must acquire if they are to survive and succeed in their world.

In Japan the design of political control is neither dictatorial, centralized, nor decentralized. It is more of a collective mutual-assistance system. Conservative politicians and big-business leaders form a mighty coalition. This is natural, for in capitalism money is power. Conservative politicians stay in power because they win elections. They win elections because their campaigns are supported by large contributions from big business. A marriage between political and economic powers, of course, is not the only reason for the strength of the conservative party. The position of power tends to attract many talents from all segments of the country, including the bureaucracy, local political districts, and the mass communications industry. The conservative party supports, and is supported by, numerous political organizations throughout the country. And the philosophy and style of conservative politicians are more compatible with the temper of the masses than are those of the leftist opposition leaders.

The bureaucrats join the conservative politicians and the big-business leaders to form a three-sided power structure. Their alliance is almost inevitable, since it is dictated by the requirements of modern society. Classical capitalism, based upon the economic philosophy of laissez-faire, is no more. The dictum that the government is best that governs least no longer applies. Advanced society is highly managed. The output of public administration expands annually, and the state has to cope with increasingly complex problems. Governmental jobs proliferate, as new laws are designed and drafted and new budgets planned and programmed. Public administration projects become elaborate and voluminous; only the experts can handle them.

The more specialized and difficult the task of public administration becomes, the more authority bureaucrats are bound to assume. Thus the weight of the bureaucrats in the total power structure will inevitably grow. No matter how imperfect and unsatisfactory their performance may be, everyone agrees that only they can do the job. Party politicians cannot function without them. A dignified political leader who speaks in haughty language on the floor of the Diet, once behind the door, may have to beg a bureaucrat for help on legislative technicalities. A bureaucrat-turned-politician can command respect and influence, for his background places him in a position of advantage over straight politicians who lack his expert knowledge of lawmaking. Businessmen cannot afford to offend a bureaucrat under any circumstances, because their future business ventures may require his official stamp of approval. The bureaucrats as a group are always exerting power from behind the scenes. Invisible as they are, they hold a master key to the ruling of Japan.

Before World War II, under the Meiji Constitution, the emperor was the sovereign. In principle, absolute power was in his hands. In practice, political decisions of import were made by the elder statesmen, the prime minister, and the heads of the ministries. After the war, the emperor became the mere "symbol of the State." Article 1 of the new postwar Constitution of Japan states: "The emperor shall be the symbol of the State and of the unity of the people, deriving his position from the will of the people with whom resides sovereign power." Thus, in postwar Japan, the people are the sovereign. But to interpret this to mean that now it is the people who rule the country is an exercise in metaphysical daydreaming. There are too many of them. It is not technically feasible for the masses to participate directly in the ruling of the country. A few may rule many, but not vice versa. If we follow Joseph Schumpeter, the distinguished Austrian-American economist, political democracy at best amounts to the people's right to choose those by whom they shall be ruled. Of course, there have been fundamental changes. Life in postwar Japan is freer and more open than in the past. You can judge politicians for yourself in each election, although the top leaders are not directly elected but are chosen by the ruling party. You can choose your own newspaper to read. No one forces you to watch a particular television program. If you cannot stand a corporation, you need not buy its products. To end the career of an author-intellectual, the only thing people have to do is stop reading his articles. In postwar Japan, freedom and democracy have made the position of those inside the power structure more vulnerable to the will of the people than before. It may be said that freedom of choice enables the masses to rule their rulers indirectly.

The bureaucrats, however, are the exception. They are immune even to an indirect check by the masses. They are the untouchables of Japan. There is no way for the common people to reach and shake the tower of bureaucracy. It is next to impossible for anyone or any group of individuals to recall or censure functionaries whose interests and status are carefully protected by the thick walls of their huge organizations and the complex rules defining their prerogatives. People may complain about their misconduct and irresponsibility. But assuredly there will be no reaction. If the people were to lose patience, organize a mass protest, and march into public offices, only one thing would happen: the marchers would be arrested immediately, for violating the Public Works Obstruction Prevention Law.

After World War II, the bureaucrats came to be fondly called "public servants." The truth is they have been servants in name only. Protected by their secure status, they are prone to abuse their positions of public power. Prefectural governors and representatives of local governments must bow low and beg central government officials for transfer funds as though the money were coming from the officials' own pockets. And, while the politicians play out the political drama, all the techniques of production are in the hands of the bureaucrats, who write the scenarios and direct the plays. It is the people, the audience, who pay the high admission charge—taxes.

Many late-19th-century promoters of the modern state

of Japan had been low-class samurai under the Tokugawa regime. With the Meiji Restoration and the relinquishment of the feudal order, they suddenly found themselves the core of the new ruling class. The building of a new Japan began under the restored imperial order and the emperor became the new head of state. The door to social ascent was opened to people of all classes and backgrounds. With courage, talent, and effort, any status seeker could now climb up the ladder. Under the new order, one's relative status was set by the distance between one's position and the imperial chair at the top—the closer the distance to the emperor, the higher one's status. The standard formula for success, therefore, was to enter the civil or military service.

Many political leaders and bureaucrats of Meiji Japan knew that had the feudal order lasted longer, they would have spent their entire lives in poverty and humiliation as samurai of the lowest rank. They understood that respectability was not a matter to be determined by the social status of the family into which one happened to be born. To them, truly respectable status was something to be earned through capability and endeavor. The Meiji government, still in an embryonic, insecure condition, had hastened to mobilize all talents from every corner of the land and had let the possessors of those talents nurture the emerging modern state, with the idea that those supporting and promoting the new state would be the most capable officials in the country.

Two standard routes of social ascent were established. A network of imperial universities was built to produce career bureaucrats in the civil service, and army and navy academies were established to train professional military personnel. Those who managed to negotiate these routes were to become the elite of the new Japan. Under the new scheme of ladder-climbing, the fundamental requirement for becoming a member of the elite was to study—and study very hard—to pass entrance examinations to the key schools. In the context of the time, to study meant to master things Western: science, technology, jurisprudence, languages, or whatever else was useful to the state. Few students ever questioned whether the subjects they had to study were relevant to their personal lives. What they knew was that mastery of these subjects was indispensable to their careers and that the rule of the game was to pass all the tests with the highest grades, no matter what. This was the only way they could demonstrate the superior quality that was required for entry into the new privileged class.

The ambitious and bright, then, rushed to the imperial universities where competition for admission was the keenest. Their family backgrounds and personalities made little difference. There was no discrimination on the basis of creed or prefectural origin. The only thing that mattered was the number of points they scored in the entrance test. Admittedly, test scores may not reveal everything about human qualities; nevertheless, they were considered the least subjective criterion available.

To succeed, these students had to be tactful and shrewd, even-tempered and disciplined, and they had to conform to the ready-made curricula. They were expected to excel at all subjects. The eccentrics and the temperamental students who did exceedingly well in only one field did not have a chance. There was no room for the erratic. The worth of the youthful aspirants was to be determined solely by their performance in all the crucial entrance examinations.

How good was a good student who made it through all the hurdles, and what was he like as an individual? The assumption was that facets of a person other than learning were of secondary importance. One's academic excellence might not be sufficient for acceptance into the elite—yet a person without learning was out of the question. The best would necessarily be found among the brightest. Under this highly regimented scheme, it was inevitable that a youth who succeeded was, in all probability, one who seldom played as a child, who had studied long and hard since his early days—a creature of continence, a paragon of self-denial and abstinence, a technician capable of writing a test that would make him look better than he really was.

Once he passed the entrance examination to an imperial university and the civil service examination, there was no more competition to speak of. Under the seniority rule, the escalator would steadily move him upward within the hierarchy of bureaucracy. Each ascent meant a step closer to the emperor and away from the people. Those who chose a career in the army or navy followed a similar upward path. In either case, each promotion stretched the psychic distance between the masses and the chosen people. As these latter looked down from their high seats, those below them appeared more and more marginal and contemptible. The ordinary people were the leftovers, the failures, the scum of the Japanese earth.

According to the Meiji Constitution, the emperor was the sole ruler of Japan, and the task of the prime minister was to assist the emperor in his rule. The higher and closer to the imperial crown one's position was, the greater was one's responsibility. However, one was responsible not to the people but to the emperor. In actual practice, as a person climbed up the ladder, he became less responsible for his errors. A higher official could get by through shifting his responsibility to someone below him. For a mistake committed by the prime minister, a minister might be held responsible, and the minister's faulty decision was due to the vice minister's misjudgment, which in turn was caused by the bureau chief . . . and so on down the line. In prewar Japan, there developed a peculiar logic for sustaining the political-bureaucratic structure. This rationale might be termed the system of nonresponsibility. Under this system, for every error someone below was always responsible. The extension of this logic was that nobody involved in political decision-making was responsible for anything, and it was the people at the bottom who were ultimately responsible for the fate of the nation. Not surprisingly, an expression that widely circulated in Japan right after World War II was the "collective penitence of all one hundred million Japanese"—who were presumably responsible for the crime and tragedy of the war.

The logic of nonresponsibility was inherent in the prewar emperor system. In the beginning of Japan's modernization, political reforms were carried out by former samurai of the feudal regime. They had had their topknots cut off to celebrate the dawn of the new era, but the insides of their heads had not changed very much. Intellectually, they were all for modernization, for organizing human relations on the basis of reason. What appealed to their hearts, however, were the feudalistic human connections, based upon precepts of loyalty, obedience, authority, and benevolence. In traditional society, the sense of obligation runs vertically. You belong to a clique and devote all your energy to the cause of your clique. Those belonging to other cliques are enemies, actual or potential. In the early phase of Japan's modernization, the destructive elements of cliquism were rampant within the political and bureaucratic structure of the Meiji government. Not infrequently, there was open, naked hostility between the adversary groups. Bureaucrats who went to the Imperial University of Tokyo formed an interest group opposed to those who graduated from the Imperial University of Kyoto. Politicians from Kyushu did not get along with those from Tohoku. The navy officers refused to cooperate with the army officials.

The emperor was the only being who held enough authority to minimize and control the internal attrition. The imperial crown was a means of unifying the split groups around a common objective: striving toward the glory and prosperity of the new nation. In actual fact, however, the emperor was not the true ruler of Japan. He was a symbolic, ceremonial entity who made few political decisions. Specific political decisions were made by the senior statesmen, but, technically, the prime minister was responsible for those decisions. Ambiguity was the substance of politics in prewar Japan. The formal line of political responsibility moved upward; yet, toward the end of the line, the imperial mist blurred the whole matter of responsibility.

The contradictions of the prewar system did not surface during the early decades of Japan's modernization. The bureaucrats of Meiji Japan had, at least, a personal sense of mission. It was later, in the 1920s and 1930s, that the pathology of the prewar system began to reveal itself. More and more public officials became bureaucrats in the worst sense of the term—technocrats who carried out their duties perfunctorily and competently without accounting for the effect on the nation's destiny. When the tentacles of Japanese imperialism began to reach Korea, Manchuria, and China, no one seemed responsible for the political decisions behind this military expansionism. In the late 1930s Japan became increasingly totalitarian, and embarked on a disaster course toward the Pacific War. The system of nonresponsibility degenerated into a system of irresponsibility. The bureaucrats who manned the system could not avert the historic catastrophe that awaited the entire nation. The people learned the hard way that the prewar system of ruling, whatever its merits, had some serious limitations.

*

The old order crumbled with Japan's unconditional surrender in World War II. The major changes that took place during the occupation period were revolutionary in character and far-reaching in scope. The occupation directives rolling out of General MacArthur's headquarters were stringent and uncompromising. The Imperial Army and Navy were disarmed. Ultranationalistic organizations were abolished. The political and military leaders of imperial Japan were tried as war criminals by the Far Eastern Military Tribunal. The *zaibatsu* corporations, giant, family-based financial combines like Mitsui and Mitsubishi, were dissolved. The land reform broke up concentrated land ownership. Shinto was no longer recognized as the national religion. The divinity of the emperor was denied.

The newly adopted postwar constitution emphasized the importance of political freedom and civil liberties. Many institutions supporting the old order had vanished from the scene. The armed forces, the Ministry of Internal Affairs, the secret police, the Privy Council, the House of Peers, the titles of nobility, and some aspects of the traditional family system . . . all became things of the past.

What did the demilitarization and democratization of Japan do to the prewar ruling classes? The effects were uneven and varied. The high-ranking military officials were summarily dismissed. The Ministry of Internal Affairs, a bastion of the imperial order that included the largest number of the intellectual elite, received the severest blow. The ministry was dismantled, its highest officials purged, and the lesser ones transferred to other ministries. The top-level *zaibatsu* executives were purged, and few of them managed to come back after the occupation. As a result of the land reform, the landlords lost much of their influence in local politics. The effects on politicians were mixed: some disappeared for good; some others survived the ordeal of the time and made successful comebacks—like Kishi Nobusuke who, despite his stained record of membership in the Tojo cabinet, became prime minister after the war.

It was the bureaucracy that showed the greatest resilience and viability in this period of national chaos. The highest ranking officials of all ministries were purged by the occupation authorities, but like an earthworm whose head was cut off, the body of the prewar bureaucracy lingered on. Vacancies at the top were quickly filled by middle-management officials who were no less competent than their fallen superiors. The bureaucracy as a whole stayed on as solid and stable as ever. General MacArthur, the new absolute ruler of Japan, did not dare dissolve its entire structure. To do so would have meant the uncontrollable disintegration of the country he was ruling. Instead, he depended on Japanese bureaucrats as instruments of his occupation policy. The direction of the policy's administration by the Americans themselves would have been too costly. In a country whose customs and mores were unfamiliar to the Americans, such an approach would have assuredly caused much friction with the native population.

Article 15 of the postwar Constitution of Japan states, in part: "The people have the inalienable right to choose their public officials and to dismiss them." While this sounds very reasonable, the article in fact is a dead letter. No legal basis was ever established upon which someone outside the bureaucracy could initiate dismissal of an official. On the contrary, the National Personnel Authority, instituted after the war, actually moved in the direction of increasing the security of public officials. It is practically impossible for the people to fire their bureaucrats. Technically, it is not feasible even for the cabinet to displace them. In short, there is no threat to their positions from above or below. In prewar Japan, the job of the bureaucrats was to serve the emperor. During the occupation period—the spirit of the postwar constitution notwithstanding—their new master was not the people but General MacArthur. Before the war, the Ministry of Internal Affairs, the arch-guardian of the conservative establishment, was the mainstream of bureaucratic power, controlling, among other things, the national police. Right after the war, the Ministry of Foreign Affairs, with its large supply of bureaucrats who could speak English and knew how to deal with Westerners, moved to the front rank. Many of those politicians and bureaucrats who rose to the highest positions during the occupation period were former career diplomats who were pro-Western. They were known as "liaison bureaucrats," favored and protected by the occupation authorities. Thus, their heyday ended with the end of the occupation, for the other bureaucrats had viewed them as opportunists taking advantage of the abnormality of the period. The "liaison bureaucrats" were replaced by those with backgrounds in economic affairs. During the post–peace-treaty years, such familiar figures in Japanese politics as Ikeda, Ohira, Miyazawa, Kurogane, Maeo, Fukuda, Kaya, Aichi . . . all came from the Ministry of Finance.

The system of Japanese bureaucracy not only survived but also expanded after the war. Despite the territorial shrinkage of the nation after the loss of former colonies, the number of public employees in Japan continued to increase. Relative to the golden age of the imperial order, however, the prestige of the career bureaucrats has suffered a decline. Instead of being the emperor's direct servants, they are now public servants, presumably working for the welfare of the people. The bureaucrats of today assume only a secondary role in politics. The peak of their ambition in prewar Japan was to head a ministry of the national government. In postwar Japan, the peak has been lowered. The highest level to which a career bureaucrat can climb is the post of vice-minister, acting as a technical assistant to the politically appointed head of a ministry. One who wishes to rise above the rank of vice-minister must leave the bureaucracy, go into politics, be elected to a seat in the Diet, ascend within the power structure of the governing party, then be appointed a minister. The image of the professional bureaucrat has lost much of its glamour. Few school children nowadays write in a questionnaire that they want to be bureaucrats when they grow up. If fame is one's interest, a quick way to it is to become a baseball player, a movie star, a singer, or a writer. If money matters, a more reliable way is to go into business, especially to get a job in a leading corporation that pays a good deal more salary than government offices.

Bureaucrats as a group possess the instincts of chameleons. They are quick to change their exteriors, depending upon shifting circumstances. Before the war, they acted as solemn servants of the divine emperor. After the war, the emperor became a man, General MacArthur a god. To the bureaucrats, democratization of Japan meant faithfully listening to the voice of the newly arrived ruler from the West. Dutifully they followed the conquerors' directives, knowing that they were being depended upon by the victors. Superficially, they showed every sign of collaboration with the occupation authorities. Behind the scenes, they employed every means to resist any move that might possibly be detrimental to the continuance of their system. They were aware that it was impossible even for General MacArthur to destroy them and, at the same time, depend upon them to carry out his policy. After all, many members of the occupation staff were relatively young, inexperienced Americans on temporary assignments away from home. They could not outwit veteran bureaucrats of the Japanese government who had spent years in public administration.

In prewar Japan the object of the bureaucrats' loyalty was pure and simple. Loyalty to the emperor superseded any other kind of loyalty. It did not take much thought to clarify the sense of direction in one's public service.

After the war, the object of their loyalty became vague and confused in their minds. In principle, all public servants supposedly serve the people. The "people," however, are too numerous and obscure to generate a real feeling of allegiance. If you are a Japanese bureaucrat, you know you are a member of a carefully selected elite; you are above the people. But the new constitution defines your role as being loyal to those below you. After the occupation period, the party politicians began obliging the bureaucrats to support and implement their policies.

It is not always pleasant, however, to remain a mere tool. The bureaucracy today is a big, impersonal machine. Being inside it, you feel little sense of public mission. All you see around you is the monotonous working of a mechanism that rolls out tons of forms and documents, week after week, month after month, without end. You are but a meaningless cogwheel in the giant apparatus. You become dehumanized and begin to feel hopeless about the whole thing. Cliquism within the bureaucracy is as rampant as ever. Its popularity and persistence might be understood as a psychological escape-hatch, a means of adding some human elements to what otherwise would be an unbearable situation.

Almost every corner of modern society is covered by public rules and regulations. Society needs someone to administer its laws. The power of bureaucrats lies in their control of all the strings attached to the rule of law. They may inwardly feel nihilistic about their jobs; yet it is they who issue and enforce administrative guidelines, collect taxes, program budgets, distribute national funds, draft new laws, manage public employees, and place purchase orders for a myriad of goods. The hand of public administration in modern society touches one's life from the cradle to the grave. Officials may complain about their meager pay, low prestige, and diminished status. But few of them quit their jobs, for they enjoy being in the shadow of the power structure. Theirs is one of the most secure positions in the world.

Why are they disliked by the people? It is not so much what they do on their jobs as it is their bureaucratic personality that is the cause of their unpopularity. The people find bureaucrats self-righteous, inflexible, hypocritical, and obsequious to superiors, but arrogant and overbearing to subordinates and taxpayers. A high-ranking official would deny this by saying, "It is the lower officials who might be obnoxious. The higher ones tend to be more pleasant and understanding." But those at the top can afford to be relaxed, personable, and magnanimous. They themselves were once at the bottom. They know well what goes on down below. Because of the hierarchical structure of bureaucracy, the lesser officials incarnate the dislikable. The men at the top, however, do little to correct the situation.

To reach the top, a functionary must be conservative, cautious, and meticulous. A daring, theatrical personality may be an asset to a politician, but it is a deadly vice to a bureaucrat. Every day he should arrive at his office on time, work regularly, be tactful and prudent, speak in a low key, behave passively, avoid small errors, honor conventions, never do anything without precedent. He must cultivate the art of shifting responsibility to someone below. Those at the very bottom—who meet and deal with people over the counter—find themselves in a most thankless position. They have the least authority but are obliged to absorb all the blame for every error that may occur. It is understandable, if not agreeable, that many petty clerks in government offices act obnoxiously toward the taxpayers who pay their salaries.

Once I was trying to use the research library of the Ministry of International Trade and Industry in Tokyo. A man at the desk told me it was not open to outsiders. I went up to the third floor of the building to see my friend, the head of a department in the ministry. He phoned the library to make special arrangements for me. In a matter of seconds, the deskman rushed in breathless to apologize to my friend for the error he had committed.

Red tape in Japanese government offices is legendary. If an American in Tokyo is frustrated by the Japanese bureaucracy, he should not draw a paranoiac conclusion that he is being discriminated against on the basis of his color. He is merely being treated as the natives are. A long wait and no response are routine. He must be prepared for all contingencies and surprises. Before he begins to fill out forms, he had better ask them if it is permissible to use a ball-point pen instead of a fountain pen. They may not accept his application unless it is written with regular ink.

The Japanese use *hanko*, a stamp bearing one's family name, in place of personal signatures. All official papers must be stamped by a *hanko*, registered at one's bank, ward office, tax office, and other places where important business is transacted. Sometimes your application is rejected because, allegedly, you used a *hanko* different from the registered one. You tell the clerk that it is the same stamp you have been using for the past ten years. It may be an hour or two before he will get up, walk to the next room, and see if the one you are using this time really matches the registered one. He may then advise you that, since the present one looks worn out, you had better acquire a new one and have it registered—though registration will perhaps take more than two weeks. Sometimes the authenticity of a *hanko* is carefully examined; most of the time it is accepted, provided it bears your name. Once I was visiting the Ministry of Foreign Affairs to obtain a legal paper. A clerk told me that I had to use a *hanko*, which I did not have. Nonchalantly, she instructed me to go around the corner to a *hanko* shop and buy one bearing my name for 25 cents. Any imposter could have done the same, but that did not seem to matter.

The bureaucracy provides a setting ideal for the working of Parkinson's law. The number of employees increases independently of the amount of work to be done. Every official wants to have as many subordinates as possible in order to raise his status in the hierarchy. Each one asks for more budget and positions for his section. Sectionalism is strong and prevalent. Jurisdictional disputes are frequent. It is wrong to assume that though the bureaucrats may be uncooperative to civilian outsiders, they are friendly to one another. An official of one ministry may treat another official from a different ministry as coldly as he would a total stranger. Since each section attempts to get more money and personnel, duplication of jobs in different ministries becomes inevitable. Joint, cooperative ventures are discouraged. A project, perhaps vital for the public good, that faintly suggests the possibility of intersectional conflict will tend to be avoided. More important than the public good is the enhancement of sectional interest, for promotions depend upon the latter. Activities of an interministerial agency are bound to stagnate because each member tends to think and act in terms of the gain to the ministry he represents, not in terms of the interest of the agency. In this situation, you forget about your role and obligation as a public official. Your efforts and concerns are directed toward one objective: tying up with the right people for faster promotion. It is common for a young bureaucrat to marry his boss's daughter. Ikeda Hayato, while he was head of the Ministry of Finance, is said to have arranged more than 100 marriages of his subordinates in the ministry.

The constitution is written in general language and contains relatively little text and few articles. For the average person, it is an approachable document. The same is not true with the laws; there are so many of them. The voluminous old ones remain in force, while new ones are added each year. They are written in difficult technical language that sounds disconnected from human life. Below the laws, there are numerous administrative rules, cabinet orders, ministerial ordinances, departmental notices. They are numbingly impersonal. Anyone who tries to read them all, let alone understand them, will soon throw up his hands. Yet it is the job of the bureaucrats to cope with them.

The laws look flawless and watertight. Every single case, every conceivable situation, appears amply covered by provisions and counter-provisions. At least, this is the way they look to outsiders. But a bureaucrat has become a real professional when he begins to see loopholes here and there. He learns not merely to administer the laws and regulations but to manipulate them as well. He begins to feel a satanic pleasure in holding the secret of the law in his hands. He knows that he knows what others do not. At the same time, he is suspicious of any intruder's motives. Thus, an interview with a Japanese bureaucrat is bound to be an exercise in futility. He will not say anything of interest. His answers will be dry, perfunctory, and uncontroversial. Soon you begin to wonder if you are conversing with a robot wearing a human mask. But he is a victim as well as a symbol of the dehumanization of complex modern society—which is embodied in the bureaucracy. The situation will not be cured by a political revolution. It is not certain that a conversation with a Russian bureaucrat would necessarily be more animated.

People do not always mean what they say in public. We have vested interests of one kind or another, and are prone to adjust our statements accordingly. The life of bureaucrats depends upon the existing political order's continuation. With each radical change in the nation, some or many of them will vanish from the scene. It is natural, then, that they become great defenders of the status quo. Before World War II, during the days of imperial glory, most Japanese bureaucrats upheld the rightist ideology. Whether they really believed in what they professed is beside the point. Openly to reject ultranationalism would have assuredly jeopardized their careers.

After the war some bureaucrats, like Wada Hiroo and Katsumata Seiichi, became socialist politicians, but they are a distinct minority. The majority of today's bureaucrats approve political freedom and democracy, not necessarily because they firmly believe in them as a matter of personal philosophy, but rather because freedom and democracy constitute the framework of political life in postwar Japan. One thing they disdain is any radical, revolutionary idea or movement that would threaten their existence. Most of them vote for the Liberal-Democratic party. Some prefer democratic socialism, and that is as far left as they go. None accepts communism as a political system. If you ask them about deep and wide corruption in Japanese politics, they will supply a standard answer: "People elect the Diet members. Election is the heart of political democracy. Disapproval of Japanese politicians implies distrust of Japanese people."

Who, then, is responsible for the corruption? They will provide a foolproof reply: "Both politicians and voters." The bureaucrats' political consciousness is inescapably conservative with respect to the nation's power structure. Their conservatism acts as a strong built-in stabilizer of social order, for good or ill. It may restrain a reactionary trend, or stand in the way of healthy, democratic progress. No wonder the bureaucrats are despised by both ultrarightists and ultraleftists as sly, lukewarm opportunists.

Salaries of public officials are considerably lower than those of business executives who have comparable background and experience. Yet bureaucrats seem to lead a materially comfortable life. They live in decent houses, own automobiles, travel with their families. At first glance, there is something mystifying about their standard of living, which looks too high to be warranted by their officially quoted salaries. The secret lies in perquisites of all sorts to which they are, *ex officio*, entitled. They are provided with public housing for which they pay nominal rents. The higher officials have access to chauffeur-driven government automobiles. When they travel with their families, they can stay at special inns that are heavily subsidized by the government. Expense accounts may be used for other than strictly official purposes. Not infrequently, when functionaries make official trips, local businesses offer to take care of travel expenses. At the end of each year, they receive gifts of all sorts from business interests—but not in amounts large enough to arouse suspicion of bribery. They manage to live well, for their low salaries are matched by low living costs. Their retirement normally comes early, in their mid-fifties, but they are entitled to good pensions. After retirement, a second employment in private business or public corporations is more or less guaranteed. Political scandals abound, but top-level bureaucrats seldom get caught. They are too cautious to commit clearly illegal acts. They are familiar with loopholes, provide themselves with escape-routes, and, in the last resort, have access to political protection. It is the lower officials—the less tactful ones—who get caught and face criminal charges.

In modern society, one's status is usually measured by occupation, education, income, and residence. The more professional one's job is, the greater the respect it commands. Those who manage people generally fare better than those who manage things. Despite the stigma attached to the bureaucracy, officials in Japan still receive substantial respect from the public, for they are professionals in law and public administration who manage a large number of government employees. Japanese society provides added advantages to their status. Most high-ranking Japanese bureaucrats are graduates of the University of Tokyo, and in Japan anyone who went to the University of Tokyo is respected automatically irrespective of his real worth. Furthermore, in Japan high income and high social status do not necessarily go together. In fact, people tend to look down on those who comfortably live on interest, dividends, and other property incomes. Those who live in enormous houses—even if they are not living beyond their means—tend to be despised or laughed at. Therefore, the bureaucrats who reside in decent but hardly luxurious public housing do not lose respectability on this score. In the United States, status-seeking is severely constrained by one's race, religion, and nationality-origin. In Japan, on the other hand, ethnic minorities constitute a tiny fraction of the total population. As long as you are a Japanese living in Japan, your status can go up as high as you wish solely on the basis of the level of education and professional status. The bureaucrats continue to be respected in Japan because by and large they meet the respectability criteria of Japanese society.

At the top level of Japanese politics, the ex-bureaucrat politicians assume influential positions. Throughout Japan's modern history such men have outnumbered those who were wholly politicians, and have greater longevity than those from non-bureaucratic backgrounds. During the early postwar years, there were three prime ministers from private backgrounds: Katayama Tetsu, Ishibashi Tanzan, and Hatoyama Ichiro. Their reigns were all short-lived. All other premierships, prior to 1972, had been held by former bureaucrats. Tanaka Kakuei, a self-educated man with no bureaucratic past, became prime minister in 1972, but this was an outstanding exception.

The prewar pattern was more striking. Only one prime minister during the entire prewar period, Inukai Takeshi, came from a purely private background. Pure politicians do better in popularity contests among the masses. They tend to be old-fashioned, theatrical, spontaneous, vulnerable, and, at times, odd. These traits are the very reasons for their popularity. In contrast, the masses find the bureaucrats-turned-politicians too tactful, too flawless, too perfect to be likable. They also fail to entertain the favor of the Japanese press. Many Japanese journalists are graduates of private universities, rather than the University of Tokyo. Subconsciously or otherwise, journalists suffer an inferiority complex toward those who rose to power through the orthodox channel of Japanese meritocracy, and over the years their complex has fermented a certain anti-bureaucratic tradition. Criticized and disliked by the masses as well as the press, the bureaucracy thrives on. It continues to be a breeding ground for powerful political figures.

Why are the ex-bureaucrat politicians so strong? That they are backed by the power structure is only a partial reason. The fundamental explanation is that their strength rests on their true capabilities. They may not have likable personalities. But their technical competence is unquestioned. As members of the Diet, they can freely and effectively utilize their expert knowledge—cumulated over years of professional training—of legislation, budgetary proceedings, and administrative technicalities.

While at the University of Tokyo, where most of them studied, these men were already a select group. Their university background has increased their acceptability as candidates for important positions. Over the past century, the University of Tokyo has supplied the leaders in government, politics, business, academia, science, and education. And it has been training not only the establishment elite but the antiestablishment elite as well.

Many communist and socialist leaders went to that
university. Since the mid-19th century, it has contributed to the snobbery and self-righteousness of the power
elite. At the same time, however, it has served as an
efficacious mobilizer of the nation's talents. Those who
pass the entrance examination to the university are high
school graduates with the highest scholastic records in
the country. They are screened again when they take
the civil service examination to qualify for a bureaucratic position. After being assigned to various ministries
of the national government, they receive training on the
job, and attend specially programmed seminars. During
the tenure of civil service, the bright ones become brighter. It is only natural, then, that their knowledge and
training in law and public administration become
uncontestably superior to that of any other group,
including the political parties *per se.*

Japanese political parties do not maintain their own
well-developed professional staffs. Practically all technical matters are handled by career bureaucrats. Each
party is torn and split by factions. Ideological differences between the conservative ruling party and the
opposition parties are deep and wide. The Japanese
Diet is far from a showcase of political democracy; it
is more a display-window of political inefficiency and
disorder. Occasionally, violence erupts on the floor of the
Diet, and such eruptions are sure to be telecast to the
rest of the world. Because of this apparent instability,
uninitiated foreign observers may assume that Japanese
political democracy is a fragile blossom that may fall
at any moment. This, however, is to see only the surface.
Actually, the bureaucracy's rocklike presence provides
Japanese politics with a psychological environment of

basic stability. Without such an environment, it is not unlikely that Japan would have witnessed the rise of uncontrollable confusion in politics, followed by revolution, counterrevolution, wholesale corruption of all sorts, the emergence of a military dictatorship, and neo-fascism. The Japanese bureaucrats, however, are "trustees" of the nation's democracy. And, notwithstanding the opposition parties' charge to the contrary, the bureaucracy maintains, at least on the surface, a position of neutrality vis-à-vis party politics. It exerts quiet, restraining influence from the rear. The power it represents may be an evil, but it is a necessary evil.

Many less-developed countries in Southeast Asia and Latin America suffer from chronic political instability because, while there may be able politicians, those countries lack a well-developed, competent bureaucracy that serves not only as intermediary between the government and the people, but also as a preventive against any extremist movement at the top. The bureaucracy does generate its own problems, but in its absence a nation—like a car without a carburetor—will break down. In Japan, bureaucrats are respected, disliked, and depended upon all at once. Most of us choose to vote for someone who is unpleasant yet totally capable, rather than a likable but inept and incompetent candidate. The bureaucrats who run for political office have all the credentials, and the average Japanese votes for them because he or she feels that they can be trusted and relied upon in the management of the nation's political affairs.

Except for a brief period of coalition government under socialist premier Katayama shortly after World War II, the conservative party, now known as the

Liberal-Democratic party, has stayed in power through-out the postwar years. Japan has maintained a *de facto* one-party system—which is fondly referred to as a one-and-a-half-party system. If the ruling party were to change periodically, it would, in the long run, be in the best interest of the bureaucracy to maintain strict neutrality toward party politics. But neutrality can be dangerous to the self-interest of the bureaucracy if the ruling party is always the same. In Japan, ambitious, high-ranking bureaucrats have found it more advanta-geous to cooperate closely with the conservative politicians in power than to observe a true neutrality, despite the harmful effects such close cooperation may have on the quality of the nation's democracy.

Nowhere does personal connection count more than in the world of politics. After retirement, a bureaucrat may join the Liberal-Democratic party and run for political office, obtain an executive position in private business, or seek employment in a public corporation. The prospects for all these alternatives, directly and indirectly, depend upon keeping a friendly relationship with conservative politicians. Thus, the allegation of a neutral bureaucracy begins to lose its substance. The adhesion of the two power groups—bureaucrats and the ruling party—is inevitable. "Public servants" be-come "private servants" of whoever happens to be in power at the top.

Before the war, the bureaucrats served the emperor well; during the occupation, they were obedient servants of General MacArthur; after independence, they have in fact been guardians of the conservative cause. They have demonstrated a formidable talent for self-preserva-tion and have been remarkably effective in serving the power structure. Yet they have shown little positive interest in correcting the defects of that structure—be it the system of nonresponsibility, red tape in government offices, corruption among lawmakers, or inefficiency and disorder in the nation's political processes. These problems, of course, are not uniquely Japan's. They exist, to varying degrees, in all other countries. Perhaps it is too much to expect the bureaucracy—Japanese or otherwise—to guard the power structure and repair it as well, just as it is too much to expect individual citizens to assume full responsibility for the malaise of their society.

✦ WHAT IS AND WHAT IS NOT

In the islands of Japan nature fashioned a favored spot where civilization could prosper and a people could develop into a strong and great nation. A happy combination of temperate climate, plentiful rainfall, fairly fertile soil, and reasonable proximity to other great homes of civilized man predestined the ultimate rise of the inhabitants of these islands to a place among the leading peoples of the world.

—EDWIN O. REISCHAUER

The Japanese women are white and usually of goodly appearance; many, indeed, are extremely comely and graceful.

—BERNARDINO DE AVILA GIRON
(came to Japan in 1594)

Of all the races of the world, the Japanese are perhaps physically the least attractive, with the exception of Pygmies and Hottentots.

—KAWASAKI ICHIRO

6 ✦ The Importance of Being Dependent

*The Japanese did away with nomadic life early, and
settled down to cultivate rice fields. People living on
rice must inevitably settle permanently in one place.
In such a society families continue generation after
generation. Genealogies and kinships of families
through long years become so well known by their
members that the society as a whole takes on the
appearance of a single family. In such a society,
individuals are closely bound to each other, and they
form an exclusive human nexus. Here, an individual
who asserts himself will hurt the feelings of others
and thereby do harm to himself. The Japanese learned
to adjust themselves to this type of familial society.*

—NAKAMURA HAJIME

No man is an island. We are fated to be born, grow up,
live, and die within the confines of society. Life is like
a long thread tied to numerous other threads. A few
hermits may hide in remote mountains where there is no
trace of man, and a few recluses may sever the spiritual
bond with other men while continuing to live, physically, inside a human community. But most of us choose

to lead lives that depend upon and are depended upon by others.

Japanese culture has long viewed the intricate web of interdependencies as a fundamental fact of human relations. In the Japanese language, the word "individualist" suggests an egotistical man. To the Japanese ear, the phrase "independent personality" connotes an attitude of defiance, a lack of concern for others. Not that Japanese culture necessarily stresses the importance of being dependent, in the way the importance of independence is encouraged in America. What is stressed in Japan is the art of being dependent. The fact of mutual dependence is taken for granted. It is a way of life that no Japanese can escape. The customs, habits, language, traditions, mores—which every Japanese has to learn and cope with—are all intermingled in reinforcing the system of dependence. So stringent and thorough is the system that the personality is bound to be conditioned by it.

The total dependence of a newborn infant upon its mother is viewed by Japanese as the purest form of human dependence. It is pure because there is no cunning calculation involved in the relationship. The infant's life is completely in its mother's hands, and its needs are affectionately fulfilled by her. In the early days the infant is not even conscious of being a self, physically apart from its mother. Its life is saturated with mother's love. At the same time, the mother derives an immense pleasure from the child's total dependence upon her care. The joy of her giving love is no weaker than the joy of the child's receiving it. There is a reciprocity of happiness; yet happiness of the infant comes from total dependence, the mother's from being depended upon.

A couple truly in love is another example of ideal human dependence. A man and a woman totally identify themselves with each other. They are still two physical beings but, psychically, the two become one. The act of giving and sacrificing is magically transformed into an act of spontaneous pleasure. Willingly, each does, for the other, things that would otherwise be boring chores. They become spiritual Siamese twins. Life apart becomes inconceivable, for the happiness of the two rests upon their mutual and simultaneous dependence.

The mother-infant relationship and that of a couple in love, admittedly, are ideal cases of human connections. As people grow older, they discover much to their dismay that human dependence is not always pure, and that people's motives can be devastatingly ugly and wicked. They are faced with a terrible dilemma. They cannot live alone in this cold world. They want to rely on others for their happiness but their attempts to do so are not always favorably reciprocated. The voice of Western culture would then suggest: ''Be independent. Be an adult. Do your own thing and go your own way.'' Japanese culture says it differently: ''Search for the ideal. The ideal may be rare, but the rare is not impossible. Find your group and belong to it. You and the group will rise or sink together. Without belonging, you will be lost in the wilderness. Apart from dependence, there is no human happiness. Contentment through independence is a delusion.'' In the context of Japanese society, this is a persuasive voice. As a Japanese looks around, he realizes that he has no other alternative.

Japanese society is very group-conscious. There are thousands of groups, formal and casual. Each person is conscious of which group or groups he or she belongs to.

Each person is either an insider or an outsider of a given group. Those inside a group feel a strong tie with one another or try to believe that there is one. A "we-feeling" may be an illusion, but it is an illusion capable of profoundly affecting the human mind. It gives one a sense of security, and it does not matter if such a sense is false. What matters is that one feels it. The sense of security provided by the group is better than the horror of being left alone in the cold universe. Each person becomes acutely concerned with his group's welfare. He may not get along with some other members of the same group, but he does his best not to disturb its solidarity. It is like riding a submarine. The captain reminds his crew—and each member of the crew understands—that if the ship goes down, so goes everyone. To ask, "Granted the group is important, should it be more important than its individual members?" reflects a Western mode of thinking. The ideal in Japan is that members can identify themselves with their groups so thoroughly that they and the group are fused into oneness. All petty differences among individual members are washed away. Each member is rid of his ego and dedicates his total self to his group. As a result, the group triumphs and so do all its members.

Most of this, of course, is nonsense. Saints and the selfless do not represent mankind. Many human relations are deliberate and calculated. Instead of promoting individualism as a way of survival, however, the Japanese reach out for a solution that makes the best of the group system. If they do not find a ready-made group that gives them satisfaction, they will organize a new one. For this purpose they take advantage of every opportunity. In the spring of 1969, I taught a

course one evening a week at a private college in Tokyo.
Towards the end of the semester, my students organized
an alumni club in my honor and resolved to have
"class reunions" periodically in the future. The fact
that I was soon returning to the United States was not
important. I was merely a catalyst for forming a new
group. Six months later, a member of the club came
to the United States on business. He called my Berkeley
residence from Los Angeles to wish me well and send
me regards from all the club members.

The code word in the Japanese language to describe
the intricate web of human connections is *giri-ninjo*.
The manner in which this term is used in Japan and the
subtle variations in its meaning are unfortunately not
translatable into English. It is a compound noun:
giri roughly means indebtedness, duties, obligations;
ninjo stands for human feeling, kindness, a warm heart,
spontaneous generosity. Sometimes the two words are
used separately, or they may be put together to form a
compound noun. The central implication of this code
word is that every human connection is some variation
of *giri-ninjo* and no one can escape from its shadow. A
mother's acts of affection to her child and one's deeds
of generosity for a close friend are all spontaneous and
pure. What a man does for his colleague or superior is a
matter of *giri*. Ideally, we should do for others as a way
of manifesting our honest desire and spontaneous feeling
toward them. But we are all stuck together within circles
of dependency. We must learn our duties. We must cultivate our sense of obligation to others. Courageously
and willingly, accept others' attempts to depend on you.
Learn how to depend on others properly and how not
to depend to the point of annoying others. In any event,

a person who has no warm feeling for another and no sense of obligation to anyone else is the worst and the most dreadful. Such a person is as good as dead.

Much of this corresponds to the Christian concept of brotherly love. Yet there are differences. A Japanese learns to be keenly conscious of his loyalty to his group— particularly, his family, relatives, classmates, teachers, and colleagues. However, his sense of concern and collective responsibility stays essentially private and particular rather than public and universal. A sharp line of demarcation is drawn between his private groups and those to which he does not belong. To insiders, he tries to be warm, kind, considerate—not necessarily because of his inborn altruism but rather because of his awareness that his welfare depends upon his group and his inconsiderate acts may invite retaliation.

The psychology of dependence breeds a certain anxiety syndrome among many Japanese. They feel at home only when they are with members of their own groups and become awkward and ill at ease when they must deal with others. Even inside Japan, farmers go on sightseeing tours in large groups—not a group of 10 or 15 but of 50, 100, or 150. When they go overseas, few prefer to travel alone, and the cost difference is not the primary reason. They are too apprehensive to walk alone on foreign soil. Before leaving Japan, they frantically try to get hold of as many connections as possible abroad. A man will write to his friends and acquaintances who happen to be abroad. He will probably write to his friends' friends as well as to his friends' friends' friends, asking if they can help him when he comes to Paris.

Language and manners reflect the same anxiety. The Japanese word *tanin,* "stranger," carries the chilling connotation of someone who has totally disconnected himself from the human community and toward whom you experience no feeling. This is the feeling the Japanese dread. They tremble at the thought of being ostracized by their group and of becoming *tanin* whom no one cares about any more. Many Americans who have met Japanese with a limited knowledge of English note that they often say ''I'm sorry'' when they are expected to say ''Thank you.'' The Americans do not understand why Japanese have to feel ''sorry'' for the favors they receive. At a superficial level, this is a humorous instance of mistranslation. ''Thank you'' in Japanese is *sumimasen,* which literally means ''I'm sorry.'' The sense of this expression, however, has deep cultural roots. When a Japanese receives a favor, his feeling of gratitude is inseparably mixed with a sense of guilt or shame. He is grateful but feels ashamed that he has inconvenienced the person from whom he has received the favor. He wishes to apologize because he hopes to continue his dependence upon the other person in the future. He is saying in effect: ''Please forgive my selfishness in having asked you to do me a favor. I am a weak, dependent soul. I really appreciate your kindness. You may inwardly be annoyed and disgusted with me. I hope you will understand my weakness and let me continue to depend upon you in the future as well.''

Under the dependence system, there is no automatic assurance that warm feelings will be reciprocated. The naked truth is that being depended upon by others is more frustrating than pleasurable. For every act of depending, there is a person being depended upon. Mathematically, it is impossible to organize a society where people can only depend on others. If a child refuses to grow up and continues to sulk and depend upon his mother, what was once pure joy to her will soon turn into displeasure. A human relation is vulnerable; it can move in unexpected directions. A father-son relationship is severed. A brother becomes a stranger. A longtime friendship comes to an end. A professor refuses to accept a student as his disciple. A boss shows favoritism toward another fellow whom you cannot stand. You are stuck with your group, but the group's interest does not coincide with yours. Japanese psychology is ill-equipped to deal with these situations of disappointment. The system of dependence is the antithesis of individualism. A Japanese is conditioned to look for a source of contentment from without, instead of from within himself. If he expresses his dissatisfaction with his group when it fails to fulfill his personal desires, the group will either ostracize him or force him to suppress his selfish wants. This will only intensify his anxiety. He will develop a hypersensitivity toward others, though he may not show it externally.

Interpersonal relations in Japan tend to be sticky, wet, and delicate. To avoid offending others, every word and move must be carefully watched. The angle and frequency of bowing ought to be tactfully measured. A letter of rejection has to be written with utmost care and in a vague, roundabout manner. A verbal request must begin with a long monologue that has little to do with the request, since exposing the real intent at the outset will be considered rude. The way for a university committee to reject a submitted thesis is not to say no, but to hold it indefinitely until the degree candidate gets the right idea. When a husband asks his wife, "I'm free this evening. What would you like to do . . . go out some place?'' her typical answer will be: ''Well . . .to a movie, perhaps . . .'' She deliberately makes her response vague and open-ended and carefully avoids too definitive an answer, since it may not coincide with the husband's. In Japan, a person in a position of leadership (e.g., a school principal or a head of a government agency) often resigns for a crime or an act of misconduct committed by someone below him. He resigns—even if he is not technically responsible—as a symbolic gesture to cleanse the shame brought upon his group.

When a Japanese with an imperfect knowledge of English is visiting an American home, he will likely be turned off by the host's remark: ''Please make yourself at home.'' Literally translated into Japanese, the remark sounds as if he is saying, ''I don't know your particular wants, and I don't really care. Instead of my bothering to make you feel comfortable, why don't you go ahead and help yourself?'' When Japanese meet their superiors, strangers or foreigners, their manner tends to become overly polite and formal, their attitude rigid and reserved. This is an instance of cultural conditioning, a byproduct of the dependence system. The human relationship in which one can say and do anything as he pleases with absolutely no fear of committing an offense is rare. One wrong phrase may sever the human connection. One inappropriate gesture may turn out to be a fatal mistake, the beginning of the end of a warm friendship. In Japan, no one can afford to take a chance. A Japanese is compelled to be polite and reserved. He does not particularly enjoy being rigid in his manners but, after a while, reserve becomes a reflex. To the Westerner, all this may sound suffocatingly inflexible, but this is an outsider's reaction, just as it would be an out-

sider's reaction for a Japanese man to be overwhelmed
to learn the range of things that American men must do
for women in American society. Those inside the dependence system do derive a sense of security from it.
To the Japanese eye, it is the so-called individualism of
the West that looks cold, dry, exclusionist, and mortally
inhuman.

Most of us require some degree of dependence upon
others for the sake of our own mental hygiene. Those
who deny this are deceiving themselves. Left in complete
isolation from the rest of humanity, one's psychic equi-
librium will eventually break down. A child with a de-
pendable father is happier than an orphan. A daughter
who can rely upon her mother for spiritual comfort is
better off than a motherless girl. A wife who can count
on her husband in a moment of crisis is more fortunate
than a spinster. Retired parents with supportive sons
are more contented than those on welfare. With no dependence available, life quickly becomes barren.

Postwar Japan has had her share of problems common
to all other modern societies: generation gaps, the death
of traditional values, increasingly impersonal life-styles,
alienation, nihilism. Symbolic of the trend of social unrest, the radical student movement in Japan reached its
peak in 1968–69. Thousands of students marched, snake-
danced, threw rocks, burnt auditoriums, and forced the
closing of numerous campuses across the country. Ironically, many of those violent students felt that they were
the victims, rather than the offenders. They felt persecuted by a society that had become purposeless. They
could depend upon nobody, neither corrupt government,
nor professors too busy to talk with individual students,
nor parents who continued to live according to values

in which they themselves no longer believed. Japan was fighting no war they could join in. Nobody challenged them or offered them new values they could accept. To receive attention and gain some sense of living, rebellion was the only recourse. While they decried the hypocrisy of the old generation, they did not provide any new values, either, that could satisfy everyone in society. The new values would presumably emerge from the ruins of the old world.

The vehemence and magnitude of the radical student movement in Japan is to a large extent an inevitable consequence of a huge crack which World War II left in the structure of Japanese society. The cult of the divine emperor was gone, the glory of militarism had vanished, and filial piety was passé. The lessons in ''freedom'' and ''individualism'' that the Japanese received from the occupying Americans after the war added further confusion to their minds. The word ''freedom'' did not exist in traditional Japanese language. It had to be invented in the 19th century. Prior to 1945, the Japanese interpreted the word to mean ''lack of discipline, selfishness, disorder, self-interest at the expense of group interest''— in short, it meant something antithetical to their traditional values. Then the Americans marched in and taught the Japanese that the freedom of each individual must be defended at any cost, for it represents human dignity and constitutes the core of democracy. The lesson from the conqueror was duly accepted. The good meaning was now added to the bad meaning of the word.

During the postwar period the word ''freedom'' has been used in both ways, causing a great deal of confusion. The confusion has not been merely terminological. Japanese thought has suffered a schizophrenic derangement about the question of man versus society, freedom versus collective responsibility. The Western doctrine of freedom holds that the rights of each individual are inalienable and that individuals always come before society. Projected in the mirror of the Japanese mind, this doctrine reads like a statement of an ideology, a secular religion, a fiction, not an expression of truth. To the Japanese, asking ''Which is more important, man or society?'' is like asking ''Which comes first, mind or body?'' The two are inseparable. To believe that a man can legitimately claim his rights beyond and above those of the community of which he is a member takes an act of faith. A Judaeo-Christian proverb, ''God helps those who help themselves,'' sounds strange and disagreeable to the Japanese ear. It does not seem an ideal suggestion for a community of men.

*

The Japanese dependence system is rational and efficient from the standpoint of social control. Each member is trained to be selfless and think of others first. The virtue of being selfless is reflected even in the structure of the Japanese language, which frequently drops a subject from a sentence. The subjects—I, you, he, she—that emphasize the identity of each acting individual are discounted. Who does what is less important than what is done for the collective will and communal interest. The dependence system can be an effective means of mobilizing people toward a national goal. Each group exerts pressure against the dissident views of its members. Members agree to behave in accord with their common goal.

Unfortunately, the system can transmute itself into fanaticism and drive the whole nation into a state of hysteria. When only one individual becomes hysterical and starts acting irrationally, he may be sanctioned by his group so that the group as a whole manages to retain its sanity. It is not difficult for the group to single him out as an unacceptable person and punish him accordingly. The situation changes, however, when the group becomes hysterical. It will be increasingly difficult for the originally rational members to resist the new mood. It is simpler for them to join the crowd than to keep opposing the trend at the risk of being persecuted for their disloyalty. The psychology of dependence only encourages the snowballing effect of collective madness. It pushes each member to ''selfless'' action, for good or ill. The gathering storm of Japanese fascism in the 1930s and the fanaticism of Japanese soldiers in World War II are cases in point.

The presumed virtue of being selfless precludes autonomous thinking. In practice, it points to a certain intellectual indolence and a susceptibility to extraneous thoughts. People become impressionable, and an element of docility seeps into their minds. What they think and believe at any one time is not the result of their long, hard, independent search for the truth, but simply what they have been hearing from others lately. They will grab any idea which happens to be currently fashionable. Of course, in any society, the so-called ''silent majority'' does not consist of those who can aptly be described as independent thinkers. Anywhere in the world, public opinion, to varying degrees, is manipulated by the mass media and the establishment. What distinguishes the Japanese is that their psychology of dependence intensifies the tendency toward intellectual changeability, toward a fundamental skepticism about the universality, permanence, and absoluteness of all things in life.

What is not truly your own may be accepted or abandoned with ease. In the 1930s, most Japanese went along with the cult of the divine emperor, the magical superiority of the Japanese armed forces, their mission to establish a new world order, and other mental paraphernalia of the day. Few objected to the Ministry of Education when it began circulating the standard elementary textbook of Japanese history in which mythology and facts were all mixed up. Just before World War II there was a tremendous fad of Nishida philosophy in intellectual circles. Almost every educated Japanese talked about Nishida philosophy. Despite the extreme difficulty of Professor Nishida's original writings (mainly concerned with a synthesis of Eastern and Western philosophies), long lines of university students would form in front of bookstores before sunrise. Patiently they stood in the still dark streets to snatch the remaining copies of the Nishida books as though those books contained the final truth.

The changeability of the Japanese can cut through the wall of resistance against desirable social change. But it may also sever the cord of reason. Stubborn adherence to old ideas can constitute a formidable barrier to the necessary transformation of a society. At the same time, the lack of autonomous thinking can hold the seed of disaster—as the Japanese learned the hard way in their recent past.

As long as a society is small and simply organized, the dependence system may work effectively. The same system, however, faces rising frictions and contradictions when a country becomes industrialized and its social organization more complex. The required degree of mobility must necessarily rise. Each social organization can no longer afford to respond to the dependence needs of each member. More and more people discover that their loyalty to the group is not sufficiently requited. They sense a growing disparity between their needs and those of their group. This should not cause much mental strain to a person accustomed to individualism. If he does not like his present group, he moves to another or goes independent and cultivates his own garden. His premise is that he never needs a group as much as the group needs him.

The matter of unrequited group loyalty is not quite as simple to a person who has grown up in a culture saturated with the ethos of mutual dependence. He remains an eternal child. When his innocent attempt to depend upon others is coldly rejected, he is prone to be hurt like a child unexpectedly scolded by his mother. The dependency system particularly affects attitudes toward women. Since there must be some relief for Japanese men who struggle in the chilly waters of human relations, many Japanese women, after growing up, remain baby-ish, sweet-voiced, soft-mannered, delicate, and doll-like; girls whose inborn personalities are of the opposite kind try or pretend to be so. This is their subconscious response to the need of Japanese men who, in their mature years, retain their mother-complexes and seek spiritual as well as physical comfort in playing the baby to their women.

The way the dependence system works in practice often deviates considerably from what it is supposed to be like in theory. The Japanese perenially suffer from guilt and shame about their conduct. Their minds are

caught up in an intricate network of duties and obligations, the questions of how to be proper, how not to say
certain things, how to return favors without insulting
the other party. At times, the substance of human relationships is lost while a disproportionate amount of
care is devoted to the manner of fulfilling one's obligations. Wives constantly worry about the correctness of
what they do and say to their relatives and in-laws. Husbands are continually concerned about protocol toward
their superiors and colleagues. To be sure, wives and
husbands around the world worry—more or less—about
people in their lives. What distinguishes the Japanese
is the degree of their anxiety, the intensity of their concern. Propriety becomes a compulsion.

When a family is visited by a relative who has not
been seen for many years, the wife goes overboard to
prepare a feast. Enormous amounts of time and money
may be spent to demonstrate the correctness of her
hospitality. The wife may keep herself so busy serving
the relative with one thing after another that she scarcely
talks with him before he departs.

In America, gift-giving in general—to say nothing of
the onrush of the Christmas season—is bad enough. In
Japan, it is a mad race. Each visitor to a private home is
expected to bring a gift. The correctness of the gift
depends upon the nature of the visit and the age-status
relationship between the giver and the receiver. Later,
the receiver is supposed to deliver a return gift appropriate in value and kind. It is not easy to keep finding
appropriate gifts. Out of desperation, one would pick
anything to get the task over with. A Japanese professor
once showed me a cabinetful of junk—cheap dishes,
baskets, fans, trays, and other gifts of dubious utility—

that he had received from his students. "I don't know what to do with them," sighed the man. During my visit with the professor at his home, I witnessed a scene which would not have occurred in America. He happened to be lending some money to a distant relative in financial trouble. The relative, a young man in his late twenties, came with his mother to pick up the money, and they brought with them a huge, elaborately decorated cake made by one of the most expensive bakeries in Tokyo. Evidently it was not proper for the young man to borrow less money and forgo presenting the cake.

The tyranny of gift-giving is intensified when a Japanese goes overseas. Once the news is out, he begins to receive congratulatory bon voyage gifts from his friends, relatives, colleagues, and business associates. The poor man has to keep a meticulous record of who gave him what, so that he will be sure to buy the proper return gifts abroad. It would be unpardonable to come home and face these kind people empty-handed. The Japanese have already established a global reputation as great buyers of expensive souvenirs. As early as 1961, the Amsterdam airport displayed a sign in Japanese, wooing tourists to the city's diamond shops. Gift shops attended by Japanese-speaking salesgirls have been proliferating in Paris, Rome, London, New York, Chicago, Los Angeles, San Francisco, and other major cities of the world. But it is duty toward friends and relatives, not love for gifts, that compels Japanese tourists to spend hard-earned cash on foreign-made souvenirs. Inwardly, they are sick of the awesome burden of gift-hunting that diverts so much of their time, energy, and money from the more pleasurable aspects of travel.

The psychology of dependence tends to induce feelings

of persecution. Emotional life hinges on the care, guidance, and spiritual comfort provided by others, and
if dependence needs are rejected, the rejected person will
blame the other party for his or her anguish. Dependent
people stand, as it were, on other people's feet. If such
people fall, it is the fault of those who suddenly pulled
their feet away. If you ask the Japanese who are their
favorite figures in Japanese history, many of them will
cite Kusunoki Masashige, Minamoto no Yoshitsune, the
Forty-seven Ronin, and Saigo Takamori. It is no coin-
cidence that these were all ill-fated individuals, heroes
who lost their lives tragically. Losers are popular in
Japan, and the sense of sympathy with them tends to
run deeper than feelings of respect for those who win.
Many Japanese secretly enjoy a feeling of identity
with the radical students. All Japanese—particularly
those whose shop windows were broken—deplore the
students' violence. Nevertheless, they feel for those who,
before everyone's eyes, are destined to lose to armored
police cars, and they cannot entirely conceal their admiration for these youngsters fighting a heroic battle
against the corrupt establishment.

The persecution complex of the Japanese conditions
their image of the outside world. In international conflicts, they tend to think of themselves as the injured
party. In this respect, the Japanese are not much different from all other peoples; every war, to those who fight,
is more or less a defensive war. Americans believe that
their country was drawn into the Pacific War because
Japan suddenly attacked Pearl Harbor in December,
1941; certainly the United States did not start the war.
In Japanese eyes, this is a magnificent oversimplification,
a grand confusion between symptom and cause.

Throughout their modern history, the Japanese had felt threatened and humiliated by the Western powers. Their attitude toward the West had been permeated with ambivalence—a mixture of love for the superior accomplishments of Western civilization and vexation at being unfairly treated by the arrogant Western states. Western guns had forced the opening of Japan in the mid-19th century and Japan was impelled to swallow humiliating demands for extraterritorial jurisdiction and unequal commercial treaties. The West had taught her that, in international power politics, might is not right but it surely helps. She learned the lesson too well. As Japan began her colonial expansion in Korea, Manchuria, and China, the Western powers in unison condemned Japan while they themselves were doing the same thing in Asia, Africa, and Latin America. The United States in the abstract was the land of freedom and opportunity; but this image was hardly reconcilable with the naked discrimination that awaited Japanese immigrants to California. In 1940 and 1941, there was a steady buildup of tension in U.S.–Japan diplomatic relations. The United States terminated shipment of petroleum and scrap iron to Japan, then froze Japanese assets held at American banks. Toward the end of 1941, the atmosphere in Japan became so tense that everyone felt some kind of blowup was inevitable, though no one could say for sure when, where, and how it would happen—let alone foresee the national disaster in the making. They felt they had been humiliated enough . . . had run out of the last drop of patience. The news of Pearl Harbor gave them a great sense of relief that the moment of truth had finally arrived.

The persecution complex of the Japanese breeds a

certain naiveté in their views of other countries. This was graphically revealed in 1971 in their highly emotional reaction to President Nixon's new economic policy which, in part, was aimed at curbing Japanese exports to the American market. The United States had been suffering from a high rate of unemployment, inflation, chronic balance-of-payments deficits, and depression in an increasing number of American industries hard hit by foreign competitors. Any president of the United States has to think of America before any other country, and Japan's export surplus vis-à-vis the United States was growing at an alarming rate. Nixon imposed a special import surtax and forced Japan to revaluate the yen upward. In a way, Nixon's new economic policy was something Japanese consumers should have been grateful for, since the yen revaluation meant that they could buy American goods at lower prices and that Japan's huge holdings of U.S. dollars, resulting from her export surplus, could be used to buy more from the United States.

The Japanese reacted with anything but gratitude. Nixon's policy came as a shock, a shameless declaration of economic war against Japan, a blatant attempt to shut Japanese goods out of the American market. Prior to 1968, Japan had been running a trade deficit vis-à-vis the United States. But when Japan had been struggling to improve her export capabilities through hard work and austerity, the United States had not criticized her own failure to buy more from Japan. Then, when the trade balance was finally reversed, the same country that had ignored Japan's difficulties began accusing her of not importing enough from the United States. Nixon's subsequent announcement of his China visit, without prior consultation with Japan, only added oil to the flames.

Why all this hysteria? In order to understand Japanese emotionalism, we must return to their psychology of dependence. In 1945, Japan lost the war to the United States. Ever since, the two have been close allies, the United States being the big brother. Japan had been playing the proper role of a little brother by being a passive, polite, and even timid partner of the alliance. After the defeat, Japan accepted the position of sub-servience to the United States, a nation of great power and wealth, a symbol of trust and benevolence. In short, Japan decided to depend upon the United States. In Japanese cultural tradition, once a master-follower relationship is established, it is presumed to remain harmonious for good. The follower expects permanent comfort in depending upon the master for spiritual guidance as well as material needs. It takes the Japanese psychology of dependence to apply this sort of expecta-tion even to the sphere of international power politics. In 1971, Nixon did only what he had to do as president of the United States. To the Japanese, his was an act of betrayal and disgrace, a sudden stab in the delicate tissue of the heart.

7 ✦ Longing for Belonging

> *In nearly all activities and issues the Japanese traditionally think of themselves as members of a group, and their satisfactions are largely expected to come through group fulfillment of group objectives.*
> —HERMAN KAHN

> *The Japanese have had to develop a society like that of herbivorous animals, not like that of carnivorous ones.*
> —YONEYAMA TOSHINAO

The Japanese are fond of introducing themselves in terms of their institutional affiliations. A man you meet in Tokyo is likely to tell you first, "I work for the Mitsubishi Heavy Industries," "I'm from the Sumitomo Bank," or "I belong to the Mitsui Trading Company." The disclosure of his occupation—what he does on his job—usually comes much later. For a long while, you may not know whether he is an accountant, a salesman, a lawyer, or an engineer. It is possible that a man in a gray flannel suit who introduces himself as "Fuji Television" turns out to be a company chauffeur rather than an executive producer. When two Japanese meet for the first time, they try to find out, before anything else, what the other's "affiliation" is. In assessing a man's social position, his occupation, technical training, or particular skill counts less than which company, university, bank, or government office he is associated with. In Japan, a place of employment is not considered merely an organization with which one is related through a contract, but is viewed as a place to which one belongs. Attitudes toward it are highly emotional and subjective. It becomes "my firm," "our corporation," and even "my life" itself.

Group consciousness is deep-rooted in Japanese culture. Its prototype is found in the traditional concept of the household (*ie*), which does not necessarily coincide with a blood-related family. The traditional household in Japan is a communal grouping of individuals who share residence and jointly participate in a common enterprise. Interpersonal relations as members of the same household take precedence over any other kind of human relations. Being a member of the present household is more important than being a member of the original family. A son who is adopted into another household thus becomes a "stranger" to his own family. A daughter-in-law matters far more than one's real daughter who has been married to someone in another family. A great psychic distance quickly develops between two real brothers once they start managing separate households.

To organize a household not by kinship but by including anyone who could fulfill its needs had been a practice for so many centuries in traditional Japan that even the present-day Japanese do not see anything unnatural

about it. It was common for a family business to be run
by trusted employees who were treated like real members
of the family. It was not unusual for the family head to
marry his daughter to a young, able foreman, and make
him his successor as head of the household. The expression "family business" in Japan requires careful interpretation. "Family" does not really refer to a collection
of kin and siblings; it pertains to the way in which members of the enterprise interact and identify with one another. The traditional ethos of the "household" thrives
in modern Japan as well. The management of the Japan
National Railways, one of the finest and most advanced
train systems in the world today, fondly describes its
vast organization as "our railway family." Japanese
labor unions are basically enterprise unions. Each union
operates within a company and regards itself as an integral part of one corporate family. Not only employees
but also their families are perceived as belonging to the
company. Thus, while radical historical events, such as
the fall of the Tokugawa regime and the total defeat in
World War II, may alter the exterior of social organizations, the pattern of group behavior in Japan stays
essentially the same. The old institutions crumble, new
ones emerge, and names and slogans change, but the
ethos of the traditional household lingers on, its logic
and its moral codes adapted to the requirements of each
new era.

A company, a government agency, a musicians' guild,
a school of flower arrangement, or any other organization in Japan develops familylike characteristics. While
each group contains individuals whose backgrounds
may be diverse, the members of a group tend to cultivate
a strong rapport among themselves. This differs from a

"we-feeling" that prevails, say, among professionals during their annual conventions. The group feeling among pediatricians, anthropologists, or mechanical engineers stems from their occupational identity. The basis of their rapport is impersonal, rational, and abstract. A chemist experiences a sense of affinity toward another chemist, not for personal reasons, but because the two share a common professional interest. The basis upon which the Japanese develop their group identity is predominantly a personal and emotional one. Every employee of the Hitachi Corporation—from janitor to assistant manager—is deeply conscious of his belonging to the same corporate family. The pathos and the pleasure of the house are to be shared by all of its members. What accompanies such an emotional approach is the spread of a collective life-style. Each member's language, manners, beliefs, and way of thinking become group-oriented. The distinction between business and personal matters gets blurred. Affairs of the company begin to take over, more and more, the domain of the employees' private lives. Employees are expected to work extra hours. The company sponsors a vacation trip in which not only the employees but also their families participate. Many workers in Japan regularly wear a company badge. Some may consider this group orientation a private totalitarianism, but others find a profound sense of comfort and security in their total involvement with the group. The importance of institutional affiliation in Japan indicates that more Japanese take the latter view than the former one.

According to the moral code of traditional Japan, all problems—personal or otherwise—are expected to be solved within one's group. A bride who cannot get along

with her husband or mother-in-law may not be helped
by her own parents, brothers, or relatives, who are now
outsiders. Unity is always emphasized. A junior faculty
member refrains from raising an objection to a scientific
argument of his senior professor. A line from *Hamlet,*
"Man and wife is one flesh," summarizes the ideal of
Japanese marriage. It accords with a Japanese saying,
"Husband and wife speak in one voice." A wife will
vote for the same candidate as her husband. Everybody
thinks of his action in terms of what it does to his group.

A modern Japanese corporation is a closed world.
Employees are expected to stay there permanently. New
recruits, just out of school, are like brides who have been
brought into a new house. Their loyalty to the firm is
taken for granted. The company enters into their personal lives. It maintains funds to give monetary gifts to
the employees and their families on such occasions as
weddings, births, and deaths. These highly personalized
fringe benefits are more common and better developed in
large, leading corporations than among small, marginal
firms. The management-labor relation is viewed, not as
a contractual matter, but as something like the relation
between a husband and wife brought into union by the
guiding hand of fate. The company embraces the men
themselves instead of the work of the men. It is only a
logical extension of this philosophy to include families
of the employees in the greater circle of the company.
This is the ideology of management that has persisted
throughout Japan's modern history. It was popular in
the late 19th century, was prevalent during the prewar
decades, and was effectively utilized in World War II
by government and industry as a means of keeping high
morale among workers. During the postwar years, the

popularity of the ideology has hardly waned. On the contrary, it has been one of the significant factors in Japan's economic growth.

A Japanese labor union is an enterprise union whose membership covers all trades, skills, and types of work, production workers as well as clerks in the same company. It is difficult for a Japanese worker to move to another firm. He is stuck with his company. Since every firm uses the seniority-based wage system, he will suffer a substantial wage loss by moving to another company. There is no reliable channel of information about his trade to consult, and he can count on little help from someone in his trade who is outside his company. Emotional involvement in group activity nurtures isolation from the rest of the world. It ferments a distinct (or supposedly distinct) style, mood, tradition, and "way" associated with the company—which in turn reinforces the "we-feeling" among the employees. Those inside become closer, those outside stranger. The psychic distance between "us" and "them" widens. Men of the same craft experience little rapport with one another if they work in different companies. The more stable the society, the more intense will be the sense of discrimination each person develops toward others who are not members of his group. The Japanese can even drive themselves to the point of treating outsiders as subhuman. In a crowded train, a man may push a stranger to gain a seat; yet the next moment, he will get up to give his seat to his superior who happens to come by.

It is only natural, then, for the Japanese to be unsociable. Here we are not speaking of a sophisticated, highly cultured person like a diplomat, a professor who has spent many years abroad, a trading-company executive who constantly deals with foreigners, or a pianist who studied at the Paris Conservatory of Music. We refer to ordinary people with modest backgrounds. They become tense when they meet other Japanese of different backgrounds. For a Japanese, to be sociable is an ordeal. Confronted with an outsider, he does not know what to say or how to behave. It may be that the custom of bowing was invented to alleviate the pain of first encounters with strangers, for it is perfectly polite not to say anything as long as you are bowing. It is not an uncommon sight to see two Japanese bowing on the street apparently endlessly. The unsociability of the Japanese is a result of the basic rules of human relations in their country. The rules leave little room for training in the art of meeting different people easily under varying circumstances. In Japan, members of a group are forced to keep close contact with one another for the sake of group solidarity. To do so is a matter of necessity, for a stable, unified group is the source of each member's sense of security. Knowing your colleagues is all that is required. There is no need to be sociable with outsiders. As if you were living aboard a ship that never sailed, that was permanently sealed off from the ocean, you can spend your entire life without experiencing the stormy seas outside the harbor.

Seniority is the iron rule for placement in the group hierarchy. In almost all cases, the newcomer is assigned to the bottom of the totem pole. A person's ability and skill do not count as much as the length of his or her affiliation with the group. This is one more reason why a Japanese employee does not readily move to another firm. To quit means giving up all the seniority rights accumulated over the years. The employee has to start from scratch again. And even so, another company, knowing that a man has had many years of work experience elsewhere, will hesitate to hire him. To place him at the bottom is insulting, but to give him an equivalent position would jeopardize the morale of its own people. In other words, the company does not know what to do with him.

Among high-level executives, moving from one company to another—a common phenomenon in the United States—is extremely rare in Japan. Wages and salaries go up in proportion to the number of years served, and during the early years, an employee tends to be underpaid relative to the amount of work performed. A premature resignation results in a loss of large sums of earned but unpaid salary. Severance pay, in any substantial amount, can only be expected after a lifetime of employment with one company. In Japan, affiliation with a company constitutes capital that remains valuable as long as one stays in the same company, but is either not transferable elsewhere or will lose much of its value after the transfer.

To complicate the matter, the quality of affiliation also counts. The sheer number of years of work does not necessarily assure promotion. One has to maintain intense contact with the right people in the company, and such contact can be maintained only by being physically close to them. When a man goes away for a year or two on a temporary assignment, the geographic separation tends to sever the human contact with those at the main office.

For a Japanese, going away from the regular place of employment is like being an exile in a strange land. A man who is transferred from Tokyo to a local branch in

Hokkaido will develop paranoiac fear that this signals his removal from the mainstream of the central office staff. An engineer, sent to Brazil on a three-year assignment, will spend sleepless nights pondering the possibility that by the time he goes home his colleagues will have moved up several steps ahead of him. The Japanese quota of staff positions at the United Nations and other international organizations often remains unfilled—not because Japan lacks qualified people, but because the talented and ambitious Japanese have second as well as third thoughts before accepting overseas assignments. Those young people who do not graduate from Japanese universities but go abroad to study will have a hard time landing attractive jobs when they return to their homeland. Their credentials, earned overseas, do not fit the Japanese scheme of things.

At Princeton, there was once a brilliant Japanese graduate student in physics. Many American universities tried to grab him when he completed his Ph.D. For personal reasons, he wanted to return to a university in Tokyo, his alma mater. It offered to hire him at the rank of assistant, the lowest of all faculty positions, because he was too young to be given anything higher. The NHK symphony (the Japanese counterpart of the BBC symphony) once refused to play with Seiji Ozawa, who had studied conducting in France instead of in a more correct place such as Germany or Austria. Allegedly, he was too young and immature for the orchestra. A young Japanese who earned his Ph.D. in management sciences from a major American university was interviewed by a Japanese corporation that was looking for someone like him. He was told that his salary would be the equivalent of what he would have earned had he gone to a Japanese university and upon graduation immediately begun working for the company—plus a gratuitous 5 per cent extra for his doctoral degree. He did not take the offer, which was far below what some American firms operating in Japan were offering him.

A small organization may be able to function well and sustain its cohesiveness without formal rules on the role and status of its members. Their dogged devotion, unconditional loyalty, and emotional participation in the affairs of the organization are sufficient to generate tremendous group energy. A larger organization, however, requires some explicit principles to control the concerns and aspirations of its members. In Japan the name of the game, of course, is seniority. Two mechanics with comparable skills may have vastly different status within the same company. One's rank depends upon his age, the year in which he was first hired, and the number of years he has worked for the company. Full professors in the same department are conscious of who stands above whom in terms of length of service at the university. Officers of the same rank in the former Imperial Army and Navy were given different treatment in accordance with the year in which they received their commissions. When men get together and talk about their colleagues, friends, and new acquaintances, one of the most frequently raised questions is about the chronological ordering of those individuals—"When did he graduate from the university?" "In what year did he pass the civil service examination?" "Was it two years before Tanaka that Yamazaki entered the company?"

Each employee is more conscious of where he stands in the seniority-based hierarchy of his organization than of his formal job classification. Whether or not A is a better latheman than B means a lot less than who has more seniority. Nobody can escape the above-below classification of his standing relative to his colleagues. In America, when you say, "Harry Brown graduated from Yale two years ahead of me," it is a statement of plain fact—no more, no less. As far as social ladder-climbing is concerned, a two-year difference in graduation time means less and less as years go by. Twenty years later, you may stand far ahead of Harry Brown in income and status. In Japan, on the other hand, the senior-junior distinction stays with you for the rest of your life. Once a senior, always a senior. Thirty years after graduating from the same university, a junior man may have a much higher position than his senior. Still, the former switches to appropriate, honorific language when the two meet. I have a Japanese friend who is president of a medium-sized advertising firm in Tokyo. I once asked him, "What is the most difficult problem you have to deal with?" "My employees," he replied. "You see, some of them are my seniors, who graduated from the same college several years before I did. Psychologically, it's so hard for me to use them as my subordinates."

As long as it is seniority that is used to place employees in the personnel structure of the company, it is difficult for management to introduce any kind of incentive system. The tenacity of the seniority system is not rooted, however, in the vigorous support it receives from hardheaded executives with minds dwelling in the feudal past. On the contrary, seniority is preferred by the employees themselves. In many companies, those who were hired in the same year organize a "classmates club." The presence of numerous such clubs heightens everyone's consciousness of seniority. If a member of the club is promoted faster than the rest, the other members will be outraged at this atrocity. If someone gets an accelerated "jump" promotion, the resulting commotion will verge on a riot. "If he deserves it, why not me?" is the inalienable attitude of Japanese workers. Anywhere in the world, true talents are a minority. Thus, Japanese companies are beset by the tyranny of the majority. The management hesitates to promote a man strictly on the basis of merit, for such a promotion will surely stir up massive opposition from the majority of workers. A man with a meritorious record will himself be reluctant to jump to a higher position, surrounded by hostile colleagues—above, below and all around—who would consider such a promotion "undemocratic."

The "why not me?" principle is deeply imbedded in the minds of Japanese workers. They do not accept any method of work evaluation suggested by the management. The company is compelled to promote all members of the same "class" at more or less the same pace, regardless of their productivity. To absorb all the upcoming aspirants, new posts of dubious value must be created. The single seat of a section chief is not enough. The chief must be accompanied by a deputy chief as well as associate deputy chiefs. This tendency is stronger within large, modern corporations than among small firms. For the management of a small, shaky company operating in the backward sector of the economy, it is much easier to impose a productivity-based wage scale than it is for the managers of a large, stable company with a long history and tradition.

The Japanese company does not hire a new worker right out of school on the basis of a specialized job category. The company will assign him a particular job and then give him the necessary training. Typically, he will be shifted to different types of work from time to time. Under this scheme, it is hard for him to develop a consciousness of his position in terms of a particular level or type of skill. He would rather perceive his status in the company in accordance with the number of his years of service.

Despite the problems related to promotions, it is obvious that some workers will rise through the ranks and that the promotion ladder must get narrower as they move upward. In Japan it is not demonstrable ability that decides the game, but the right personal relations with superiors as well as subordinates. Colleagues are a worker's arch-enemies, rather than those with whom one can relax and enjoy a feeling of comradeship. Though a surface rapport may be maintained with them, the ambitious employee is continually aware that he must beat them to advance, or else they will beat him. Tension over promotions drives some people to madness. In the summer of 1973, an employee of a prestigious shipping company in Tokyo, a graduate of a leading university, beat his boss to death with a baseball bat for alleged discrimination against him.

A Japanese employee has to be extremely cautious in dealing with colleagues as well as superiors. He spends many tense hours at work every day. In the evening, thoroughly exhausted, he frequents one of the numerous bars in Japanese cities. He goes there not so much for the taste of alcohol as for the atmosphere—in which he is allowed to speak incoherently. In Japan, you are pardoned for whatever you might say while drinking. This unwritten code has a therapeutic effect. You can air all your inner frustrations under the pretense that you are drunk. In Japanese bars, hostesses are well paid—many of them earning more than the junior executives they entertain—to listen to the incomprehensible and often ludicrous conversations of their highly educated, expense-account customers. Thus the efforts of these girls, most of them from humble backgrounds, have great, socially redeeming value. Thanks to them, Japanese wives are liberated from the not-too-pleasant task of mothering their frustrated husbands every night.

While each employee is very much aware of his company affiliation, the company, in turn, is likely to belong to a certain set of vertically integrated firms called *keiretsu*. A businessman, after identifying his company, will be keen on mentioning its *keiretsu*. "My firm belongs to the Mitsubishi group," or "My cousin owns a subcontracting firm affiliated with the Sumitomo group" is the sort of statement you often hear from Japanese businessmen. *Keiretsu* should not be confused with prewar *zaibatsu*, a handful of family-owned business combines whose holding companies controlled most major industries in Japan before World War II. The *zaibatsu* corporations were dissolved after the war and, under the 1948 antimonopoly act, holding companies became illegal in postwar Japan. Some leading corporations in present-day Japan bear the well-known *zaibatsu* names such as Mitsui, Mitsubishi, and Sumitomo; these names, however, were revived after the occupation period for their trademark value and do not signify the return of prewar-style family control.

The organization of a *keiretsu* occurs when a major (so-called parent) corporation maintains close ties with a group of city banks that supply credit to the corporation. Then there is a set of subcontracting firms, known as "child" companies. Below each subcontracting firm is yet another set of smaller, sub-subcontracting firms. All these form a pyramid of companies, distinct from other business groups. The relationship between the firms belonging to the same *keiretsu* group is not strictly one-to-one. When a certain bank is said to belong to the Toyota group, that does not mean that the bank provides credit exclusively to Toyota Motors. Rather, it means that Toyota is the main customer of the bank and that the two maintain an informal but close relationship with one another. The pyramid is an extralegal arrangement. The child companies belong to a certain parent corporation, not because their stocks are controlled by the latter, but through a strong emotional bond developed between the two over the years. The arrangement gives tremendous resiliency to the operation of all firms in one group. Business is run by people; it is not solely a matter of rational calculation. The emotionalism that holds the member firms together should not be underestimated. If necessary, a child company is quick to come to the rescue in response to the predicament of its parent company, or vice versa. In times of stress, member subcontractors will courageously absorb losses for the sake of group solidarity in a manner that can scarcely be expected of a firm without any emotional sense of affiliation. But the pyramid also has its drawbacks. Loyalty may turn into rigidity. Business dealings can become increasingly inflexible. The parent company may not, without risk of inviting adverse consequences, purchase better parts at lower prices from a firm that belongs to another *keiretsu* group. A bank may be obliged to cater to a member firm and neglect better outside customers.

In Japan, a man belongs to, and serves, one, and only

one, group. The spirit of an old proverb, "No man can serve two masters," lingers on. It is either "us" or "them." The group orientation inevitably breeds an exclusionist mentality. A mechanical engineer in company X experiences little rapport with a mechanical engineer in company Y. Rivalry between government ministries is well known, and the lack of cooperation between the former Imperial Army and Navy is legendary. Each of Japan's major trading companies handles just about all conceivable products from instant noodles to missiles—often causing themselves to cut each other's throats in overseas markets.

The labor unions are no exception. Each union identifies itself with the company and not with other workers. "Workers of the world, unite!" is an empty slogan before the powerful force of Japanese culture. The union may demand higher wages but never so high as to ruin the company. In the United States a major newspaper, the *New York Herald Tribune*, was dissolved by reckless union demands. In Japan, a similar event is unthinkable. Union membership is restricted to "permanent" workers, and the Japanese labor union can even be hostile and indifferent to nonmember workers in the same company. "Temporary" workers—those who may be hired or fired, depending upon the needs of the company—are completely ignored. The permanent workers consider themselves the aristocrats of labor. To them, the temporary workers are the untouchables of the working class.

The sense of loyalty and emotional participation in group activities may generate a powerful energy. For this to happen, however, group cohesion must somehow be sustained. If the source of unity is lost, the group is likely to disintegrate rapidly, and former members may join mutually hostile subgroups. The bloodiest battles fought by students often take place between factions of Zengakuren, the radical leftist student organization, rather than against the police. In World War II many Japanese soldiers celebrated for their discipline turned into mobs once their platoon leaders were killed. Group orientation, Japanese style, dictates that each group has one—and only one—leader. It is unthinkable for members of a group to stay intact when there is more than one object of devotion. Throughout the long history of Japan, there never was a single case of oligarchy. The Katayama cabinet, the only coalition government in Japan after World War II, was formed on June 1, 1947; it collapsed only eight months later, on February 10, 1948.

To approach one's work strictly as a contractual matter makes many Japanese uncomfortable. It is too dry and inhuman. To report to work no earlier than is required, to go home as soon as the official work hours for the day are over, even if there is an unfinished job lying on the desk . . . seems to indicate, to the Japanese eye, that you do not identify yourself with your company. Managers of the steadily increasing number of Japanese firms operating in the United States take a long while to get used to the work attitudes of American employees. Americans adhere to the contract in deciding what to do and what not to do on the job. They will not perform tasks not expected of them and may openly refuse to do a bit of extra work unless it is stipulated in the contract. All these attitudes are new to Japanese supervisors. To an American, the way Japanese employees devote themselves to their company by working late hours or willingly undertaking extra chores looks premodern—a legacy of the feudal era. To a Japanese, the American way appears overly rigid to the point of hampering the efficiency of the firm, which Americans are supposedly so fond of; it almost resembles a system under which the tasks of different castes are inflexibly regulated. A contract is signed so that the employees will not be exploited by the employer. But this notion presupposes the presence (actual or potential) of alienation, a class conflict between management and labor. Japanese managers dread the thought of such alienation within their companies.

The Japanese emotionalism about work has its limitations. It generates its own rigidity. It creates difficulties in combining talents from different groups so as to accomplish a joint project. Incorporating new outside talents could enable groups to transcend their finite capacities, but the exclusiveness of each group precludes such infusions of fresh energy. An American basketball team to the Olympics usually consists of leading players recruited from all over the United States. In Japan, this sort of grouping often invites disaster. A Japanese volleyball team to the Olympics is typically an independent one, made up of employees of one large company. A newly elected president of the United States may appoint, as members of his cabinet, those whom the president has not known personally or those who come from the opposition party. This way of organizing a new cabinet is utterly inconceivable in Japanese politics. Not only in politics but also in all other fields, breakdowns occur easily in the collective endeavors of those affiliated with different groups.

Friction arises not when someone violates some technical clause in the contract, but when emotional conflicts arise over what, to an outsider, are seemingly trivial matters. Participants in a joint venture do not take the venture very seriously because they are aware that they belong to other groups. Their association is temporary and *ad hoc*. They are not deeply concerned with the contract that binds them to the joint project. The pressure under which they must work while in their own groups is exhausting enough, and once outside them, they tend to loosen up—like travelers who switch to less stringent codes of behavior, knowing that misconduct abroad will not jeopardize reputations back home. They become fussy and finicky, and they make undue demands on the leader of the joint project. They become overly critical of others—in a way they would not dare when they are with their peers. They make scenes and threaten to quit. They do not necessarily mean what they say, but they all inwardly enjoy this rare opportunity to burst out of their inhibitions without risking their careers, which are carefully protected elsewhere.

For the successful completion of a large-scale project that requires the participation of diverse groups, there must be a broad theme capable of drawing those groups toward a single goal. The theme is almost always a nationalistic one. The world-famous New Tokaido Railways (nicknamed "bullet trains" for their speed) were built with amazing rapidity because they purported to be a showcase of the new Japan for foreigners on their way to the 1964 Tokyo Olympics. Similary, numerous business groups cooperated closely in preparing the Osaka Expos in 1969 and 1970—because the nation's prestige was at stake.

A Japanese worker usually spends his whole life in one company, under an arrangement known as the lifetime employment system. It should be noted that the system is not contractual. Nowhere does one's employment paper state, "Thou shalt not quit before retirement." It is all part of an unwritten understanding between the company and its employees. Peculiarly enough, the system came into existence around the turn of the century, when Japan was still very much a labor-surplus country. Cheap labor was available everywhere. The system was first applied to skilled workers, who were scarce, as a means of holding an adequate supply of them within the company. Then the practice was extended to semiskilled as well as unskilled workers, despite their superabundance. The employers knew that in Japanese society the familylike employment system would be more effective in raising the over-all productivity of labor than the dispassionate, Western-style contract system.

The emotional approach to human relations is found in all phases of Japanese society. The businesslike approach to one's job leaves the Japanese cold. They are not content to let a contract define and specify one's duties and rights. If a Japanese works for someone, he wants it to be a total commitment. Looking only superficially we are tempted to observe that this aspect of Japanese behavior is a residue of their feudal past, and that it must disappear as Japan becomes modernized. But this observation is misleading, if not totally false, because it is not borne out by the facts of Japan's history over the past century. It may be that emotionalism in human relations was strengthened during the feudal period immediately preceding Japan's modernization, but it certainly was not invented by the feudal regime. The trait has a much more distant origin, and it now seems to exist in the very bloodstreams of the Japanese. It may come forward or recede behind the façade of historical change, yet it is always there, assuming varying designs to suit the needs of one era or another. In contemporary literature on economic development, it is often held that one of the preconditions for modern economic growth is eradication of the attributes of traditional society. This proposition is completely wrong as far as Japan is concerned. In the course of her industrialization, mobilization of human resources was, to a large extent, achieved through a traditional approach to human relations. The Japanese economy today is among the largest in the world, and her advanced products are reaching every corner of the globe. The philosophy of total participation in the group, however, and emotional identification with it continues to flourish in the most modern, progressive corporations. If nothing else, Japan's modern history shows that the modernization of a country does not necessarily imply its Westernization.

Intuitively, we are tempted to speculate that since Japanese group orientation is so thorough and extensive, the leader of each group must accordingly be a powerful figure. That, however, is not the case. On the contrary, group leaders are often far less mighty than their counterparts in such an individualistic country as the United States. Many Japanese who visit American factories are surprised to see a sharp line of distinction between a boss and his subordinates. They note with interest the commonly heard remarks, "Remember, I'm your boss" or "Well, what can I say? After all, he's my boss." Japanese visitors observe with immense curiosity that American workers obey and follow what their boss tells them to do in a way that seems un-American. An American boss can be authoritarian toward his men, but a Japanese leader who nakedly exhibits his power is sure to fail. He must have a compassionate understanding of his subordinates.

To gain their loyalty, the leader has to be able to make concessions, absorb their hopes and aspirations, listen to their personal problems. He is expected to be a man of warm heart, generosity, benevolence—a figure with whom you fall in love. Just as it is impossible for the government to teach its citizens true morality, the genuine devotion of subordinates cannot be bought with threat or coercion. It is to blossom and grow spontaneously from below.

The concept of ideal leadership, Japanese style, is reflected in the so-called *ringi* system, employed by practically every company. It is a mixture of "suggestion box" and vertically moving memoranda. Anyone in the company—even a fellow at the bottom—who has a bright, creative idea about the operations of the firm is encouraged to draft and circulate a *ringi* statement. It first moves around his immediate colleagues, then is sent to a higher post, then to a yet higher level, and so on till it reaches the office of the president. It is a means, not for top management to impose its will on those below, but for those below to voice their opinions to those at the top, and it is effective in cultivating a "we-feeling" within the company. Although most suggestions from below are not accepted at the top, the system gives employees a sense, illusory or not, of participation in the affairs of the company.

Japanese political leadership shows similar traits. Before major political events, such as a general election or a party convention, faction leaders routinely hold a series of private sessions for "adjustment of opinions" (*iken no chosei*) to minimize mutually harmful internal conflicts. To achieve a certain political objective, the government, at times, purposely avoids drafting a new law, and instead lets the bureaucracy handle the problem through so-called ''administrative guidance.'' For example, the Ministry of International Trade and Industry may extralegally attempt to discourage the production of a certain product or encourage the merger of several firms in a certain industry—with a hint of reprisal unless the industry complies with the Ministry's intent. The guidance sessions between the bureaucrats and the industry representatives are held behind closed doors. Unlike passage of a controversial law, administrative guidance receives little publicity.

In Japan, the most important quality of a leader is the capacity to harmonize his group and arouse collective enthusiasm among his men. So important is this quality that even a nincompoop can be a leader in Japan, provided that he has this capacity. Here lies the secret of the seniority system. That you are at the top does not necessarily mean you are the best and the brightest. A man who receives the highest pay need not have the greatest responsibility. Key decisions may be made by someone else. What matters is not whether the top man is the most talented but whether, under his leadership, the group is able to maximize its output. In fact, it is preferable for the boss not to be too bright, sharp-witted, and capable. The presence of a man of superhuman ability weakens the raison d'etre of his subordinates. Those below him may, in truth, be a bunch of donkeys but, like most of us, they want to feel important. The leader who is uncontestably brilliant is likely to cause more frustration and despair than admiration and respect among his men. The duller majority silently wish to depend upon their leader, but they also wish to be depended upon by him. The leader must be able to

understand and empathize with this desire of his fellow
men. Without this quality, a ton of power will not buy an
ounce of devotion. Thus, group dynamics depends not
so much upon the superb ability of the leader himself as
upon his capacity to pull the best and the most out of
everyone in the group. The subordinates respond, not to
the superior's orders *per se*, but to the human charm they
find in him. A man would dare to leap into a fire to save
a woman—provided he loves her dearly. Similarly,
genuine leadership, like magic, can transform a dull
chore or a painful duty into a labor of love. This logic of
feeling sustains the dynamism of human organization in
Japan.

8 ✦ The Language of Ah-ness

> *The Japanese way of writing is very different from
> ours because they write from the top of the page down
> to the bottom. I asked Paul why they did not write
> in our way and he asked me why we did not
> write in their way. He explained that as the head of
> a man is at the top and his feet are at the bottom,
> so too a man should write from top to bottom.*
>
> —ST. FRANCIS XAVIER
> (1506–1552)

> *I think that the Japanese language is the most solemn
> and copious tongue that exists, for it is superior to
> Latin and Greek in many ways.*
>
> —LOURENCO MEXIA, S.J.
> (1540–1599)

Language plays double roles in the lives of people who
speak it. A culture conditions the pattern of its language
and, at the same time, the characteristics of a culture are
affected by its language. In quiet seclusion from the rest
of the world over many centuries, the Japanese have
inevitably developed a deep, instinctive communal bond

among themselves. For nearly three hundred years prior to the country's modernization, they lived under the totalitarian regime of the Tokugawa shoguns. And even in Japan's modern century, state authoritarianism persisted until 1945. These and other historical facts have unavoidably influenced the meaning and role of language in Japanese life. An American visitor will soon learn that the Japanese conception of language reveals aspects of the subject that are totally unfamiliar to him.

In the West, the history of oration and dialectic goes back to ancient Greece. For more than 2,000 years, Westerners have assumed that language is *the* means of communication. This tradition has been fortified by Aristotelian logic and the concept of individualism. In order to build your position in society, you must express your thoughts as clearly and persuasively as possible. A thought unspoken is as bad as no thought at all. You must demonstrate that you are right and your opponent wrong. To accomplish this end, it will not suffice merely to declare your foe wrong. You must explain your reason to show that your logic is superior to your enemy's. In the Western world, the ability to speak effectively and articulately became an important asset; speech was elevated to the status of an art. Western history is full of political figures noted for their oratorical adroitness.

The Japanese tradition in language has been almost diametrically opposed to that of the West. In Japan, people have viewed language as *a*—not *the*—means of communication. Preference has been given to nonverbal communication. There has been a persistent tendency to believe that verbal language is not necessarily the best medium for enhancing human understanding. In Japanese history, one finds no hero celebrated for his colorful speech. On the contrary, many Japanese heroes are remembered for their verbal inarticulateness. This basic distrust of language lingers on in contemporary society. In all objectivity, no Japanese politician today—including those who hold the highest positions of power—can be commended for oratorical excellence. The same holds for the top business leaders. This is no accident. In Japan someone who speaks well and colorfully is regarded as belonging to the entertainment world, not to the realm of sublime human relations. A person who heavily relies upon verbal communication as a means of expressing his feelings is said to prove his abruptness, immaturity, and possibly dishonesty.

The theme of Japanese society is harmony, not confrontation. A family has to live in harmony. A company must operate in an atmosphere of harmony to raise its productivity and beat competitors. The factions of a political party should maintain harmony lest the party lose ground to the opposition. The nation must keep up its morale and spirit of harmony to hold its own in the tough world of international power politics.

The doctrine of harmony becomes a form of tyranny especially in regard to speech. In the name of harmony, you learn never to offend anyone by uttering one wrong word. The doctrine dictates that those who speak before they think should vanish from the earth. In feudal Japan, speaking freely often meant risking one's life. After the Meiji enlightenment people were no longer condemned to death for saying the wrong thing, but speaking out uninhibitedly remained a dangerous business till the end of World War II.

Feudalism is a thing of the past, but its ethos survives. A Japanese child is required to learn not just one Japanese language but many versions of it—dependent upon the person to whom he is addressing himself. He has to make a proper choice of honorific words, intonation, and even pitch. Soon he realizes that, in his culture, language is a ritual or, perhaps, a lubricant for the machinery of human connections. But words are not necessarily the means of expressing truth. In Japan, everything has a front and a rear. The front is decorated with formal rules, principles, and precepts, while the rear is filled with a dense blend of human feelings that cannot be neatly sorted out and arranged by a set of artificial rules. The grammar used for the front language is not interchangeable with the one for the rear. Switching back and forth between the front and rear of one's mind constitutes a strenuous mental feat which an uninitiated American might not be able to tolerate for more than two days.

Japan's preference for nonverbal communication is inseparable from her traditional family consciousness. In Japanese culture, "family" carries several layers of meaning. In the most rudimentary sense, it is a bond among those who are related by blood. It also serves as a prototype for all other forms of social organization. Furthermore, it provides a frame of reference for the ideals of human conduct.

Two members of an ideal family have no need to talk to each other incessantly. A wife understands her husband's tastes and expectations. The husband understands all her dreams and sufferings. If everything is understood perfectly, there is nothing to be explained. What is the worth of love if it cannot be felt without verbalizing it? The need to use words implies a lack of understanding. The highest form of human communication is the language of silence; as a Japanese proverb puts it, ''Silence speaks better than words.'' Nothing is said, yet everything is comprehended within one's heart—that is the ideal. All this may be a pipe dream, a grand illusion, but this is the way the Japanese feel.

One thing that strikes Japanese visiting the United States is the verbalism that, to them, borders on barbarism. The flood of small talk at cocktail parties is enough to floor them. To their fascination, they hear young American mothers scolding or explaining things, all in adult language, to their one-year-old babies as though the babies understand every word being said. They witness old ladies talking to their cats, as if cats in America had mastered the language of their masters. In restaurants, Japanese visitors will be impressed by the sight of an American couple who seem to do more talking than eating. Long-married couples in Japan tend to dine quietly or even wordlessly.

Rice farming, as a way of life in traditional Japan, was conducive to nonverbal communication. Life in the rice paddies was repetitive and routine. Members of the same family worked closely side by side, everyone knowing exactly what he or she was expected to do. Friends and relatives were all Japanese. So were strangers from other villages. So were the officials who came to collect taxes. For centuries, Japan was a single communal world in which everybody knew exactly what role to play.

Agrarian life, cultural homogeneity, the tyranny of the feudal regime all added to the discouragement of dialectics and oration. When, in the late 19th century, the formal structure of traditional Japan crumbled, the spirit of nonverbalism found its way into modern social organizations. Even to this day, the spirit thrives on in government offices and business firms. A young employee must learn how to properly keep his mouth shut. One who speaks his mind straightforwardly has little chance of success. At conferences, what is said is less important than what is unspoken. In correspondence, what lies between the lines matters more than mere written words. One of the prerequisites for promotion is the ability to read others' minds quickly and correctly. The rigid, conventional pattern of the language, set by the hierarchical order of society, persists with chilling and almost miraculous tenacity.

The principles of silent language involve more than practical technique. The same principles underlie the philosophical outlook of the Japanese, as well as their aesthetic of silence. Latent in the Japanese mind is the conviction that the ultimate truth of life cannot be revealed or grasped by words. Suppose you have discovered a beautiful wild flower on your morning walk. Beauty is there, and you want to express it in words. But language is an artificial device, classifying things under a more or less arbitrary set of rules and doing so only to the extent of man's perceptive capacity. One should not confuse real beauty with a description of beauty, and there is no reason to believe that the verbal description necessarily comes closest to the truth. At best, words may build a mirage of the thing to be grasped; yet they can only present an approximation of what is presumed to be the truth. The aesthetic of silence starts with a premise that in the beginning there were no words. It warns of the danger that the search for truth may actually be hampered by the use of words. Becoming victims of their own words, people may delude themselves with the absurd idea that whatever is not verbally described cannot be true.

The aesthetic of silence has affected many aspects of Japanese culture. It encouraged the development of haiku poems, which try to capture the beauty of things in three brief lines consisting of five, seven, and five syllables. It contributed to the rise of Noh plays in which actors wearing masks exchange little verbal dialogue. It strongly supported the growth of Zen Buddhism, which emphasizes the discovery of truth through long and intense meditation. In the more mundane sphere of human connections, its effect has been mixed. The virtue of keeping silent has been tied to the idea of sincerity in the manner of speech. In Japan, it is a sign of sincerity for a person not to express his inner thoughts candidly. Of course, in any civilized society, some restraint is expected of those who wish to speak out, depending upon circumstances. The difference is that the Japanese go to the extreme. They do not say what they want to say because they sincerely hope not to hurt others' feelings, and they say what they do not want to say, believing that their discomfort is less important than the happiness of others. Behaving this way shows insincerity in terms of American manners, and it is bewildering to a casual American visitor to realize that his sincerity may mean insincerity in Japan. But the Japanese cannot afford to judge whether their system is as bewildering as their American friend may claim. It is the system they must live with, even though, notwithstanding its intent, they themselves may feel uncomfortable as they play the nationwide game of synchronized mutual deception.

Neglect of verbal communication leads to the slighting of people skilled in argument and oratory. The model of a great leader in Japan is someone who says little and yet is capable of communicating a great deal to his subordinates. He is a superb mind reader. He knows perfectly well what goes on in everyone's mind—though he may not show it. He remains quiet, even at meetings, but when he speaks, every word carries weight. People are astonished by the shrewdness of his observations and the foresight of his decisions. He has an inexplicable charm that easily captivates the hearts of his men. Their loyalty to him is always spontaneous. He is distinctly nonintellectual, and understands that while life offers places for both reason and emotion, emotion always counts most in dealing with human problems. He lets someone else handle the legal, logistical, and intellectual affairs of his group. He is not interested in the façade of his house; instead, he concerns himself with the real drama that takes place behind it. He dislikes theorizing. Laws and regulations are man-made and he feels that anything man-made is less important than man himself. Rules and regulations may be necessary, but every one of them is more or less arbitrary. There are always exceptions, and in life the exceptions often make the decisive differences. He understands and sympathizes with the foibles of his men. He feels that those whose thought and behavior are always conditioned by pure reason and cold intellect alone should stay in an ivory tower detached from the real, human world.

Japanese politicians are fond of "belly talks." In the Japanese tradition, the truth of human feeling is stored, not in the heart, but in the belly. Speeches on the floor of the Diet or committee reports are the mere frosting on the cake. They are matters of formal procedures and rules. The cake itself takes shape behind the scenes; you cannot speak the truth before microphones and television cameras. A truly meaningful exchange of ideas, views, and offers is made in private meeting places—preferably at night, with the participants warmed by plenty of hot sakè. Ideally, the two politicians should remove their ties, suits, dress shirts, and then undershirts —until their abdomens are fully exposed. That is the moment their belly-to-belly talk begins. If one of them hesitates to strip off all his clothes, that means he still feels a distance from his opponent—he does not completely trust him. One vital leadership quality in Japanese politics is the ability to break through formal barriers and rules and, with magical ease, persuade others toward an abdominal communication.

A leader is a person who fully understands the properties of this human world, not to be confused with Heaven or some unreachable outer realm where God presides. In that unreachable world, everything may have a logical explanation and every judgment stand to reason. But to the Japanese way of thinking, that is not true of *our* world, which is a pond of muddy water contaminated with the excrement of human imperfection. In this world, it is futile to try to make sense out of anything, for there is no definitive meaning to human existence. Stirring muddy water in the pond to discover the truth will only make it muddier. Logic, symbolism, syllogism, phenomenology, ontology, Hegelian dialectics, dialectical materialism, systematic theology, critique of pure reason—all these are but word play, interesting intellectual exercises that merely provide illusions of the truth. In the final analysis, words are powerless. In this world, a pen is not stronger than a sword; each word used by man represents a grand misunderstanding.

Motoori Norinaga (1730–1801), a great scholar of Japanese history and literature, summed up the Japanese sentiment by the expression *mono no aware*, the nuances of which defy accurate translation. Literally, it means "the pathos of things." It refers to a feeling the Japanese experience at the sight of petals falling from an exquisite flower or the innocent face of a sleeping child—a feeling of wonder and sadness about this inexplicable, dreamlike world in which a flower blossoms only to return to the ground, and in which a child is born only to depart for another world. William George Aston, a 19th-century English linguist-diplomat, noted in his pioneering *History of Japanese Literature* that, at the sight of beautiful and awe-inspiring objects, the Japanese tend to sigh "Ah!" in lieu of verbalizing their feelings. He was led to translate *mono no aware* as "Ah-ness." True enough, the Japanese for ages have spoken the language of Ah-ness.

People who sense "the pathos of things" in falling petals are bound to identify themselves with nature. In the remote past, all things spoke—trees, grass, flowers, rocks, streams, hills, valleys, clouds—and signs of this ancient animism remain in the contemporary language. Metaphors and similes frequently refer to objects of nature. Expressions often suggest the intermingling of man with nature. When you dishonor your family by committing a wrongful act, you hear the souls of your ancestors weeping behind "grass leaves." Favorite names for modern express trains are Morning Breeze, Cherry, Piny Wind, Morning Star, Light, Echo, Swallow. In making analogies, the natural is preferred to the artificial. The Japanese find vegetables particularly usable. A grandfather will look for "seeds," instead of "material,'' for stories to tell his grandchildren. A tedious, verbose inquisitor is someone who never stops digging ''roots and dead leaves.'' An empty statement is like ''a plant that has lost all its leaves.'' A person who wisely keeps his mouth shut is acting like ''a silent flower.'' Kamikaze pilots whose planes were shot down over the South Pacific died like ''falling petals.'' The sense of four seasons finds its way into many Japanese expressions. ''Spring wind, autumn rain'' means ''year''; so does ''star and frost.'' The vicissitudes of life are described as ''winds and snows.''

In the Japanese world of gentle passivity toward nature, it is futile to swim against the current. It is more sane to accept things in life as they are. Lightheartedness and frank admission of human frailty are considered to be virtuous attitudes, while dogged stubbornness and blind persistence are viewed as vicious traits. The Japanese temper was too mild to build the Great Wall and the giant pyramid. Fatalism concerning the transitory and uncertain human condition, however, preserved a touch of optimism. Certain things in life cannot be helped, and many a difficulty may block one's way; but the sun also rises after the darkness of night. A stream does not remain muddy forever; fresh water will flow again after a new rain. The metaphor of water often appears in the Japanese language. Life is like ''a tiny leaf floating down the stream.'' It is ''senseless [for the leaf] to fight against the flow of water.'' One's frustrations ''should be washed away in the water.'' A game is ''like water''—meaning it is difficult to speculate about its final shape, its outcome. To disturb an opponent's talk, you ''pour water into his mouth.''

Wind, floating clouds, and migratory birds frequently

show up in Japanese poems and popular songs. They all symbolize the flow of life that has neither a beginning nor an end. Margaret Mitchell's *Gone with the Wind,* even in translation, has a peculiarly appealing sound to the Japanese ear. The mood of a bird flying away is captured by "the sound of wind left behind." In Japan, outlaws have always been viewed with a certain affection. Ostracized by society, they wandered like "floating clouds," blown by the wind of the moment. The Japanese perceived the "pathos of things" in the sight of an outlaw, all alone in the universe, walking away from a village.

No less popular than objects of nature, parts of the body are often used metaphorically in the Japanese language. A good reporter is one who covers an event not only with words but also with his "skin." You express your affectionate feeling toward an adorable child by saying, "It won't hurt to put you in my eyes." A person with an uncanny ability to dig up inside information is one "with a keen nose." Astonishment is expressed by "rolling one's tongue." Those who make remarks that leave the listeners uncomfortable have "uneven teeth which cannot cut things neatly." A ridiculously inflated statement "makes your teeth rise." A nice story to hear is one that "rubs one's ear gently." In a dire predicament you cannot "turn your neck around." All-out effort is "by hand, by foot." An unexcitable person has a "protruded abdomen." A man of determination has a "well-positioned liver." When you get angry, your "abdomen stands upright." To "move one's back backwards" means to hesitate. You caution yourself by "looking down around your feet." "Kicking sand with one's rear foot" is a sign of betrayal. A true heart-to-heart talk begins after the two "cut open their abdomens." A problem compounded by another in rapid succession is "a beebite on top of a crying face."

Tanizaki Junichiro, a well-known novelist, called the Japanese a "nontalkative" people. Their approach to the art of conversation is considerably different from that of Westerners. The Japanese place a good deal of emphasis on the shades and aftertastes of their conversation. In choosing words and manner of expression, they prefer delicacy and suggestiveness to the open and the direct. A great conversationalist in Japan is a person with an agreeable disposition and a soft voice, whose remarks are filled with tastefulness. He does not speak straightforwardly and he avoids rough and naked words. Rather than flatly stating his points, he suggests them. To an uninitiated foreigner, the master of Japanese conversation may sound a bit too vague and elusive. But such is not the reaction of insiders. It is a Japanese feeling that candid, outspoken words spoil the pleasure of conversation. If one is to enjoy a talk with another, he should eschew unsavory remarks with cutting edges. A good conversation is a tasteful conversation, possessing the body and texture of well-brewed sakè. Its flavor is brought out by controlled understatement and a finely restrained manner of expression. Yasuoka Shotaro, author of many erotic stories, was once flabbergasted by the daring mode of a German woman's confession of love for him; at first, he thought she was shouting at him in anger. Bar girls in Japan have been overwhelmed by the direct-confrontation approach of visiting American executives who, after a brief initial encounter over a drink or two, immediately propose a forward march to their private quarters.

The elegant art of Japanese conversation works well

as long as conversation is within a small circle of intimate friends and close associates. It is an art that blossomed out of a homogeneous culture, when Japan was a closed society and people led a yet more closed life within a slow-paced communal setting in which everyone knew everyone else's habits, customs, motives, tastes, and aspirations. When the world becomes modernized and complicated, however, what was once virtuous may become a defect. It is hard to conduct business efficiently when every party speaks in the language of suggestion. Obliqueness and delicacy of expression may cause misunderstanding, not joy. Tastefulness may amount to no more than awkwardness in dealing with other groups of Japanese, to say nothing of communication with foreigners.

Emotionalism may stimulate the Japanese to increase their annual output of haiku poems, but it definitely does not nurture their capacity to think rationally and consistently. Indeed, in Japanese, a ''rational'' person connotes someone who is too calculating, self-assertive, and cold to be properly human. In centuries past, fallen warriors were indiscriminately honored for dying heroically in battle, and people paid little attention to the principles the warriors had believed in or the righteousness of their cause. In the age of civil wars, many battles ended in a most baffling manner, not because one side revealed a secret weapon at the last minute, but because, at crucial moments, the supporting troops on the winning side often changed their minds and went over to the enemy.

What motivates the Japanese in such a situation is tension and not ideological fortitude. In the most fundamental sense, their philosophy is the belief in nonbelief.

What matters is that you mobilize all your resources toward action, giving little critical attention to the reasons for and consequences of your action. Once their riotous demonstration is over, radical students return to their classrooms to sit quietly and politely before the professor whose office they were ransacking only the day before. Their mentality is not much different from that of those Japanese soldiers in World War II who, once captured by the Americans, turned their backs to the Holy Emperor and began collaborating with the enemy —some of them even offering to guide American pilots on bombing missions. Emotionalism is rampant in the language of Japanese politics as well. One sees a lot of emotional slogans about ''peace'' but hears little rational discussion on the question of national security. People often pay more attention to how ''conscientious'' a politician is than to the political ideology he upholds. In all groups, the spirit of harmony is emphasized. But one who prefers the warmth of harmony to the coldness of reason is necessarily a dependent, outer-directed person—lacking self-confidence and autonomy of thought.

The Japanese always talk about the importance of suppressing and controlling ''self''; but this is another way of saying they are conformists. Unity of the group is cherished, and such unity is impossible if every group member insists on the rightness of his or her personal opinion. Thus, group decision-making in Japan is a slow process. An idea is tossed around, tucked away for a while, then revived again—until the matter finally resolves itself into a ''unanimous'' decision. The group members nervously read one another's faces to see which way the wind is blowing. Everybody votes for a ''well-rounded'' solution of the problem. The love of compromise is manifest in the popular saying ''Add and then divide by 2.'' Wartime Japan was a totalitarian state under which Japanese conformism was stretched to its extreme by stringent political control. After the war, the political control was gone, but the social control stayed on. A cultural tradition never dies quickly; it may not even fade away.

*

The cultural tradition conditions the pattern of verbal as well as nonverbal communication. Facial expressions and bodily gestures vary among different peoples. Even crying is no exception. The Japanese have their own way of shedding tears. At tense moments, a Japanese politician may show tears before television cameras. Far from constituting his political suicide, such a ''human'' reaction will probably win him more votes.

In contemporary Japan, the crying of a child is considered ''bad,'' as well as annoying to the parents. Child-care manuals accordingly talk about methods of stopping or preventing an infant's crying. This was not so in the past. ''A crybaby will grow well,'' according to an old Japanese saying. The Japanese used to hold a positive, tolerant view toward children in tears. In feudal Japan, when repression of adult behavior was the norm, society remained lenient toward the emotions of children. It was then a common rule of child care for the parents not to hit or shout at a child throwing a tantrum. People believed that the freedom to cry was good for the child's mental hygiene.

In the city of Hirado, Nagasaki prefecture, a ''crybaby contest,'' an old pastime, is held every spring. Parents take their babies, no older than two years of age, to a local sumo-wrestling arena. A pair of babies is placed in the ring. The baby who starts to cry first loses the game. The origin of the game goes back many centuries, but in the past, the rule used to be the other way around; the baby who cried first was the winner.

In modern Japan, while parents have become less patient with the weeping of their children, grown-ups are easily moved to maudlin tears. Practically all popular songs are written in a minor key. Imported songs in a major key are typically rearranged into minor so they will sound appropriately sad. In Japan, there is a distinct category of movies called "tear movies." Kurosawa Akira's cinematic art, which graphically depicts dynamic action and violence, made Japanese films famous in the West after the war, but it is very un-Japanese. It does not result in the kind of motion picture the Japanese masses approve. Rather than subject themselves to a horrifying screenful of blood, they prefer to pay their money for sentimental stories that will assuredly make them weep in their seats. To exploit the situation, the movie industry turns out a large number of soap operas each year, carefully designed to stimulate everyone's lachrymal glands. Ads are accompanied by such lines as, "With this one, you can cry four times as much," "Yes, go ahead and cry," "Your tears guaranteed or money back." One of the postwar classics in this genre was the movie *24 Eyes*, a sentimental story about twelve children and their devoted teacher in wartime Japan. Its ad read, "Even the Honorable Minister of Education cried."

At a funeral, the Japanese are not expected to cry, for tears would spoil the solemnity of the occasion. If you express condolences to your Japanese friend about a death in his family, chances are he will thank you with a smile. This is the famous "Japanese smile." In 1948, the district of Fukui in northern Japan was hit by a major earthquake that killed 3,800 people. A *Life* magazine photographer who happened to be in the area took many pictures there which later appeared in the magazine. American readers were baffled by what they saw. Half-naked women running out of public bath houses, a half-dead carpenter who fell from the top of a tall building, and other victims of the tragedy all—as they faced the camera—smiled.

Of course, it is wrong to think that the "Japanese smile" is exclusively a product of Japan. In 1971, I was attending a funeral service in Berkeley, California for an acquaintance of mine, an American woman who died in her twenties. Her all-American father, a middle-aged executive, smiled throughout the service. As he followed the coffin out of the chapel, he smiled more, nodding to the friends and relatives who were crying or trying desperately to hold back their tears. To the best of my understanding, he was smiling out of his sense of politeness. However saddened by the unexpected death of his own daughter, however touched by the presence of many outside his family who shared his sorrow, he nonetheless wanted to ease the burden of those who were troubled by the family tragedy. In effect, he was saying: "I'm OK and I want you to feel OK, too. Please do not let my daughter's death trouble you too much." If these were his thoughts, then he, the American, was unwittingly demonstrating the psychology of the "Japanese smile."

In the vocabulary of the Japanese language, the word "happiness" occupies a rather weak position. It is used sparingly. In conversation, the statement "I'm happy"

sounds unnatural, obviously playful, and even distaste-
ful. In writing, the Japanese do use expressions such as
"I was happy to see you" or "I was happy to receive
your letter," but these are formalities, devoid of real
feeling. This linguistic attribute reflects a persistent
belief that the concept of happiness is dangerous and
illusory. This theme appears in practically all the ethical
treatises written by moralists of feudal Japan. Their
books may no longer be read except by a handful of
scholars, but what the books taught millions in the past
became a cultural reflex that still survives in the contemporary Japanese subconscious.

According to the traditional philosophy, nothing is
wrong with happiness *per se*. The pursuit of happiness,
however, is futile, for it unavoidably invites self-destruc-
tion. Happiness through material possessions, for example, presents a problem that is absent for the poor.
In life, to have means to lose, eventually. The estate you
own may burn down. Treasures will probably be stolen.
All the material wealth of man is subject to destruction—
sooner or later. When you move to another world, you
must leave all your belongings right here in this world.
The more you own, the more worried you become, for
others may envy you and wish you destroyed. The accumulation of personal wealth piles up debts of one kind
or another.

The wisdom of old Japan suggests that the pursuit of
happiness is vain because, in addition to being self-de-
structive, it is a self-deceiving effort—like trying to catch
a rainbow. Yoshida Kenko (1282–1350), a great essayist
and literary critic, called life "a borrowed thing."
Within the human world, nothing lasts forever, only
change is permanent. Like a dream, life is empty and

meaningless. Therefore, any of man's ventures is illusory. What is the sense of reaching for a box when one knows it is utterly empty?

This Japanese version of nihilism, unlike its Western counterpart, does not necessarily negate the absolute in this world. Buddhist fatalism and the precepts of Confucian ethics were combined to form a nihilism that showed a peculiar moral twist. The average man cannot bear the thought that his existence has absolutely no meaning. A short life becomes insufferably long unless one can believe in something absolute. Japanese nihilism offered a solution. If life itself is empty, you can still find salvation for your soul by developing something absolute within life and believing in it. Samurai were thus taught to find satisfaction in absolute loyalty to their lords. Japanese nihilism became an ideological prop for the feudal regime. In the late 19th century, the object of absolute loyalty was switched from the feudal regime to the divine emperor, and in later decades, it was expanded into a grandiose imperial dream of world-wide hegemony. But however the object of loyalty changed, its source remained the same. Thus, without appreciating the strength of Japanese nihilism, one can not fully understand what drove many young Japanese pilots to join the suicide squadrons. The feudal lord, the divine emperor, the Japanese empire are now all gone. But the ghost of her nihilism is very much present in postwar Japan. It materializes in the nation's fanatical attitude toward economic growth, in the bloody hara-kiri death of Mishima Yukio, and in the strikingly high rate of suicide, especially among the young.

While the Japanese conception of happiness has been mixed up with nihilism in the course of history, the

Japanese people have developed a psychological tradition of their own concerning unhappiness and hardship. In contrast to the Japanese shyness toward the expression ''happiness'' is the lavish use of words carrying an opposite meaning. Popular songs are packed with words like ''sorrow,'' ''lonesome,'' ''desperate,'' ''pain,'' ''tears.'' Despite Japan's third-largest gross national product in the world, it is apparently misfortune and distress—rather than pleasure and well-being—that her people find most approachable.

Historically, Japanese books on moral improvement and how-to-live methods have stressed, as the most effective way of coping with one's frustration, the importance of accepting life as it is. Passivity is the key. Learn not to think of your troubles; uphold the spirit of resignation; reconcile your desires with the hard facts of life. Think of others who are ten times as miserable as you. If you have been unemployed for ten weeks, think of those unemployed ten months. If your wife beats you, think of wives who have poisoned their husbands. If your child is not doing well at school, think of the parents whose children are mentally retarded. If you have lost one arm, think of someone who has lost both arms and legs. Do something that will divert your thoughts from your troubles. Develop reasons for giving up unfounded dreams. Some books went so far as to expound an aesthetics of unhappiness that borders on masochism. It was held that hardship tempers one's heart. Unhappiness strengthens the psyche, so that one becomes a better, more self-reliant person. In other words, one should be grateful for—and even welcome—any hardship encountered in life.

In feudal Japan, people were told that the simplest way to acquire glorious enlightenment was to learn to

endure and overcome all difficulties that may arise. The
feudal authorities taught their subjects that infinite
patience was one of the highest virtues they could cultivate. This doctrine, highly convenient to the authorities, was eloquently discussed in *Lessons on Pleasure*
by the Confucian scholar Kaibara Ekiken (1630–1714).
The trouble is, while the book concludes that the supreme pleasure in life is found through absolute patience
with all the displeasurable things in this world, it does
not explain precisely how one is supposed to learn such
patience. Practical help comes from *Hagakure*—an
eleven-volume treatise on the moral conduct of warriors
prepared in the 18th century for the samurai of Nabe-
shima province. The treatise suggests that if you find
your service to the lord difficult, just pretend or imagine
that the service is for one day only. You can endure any
kind of service no matter how hard it may be, provided
that it lasts for only one day. If you can do it the first
day, you should be able to do the same the second day.
Repeat the process the next day, then the following days,
and so on. Thus, you will fulfill your duties all year
round.

To say that one manages to bear his misfortune by bearing it is an interesting tautology that offers little help
for most people. They need an explanation of misfortune
if they are to accept it. The explanation advanced by the
feudal authorities was fatalism. All the sufferings in this
world are supposedly predetermined. Whether or not
sufferings are punishment for the wrongdoings committed in a former life does not really matter. What matters
is the truth that all men are fated to suffer infinitely,
everywhere and in all ages, and there is nothing anyone
can do about it. If you accept this fundamental truth,

then you should also be able to accept any misfortune that may beset you.

This way of thinking was not confined to the feudal era. It was carried over to Japan's modern century. In 1935 Tomomatsu Entei, leader of a Buddhist group, wrote: "Life is suffering. It is the sign of egotism and irresponsibility to think that one can swim through the vicissitudes of life without facing any hardship."

Remarkably, however, their fatalism has not pushed the Japanese into a state of total despair. On the contrary, it has served as a source for the nation's dynamism. *Hagakure* repeatedly dwells on the importance of a samurai's accepting fatalism so that he may be psychologically better prepared when the worst does occur. The spirit of Japanese fatalism points to the expectation that an unthinkable tragedy, an untold misery, or an unimaginable misfortune may strike us any minute, and acceptance of this truth enables us to face up to any event far more effectively than when we disbelieve in the predestiny of human sufferings.

In the modern era, fatalism also provided the establishment with an ideological justification for exploiting the masses. In 1929 Ishibashi Zennosuke, a well-to-do business executive, wrote, "The fatalistic view of life teaches us the spirit of patience, and helps us improve our sense of duty." In other words, a worker with a fatalistic outlook on life can accept the hardship of his factory labor more easily than one without. Ishibashi's remark on fatalism, actually an excuse for demanding the unconditional obedience of his workers, unwittingly illustrates the peculiar origin of the concept of duty in Japan. It arose, not along with the idea of human rights, but as a psychological corollary of predestination.

✦ WORK ETHIC AND ALL THAT

The figures prosper; the people suffer.
—GEORGE PAPANDREOU

PART THREE

WORK ETHIC AND ALL THAT

The fitters prosper; the people suffer.

—GEORGE PAPANDREOU

9 ✦ Moil and Parsimony

> *If you wish to accomplish a big job, start with a*
> *little one. Small deeds shall eventually turn into an*
> *enormous work. You harvest a ton of rice, not*
> *because each grain grew larger in size, but because*
> *you have a larger sum of the same tiny grains. Each*
> *strike of a hoe will add to the cultivation of a*
> *hundred acres. With a single step, you begin a*
> *thousand-mile journey. Handfuls of mud will*
> *ultimately make a mountain.*
>
> —NINOMIYA SONTOKU
> (1787-1856)

The Japanese are said to be a hardworking people.
Many foreigners visiting Japan—journalists, diplomats,
businessmen, tourists—have noted the diligence and
perseverance of Japanese workers, the sense of dedication they seem to bring to their jobs. A Dutch engineer,
after a visit to a shipyard in Kure, remarked. ''Those
workers worked as though they were still fighting the
war.'' The correspondents of the London *Economist*
reported that Japanese factories reminded them of ant
hills.

These impressionistic accounts, colorful and entertaining as they are, do not always reveal the truth. They
tend to paint a caricature and compose a cliché rather
than form an accurate report on Japanese social psychology. It may be that Japanese are good at pretending
to look busy. According to one school of thought, the
Japanese work hard provided they are closely supervised.
Polls in Japan usually show that about 50 per cent of
Japanese think they are hardworking; the other half
do not cite ''hardworking'' as part of their self-image.
Analysis of the origin of their self-image sometimes shows
that they think they are hardworking because they
have read somewhere that that is what foreigners say
about them. Depending upon whom you interview, you
may hear the opposite view from managers dismayed
by the unreliability of their employees.

Casual impressions and first-hand reports aside, however, there is reason to believe that the Japanese are a
hardworking people. Rather, they must be. Otherwise,
how can we explain Japan's economic development and
growth from 1868 to the present? The importance of
hard work for the nation's economic growth is self-evident. After all, economic development is a human phenomenon. It does not take place in a vacuum. Factories
and roads do not spring out of a political ideology, nor
do they blossom out of ardent prayer to God. They are
built by human hands. The record of Japan's economic
growth seems to speak for itself; hard work must necessarily have been one of the essential ingredients in the
recipe.

Is it true that the Japanese, historically, have worked
more than other people? Unfortunately, we do not have
much empirical information on the question. Even for

the postwar period, internationally comparable statistics on work hours are spotty. The evidence becomes thinner as we turn to the prewar period, and for the 19th century or earlier, reliable information is hopelessly scarce.

In 1960 the number of hours actually worked per week in the manufacturing industry were about forty in the United States, and fifty in Japan. European workers put in about 10 per cent less time on the job than the Japanese. Within Japan, however, the prevailing weekly work load among large enterprises was forty-two hours, approximating the Western standard. Japanese workers in small enterprises put in roughly 10 per cent more time than those in large enterprises. In other words, as far as large-scale firms in the modern sector are concerned, there is no indication that the Japanese work more than their Western counterparts.

East and West, factory workers used to work longer hours in the past. Even in Western Europe, the eight-hour-day became a norm only after World War I. In Japan, during the 1920s, about 8 per cent of the manufacturing firms with thirty employees or more followed the eight-hour rule.

Around the turn of the century, sweat shops, long hours, and employees' quarters resembling slave camps were still common in Japan. But this work environment, which would look shocking today, was widespread even in England prior to the mid-19th century. During 1840–1870, the norm for English machinists was to be in the factory from six A.M. till six P.M., or twelve hours per day. Allowing for rest periods and meal breaks, their daily work must have come to about ten hours. Similarly, Japanese machinists used to work for about ten hours a day during the early part of this century.

When a country is poor, the average man's work hours tend to be longer than when the country reaches a higher level of economic maturity. Adjusting for time lags in development, there is little evidence to suggest that the Japanese, since the mid-19th century, have worked far more than Westerners did during their comparable historical time periods. Whatever difference may have existed over the past 100 years or so does not appear to be so great as to explain the accelerated growth of the Japanese economy.

All countries, despite their varying stages of economic development, show one common characteristic about wages. As long as a society remains traditional, wages remain low and stationary. Once industrialization starts, however, wages begin to rise, and their upward trend continues during the period of further industrialization. Japanese wages began to rise from the time of her industrial take-off in the 1890s. By this time, however, wages in the then more advanced Western countries, whose industrialization began much earlier, had risen higher than those in Japan. Around the turn of the century, English wages were about three times as high as those in Japan.

This wage difference is important in understanding how Japan managed to begin her industrialization in the late 19th century. She was a latecomer in development. Modern tools of manufacturing were virtually absent, and everything had to be done from scratch. All the machines, tools, and parts had to be imported at first from the West. To pay for imports, she had to export. At that time there was no United Nations, no World Bank, no economic aid programs of the sort to which we are accustomed today. Despite her economic backwardness, Japan had to compete with the advanced Western countries in world trade. The low prices of her products—backed by low wages—were just about the only effective weapon Japan had for improving her competitive position in the international market.

''Export or expire'' was her predicament. In avoiding expiration, the low wage was instrumental, but it does not tell the whole story. A low wage can mean a greater capacity to compete in the world market if the productivity of workers in the competing countries is more or less the same. High productivity can offset the negative effect of high wages upon the country's capacity to export. If the productivity of English workers in the late 19th century had been three times that of Japanese workers at that time, all the advantage Japan held through her low cost of labor would have been wiped out.

This apparently was not the case. A precise comparison of the quality of Japanese and English labor in the late 19th century is impossible. But the rapidity of Japan's economic transformation, the expansion of her silk exports, and the subsequent growth of her cotton textile and light-manufacturing industries provide irrefutable evidence that Japanese workers were capable of adapting effectively to totally unfamiliar Western methods and tools of production. In light of the historical context, this was an extraordinary thing for them to have done.

When Japan's manufacturing industry was just beginning, the majority of workers were trained on the job. Those entering the factories without skills were first given the simplest, easiest tasks, then later promoted to perform more skilled jobs. Those people—sons and daughters of peasants, failing merchants, and the disowned samurai—could rapidly be converted into a new industrial labor force because many of them were literate and had at least a minimal education, basic discipline, and intelligence—all the necessary ingredients for the making of a factory worker.

What is the origin of the work ethic in Japan, a country that had not been baptized by Calvinism or the Protestant ethic? To answer this question we must speak of elements in the Japanese mind that must necessarily be traced to past history. The explanation lies in two sources: one was environmental, and the other pertained to the Japanese system of inheritance.

In geography books, the climate of Japan is classified as subtropical, but this technical classification gives a misleading impression. The country has four distinct seasons. Winter can be severely cold, particularly in the north. Late spring is humid, with heavy rainfall, followed by hot summer weather. Autumn, said to be the most beautiful and comfortable time of the year, is also the typhoon season.

In many tropical regions of the world, the daytime temperature may go so high that, physiologically, the farmers cannot work in the fields too long. The summer heat in Japan, however, never reaches such an excruciatingly high level. But unlike a tropical region, Japan has had little access to an abundant supply of fruits and vegetables that may grow with little or no human care and attendance. The geographical condition of the country required Japanese farmers to work hard with their primitive tools to produce minimal foods for their subsistence. And this was not enough. For over two centuries before the Meiji Restoration, the country was under the tight control of the Tokugawa regime, and the prevailing rule was that farmers had to contribute up to 40 per cent of their total rice crop to the local lords. In Thailand, where rice cultivation was historically similar to that in Japan, the rate of contribution was only about 10 per cent. In European agriculture, weeding is not a problem. In sharp contrast, weeds grow ferociously in summer on Japanese farms. Before the coming of weed killers and modern agricultural technology the Japanese farmers had to fight a constant battle against weeds in order to squeeze a few more grains of rice out of their meager plots of land. Paddy fields had to be irrigated constantly while rice plants grew, and pushing a manual pump was another never-ending task they could not afford to ignore. For most Japanese farmers, then, hard work was not a matter of choice; it was a question of life or starvation.

The dictates of the natural environment, together with the harsh rule of the Tokugawa regime, were enough to force Japanese farmers to work hard. But there was yet another institutional setting that helped fortify their work ethic.

In China, Korea, and most other parts of Asia, the equal inheritance system was traditionally used to divide the wealth of a household. Upon the death of the head of a family, his property was evenly distributed among sons of the deceased. In contrast, what was predominant throughout Japan was primogeniture. That is, under the legal system the eldest son claimed the entire wealth of the deceased household head. This meant, for the younger children, anxiety over the possibility that they might have to leave the house without any inheritance. The extended family system of the kind that flourished in China and India as a mutual-aid arrangement among relatives never became well established in Japan. After the eldest son assumed the position of head of the household, younger sons lived in the same house as though they were mere employees of the eldest son. In practice, all the family wealth was not permanently claimed by the eldest son; typically, some of his inherited wealth was to be shared later with the younger sons. This was more a matter of privilege than legal obligation, however. The amounts the eldest son would give could be small or substantial, depending upon his relationship with the younger sons. Primogeniture thus provided a strong incentive for the younger sons to work hard for the household, in order to solicit the favor of the eldest. Primogeniture also encouraged mobility within society, for the idlers could mercilessly be disowned and forced to leave the household, or the adverse financial condition of the house could oblige even the capable ones to make a new start elsewhere.

Up to World War II, so much Japanese energy had been channeled into building modern industry and strong armed forces that the level of consumption stayed low, and this helped sustain the incentive to work hard in order to improve one's standard of living. For many years after the disaster of World War II, the Japanese mind was preoccupied with the task of recovering what was lost during the war, and this again gave the Japanese a strong motive to work hard as a matter of necessity. In the past ten years or so, the Japanese have been tasting material affluence for the first time in their history. Recent surveys, however, show that many Japanese reply to the audacious question, "What do you work for?" by meekly saying, "To make a happy home life." After the days of "Prosperous Nation, Strong Arms," ultranationalism, "Glory to the Emperor," and "Rebuilding our Motherland," the Japanese have not yet run out of purposes for their hard work. Perhaps, thirty or forty years from now, when the average Japanese family lives in a comfortable house, drives two cars, vacations abroad regularly, and has a large collection of antiques and paintings, the Japanese may start to question the virtue of hard work as a way of life. That traditional belief may slowly begin to erode—to be replaced by a massive counterculture.

＊

Economic growth means that a nation's total annual output of goods and services keeps expanding. Economic growth is induced by capital accumulation, that is, by building a larger and larger stock of plants, machines, equipment, tools, and other means of production. The nation's capital accumulates as a result of private and public investments—which, in turn, are financed by savings. A nation of spendthrifts has little chance to witness sustained economic growth, for people spend much of their income on consumer goods, and the small amount of savings they accumulate is not sufficient to finance production of necessary investment goods. The larger the amount of savings, the brighter the prospect of capital accumulation.

People's propensity to save is important and desirable, particularly when a country is operating at an early stage of economic development. There is an acute need to build factories, railroads, and ports, and this can be accomplished only by allocating as much of the limited supply of resources as possible to produce investment goods rather than consumption goods. The trouble is, economic underdevelopment implies a low per capita income, and it is not easy for a poor man to save. The country may forever be trapped in the vicious circle of low income, low saving, low investment, low productivity, and back to low income.

The mere availability of savings, however, does not necessarily assure a country's successful take-off from the state of stagnation. The rich may keep their money in a Swiss bank or invest it in a developed country rather than in their own. Idle investable funds to which entrepreneurs have no access are as good as none. The rich in a poor land may decide to use the money to build pyramids or mammoth statues of the sleeping Buddha instead of steel plants and textile mills. Thus the presence of savings is a necessary but not sufficient condition for a successful take-off. Savings must be activated and effectively utilized by the entrepreneurs. A country may borrow from abroad or receive economic aid from advanced countries and use these externally supplied funds for internal development, but this approach may or may not work. The world's postwar experience seems to indicate that, as a rule, it does not work. Borrowed funds and grants may bring about pump-priming effects, or they may quickly dissipate in the hands of corrupt bureaucrats and incompetent managers.

The Japanese are said to be not only hardworking but also frugal. Their frugality has been pointed to as one of the factors responsible for the development and growth of their economy since the late 19th century. Others who work hard may spend hard, but not the Japanese. Inconspicuous consumption has been more in accord with their temperament. They were great savers before the war, when the country was still poor, and they became even greater savers during the postwar period.

The act of saving is not simply an economic phenomenon. Many other variables and constraints, all intricately intermingled, jointly determine people's motives to save or not to save. To assert that the high rate of saving in Japan is due solely to well-reasoned economic calculations is to lose sight of the whole picture.

The majority of Japanese in the Edo period were simply too poor to save any significant amount out of their meager incomes. Influenced by the Confucian ethic for centuries, they honored frugality as a part of their lifestyle. "Bear noble poverty, despise riches" was not only a moral lesson handed down by the authorities but also a statement of the only course available to them. Frugality then carried few strategic implications for economic development. Being frugal meant taking good care of things and minimizing one's earthly desires. Whatever savings people held were primarily for weddings, funerals, festivals, unexpected events. Their actions were strongly affected by the culture of shame under which they lived. Farm wives were concerned with their husbands' saving "face" before the villagers when contingencies arose. Not to be able to hold a proper funeral was to dishonor ancestors. It was shameful to prepare an inadequate family wedding. To avoid shame befalling the house, people saved.

Savings were intended only to pay for a culturally conditioned set of consumer goods and services; frugality then carried few strategic implications for economic development. The money economy was still critically underdeveloped in the provinces. In cities, financial institutions catered to merchants and manufacturers, but their activities did not penetrate the farming communities in any significant way.

During the early years of the Meiji era, investment funds to build the very first generation of shops and factories were, by and large, provided by the wealthy merchants, landlords, and aristocrats. The masses did not participate in pooling funds for the nation's economic development, being as yet too poor to do so. The situation began to change steadily from the 1880s to the end of the 19th century. Slow as the process was, per capita income was rising, relative to what had prevailed in the Edo period. The national government—manned by a group of idealistic, forward-looking, dedicated, and generally young individuals—was vigorously pursuing a course of modernization. The Bank of Japan was established in 1882. Soon the system of national banks was instituted. As part of the government's deliberate effort to squeeze every drop of investable funds from all corners for the objective of building a nation, a highly innovative nationwide network of postal savings was introduced. Japanese farmers from Tohoku to Kyushu were encouraged to serve their country by saving at local post offices. Now that the institutional arrangements were established to channel financial funds to the investment market, even the masses could transform their traditional spirit of austerity into real savings that would serve the nation's economic development.

The Meiji government knew and understood the importance of savings. It coined and popularized such slogans as ''Luxury Is Unpatriotic'' and ''Extravagance Is Our Enemy.'' The Ministry of Finance sponsored a series of campaigns promoting savings. Private enterprises were not the sole absorbers of savings, for ''A Prosperous Nation, Strong Arms'' was the central goal of the Meiji government. While a prosperous nation was to be built through the growth of industries, strong armed forces required that large quantities of resources be diverted from alternative uses. Both necessitated austerity all around.

From the Meiji period to the end of World War II, the Japanese government was always active in discouraging consumption and encouraging austerity. The emphasis of the slogans shifted with time, but not the theme. In Meiji Japan, restraint was solicited for the sake of building a new nation. During the Sino-Japanese War (1895) and the Russo-Japanese War (1905), the ''crisis'' facing the country was emphasized. In the later decades, people were reminded of the importance of saving for furthering Japan's industrialization. Past the mid-1930s, Japan was already moving toward a war economy. Japanese children during World War II recited in unison, *''Hoshigarimasen katsumade wa* (We shall overcome our desires till victory).'' The victory never came. Instead, there lay ahead a long, rocky road of reconstruction. Emperor Hirohito, in his August, 1945, radio message pronouncing Japan's surrender, pointed toward that road when he asked his people to ''bear the unbearable.''

Japan's industrialization has been guided by the state to a much greater degree than in other capitalist countries. Her ''sponsored capitalism'' meant that while Western science and technology were devoured as a means of building a strong nation, Japan's cultural hegemony was to be preserved. ''Western Knowledge, Japanese Wisdom'' or ''Western Mind, Japanese Soul'' were popular phrases in Meiji Japan. Western-style machines were run by men and women whose hearts remained very much within the confines of native tradition. In prewar Japan, tanks, planes, guns, and warships were manufactured by men who lived in small wooden houses on an austerely simple diet of rice, vegetables, and fish.

This was fortunate from the standpoint of Japan's industrialization. If consumer life as well as production had been Westernized, this would have resulted in a much larger per capita consumption of resources and would have left a smaller amount of resources to the investment sector. As it was, consumers chose to keep their mode of living essentially Japanese for many decades after the Meiji reform—though it is hard to measure the extent to which their choice was influenced by the government's moral suasion and propaganda. It is important to note that before the 1930s Japan had, by and large, practiced free trade. Only after the mid-1930s did quantitative as well as qualitative restrictions on imports and control of foreign capital come into being and add to the notoriety of postwar Japan.

It is one thing for the state to declare to its people, "Thou must save"; it is another for the people to respond and behave accordingly. A high propensity to save implies some economic rationale, rather than a purely patriotic motive. It is hard to believe that people in Meiji Japan, most of whom were still poor, decided to save simply out of their sense of loyalty to the state. In a crisis such as war, a strong government may be able to exploit nationalistic sentiment by urging frugality. As a long-run proposition, however, it is highly unrealistic to assume that people will respond forever to the call of duty rather than serve their own self-interest.

The rigidity of the Edo-period class structure was substantially modified by the Meiji reforms. The freedom to choose one's occupation became a reality, and Japan became a more mobile society. This new possibility of upward social mobility motivated people to save for contingencies, future investments, and education. People saved, not necessarily because the government told them it was a good thing to do for their country, but because saving became advantageous to them.

The Japanese, avid readers of "how to" books, have been encouraged to save by the words and examples of their more successful countrymen. Yasuda Zenjiro, a successful financier of Meiji Japan, nicknamed the "King of All Great Savers," wrote: "The secret of a young man's success in life consists of three words—save, save, save. Diligence is the father and frugality the mother of success." Fujii Kumataro, in his book published in 1916, advocated what he called "predraft savings." He wrote: "The government pays the draftees but there are many soldiers in the service who do not find their allowances enough. Consequently, they ask their parents for more money. These parents are already hard-pressed and this is an unpatriotic sort of thing to do. In order to serve their country well, the young men ought to save enough before the draft." In a more subdued genre, school textbooks, one of the most frequently mentioned names before 1945 was Ninomiya Sontoku, a paragon of hard work, frugality, and filial piety who presumably was to be held up as an example to Japanese children.

Since World War II the Japanese propensity to save has risen above the prewar level. The trend of high saving since the Meiji era not only has sustained itself but also has shown acceleration. The rate of personal savings among white- and blue-collar workers was approximately 10 per cent before the war; it fell to 2 per cent immediately after, began to move upward during the period of recovery, and reached a postwar plateau of 16 per cent in the late 1950s. The ratio of gross savings (including individual, corporate, and governmental savings) to the gross national product has shifted from 20 per cent before the war to above 30 per cent in recent years.

The high propensity to save in postwar Japan is all the more remarkable in view of the inflation of consumer-goods prices since 1960. The economics textbooks point out that inflation discourages the saving motive as people rush to buy before prices go up. This has not been happening in Japan. Indeed, inflation in Japan is not a postwar phenomenon only; prices have shown a rising, long-term tendency throughout the course of Japanese economic development. Rising prices have not succeeded in killing the tradition of frugality. On the contrary, the prospect of development in Japan has been enhanced by inflation. People cannot buy as many consumer goods as they wish when prices keep rising. The purchasing power of savings kept for future consumption is also reduced by inflation. Strictly from the standpoint of promoting economic development, this is good because less consumption on account of inflation is tantamount to more forced savings. Inflation siphons off much of the upward pressure on consumption. Other things being equal, the less people consume, the more resources can be allocated for investments.

The traditional philosophy of frugality has survived the war, postwar chaos, and inflation. This traditional element has been conditioned and reinforced by the institutional arrangements within which Japanese must live. Prewar Japan had no social security program in the modern sense of the term. What existed then was the "family security" system. Men saved for the security of their families. The family system survives today, but it became weaker immediately after the war, and its weakening continues. Contemporary Japanese parents can no longer count on the filial piety of their sons. They must save for their own post-retirement security.

Japanese society became more mobile and competitive after the war. To ''succeed'' in life one needs a college degree, but only a few bright students qualify for the national universities, where the cost of higher education is minimal. The majority of not-so-bright aspirants must go to private colleges and universities, and the cost of going to private schools in Japan is exceedingly high. The pressure for daughters' going to college has also been rising. The daughters of the Japanese middle class nowadays have difficulty landing husbands unless they themselves went at least to junior colleges. Thus Japanese parents today are under tremendous pressure to save for the education of their children. But this is what they believe in. If you ask a randomly chosen group of Japanese family men why they save, most of them will reply that one major purpose—the need for which they take for granted—is to send their children to college.

Before the war, Japanese companies paid bonuses to white-collar employees only. Blue-collar workers received only a token sum at the end of the year, just enough to drink a few extra cups of sakè on New Year's Day. After the war the bonus system was extended to cover blue-collar workers as well. The fruits of accelerated economic growth in postwar Japan have been distributed as rising salaries, wages, and bonuses. Bonuses in Japan are paid twice, at the middle and end of each year, and their total amounts to several months' salary and wages. If bonuses increase in proportion to regular incomes, employees are likely to treat the former as part of the latter. Bonuses, however, have been rising faster than regular compensation. This relative increase in bonus income is said to have caused the formation among employees of a habit, nonexistent before the war, of saving a large proportion of extra income consisting of bonuses.

Many Japanese suffered a drastic loss of property and liquid assets during World War II, and the war-caused dissipation of wealth added tremendously to their sense of insecurity, which in turn motivated them to save as much as possible in order to recover what was lost. Despite this increased saving, in terms of the stock of wealth held by the average household, Japan still falls short of the standards of affluent society. Consequently, the desire to build a larger individual stock of wealth is likely to survive as a motive for saving for some years to come. In the not-too-distant future, of course, Japanese society will be run by those who never experienced the wartime devastation and to whom the ordeal of the prewar generations is but a remote historical tale, unrelated to their lives. It remains to be seen what will happen then to the spirit of frugality that has sustained Japanese economic development since the late 19th century.

10 ✦ The Rich and the Poor Are Neighbors

Cleanliness may have been a traditional virtue for centuries in Japan but it seems to have been forgotten, at least for most of the postwar period. Or one might say that the Shinto regard for cleanliness and purity has been submerged into the Buddhist characteristic of self-denial and withdrawal. In any case, the Japanese have tolerated pollution because they have been concentrating their efforts on rapid economic growth.

—SAKAKIBARA YASUO

Over the past twenty years, Japanese consumer life has been undergoing a revolutionary change. The sight of many a modern appliance in an ordinary household in Japan has become the norm rather than the exception. This is a result of the long-sustained growth of the Japanese economy. Yet, as we turn to look beyond appliances, we observe many striking signs of backwardness coexisting with the plethora of consumer goods.

Poverty amidst plenty is most visible in the areas of housing and social services. The majority of Japanese still live in small apartments or substandard houses.

Roads are narrow, often unpaved, typically without sidewalks. Parks are conspicuously missing. The sewage and garbage disposal systems are incredibly inadequate. Employees spend long hours commuting in packed trains. During peak hours in Tokyo, trains and subways carry three times as many people as the theoretical maximum load. The situation grows worse in winter when the same number of people try to board trains in their heavy overcoats. They are pushed in like animals on the way to a slaughterhouse. If cows were transported in the same manner, one study concluded, most of them would die of suffocation.

Although Japan is the second largest industrial power in the free world, the quality of an ordinary citizen's economic life is impressively poor. This is a grand contradiction, for economic growth is supposed to make one's life better and more comfortable. Some people maintain that economic growth in all cases is bound to be unbalanced because it is nearly impossible for a country to continue to move onto higher stages of development while continuously keeping private and social capital in a delicate balance. More likely, a developing country will follow a zigzag path. The extent of unbalance in Japan is so great, however, that the paradox cannot be fully accounted for by saying that the signs of unbalance simply manifest some law of economic development or that those signs are particularly visible in Japan because the speed of her growth has been particularly rapid. More aptly, we can say that the pattern of her growth results from the government's economic policy, which has been characterized by a single-minded concern with output expansion and a benign neglect of consumer welfare. Ultimately, government and its policy choices mirror the mind of the governed. In this sense, then, the paradox is also a product of the Japanese people themselves.

Genuine consumer welfare depends not only upon the availability of consumer goods we desire but also upon the wholesome environment of the community in which we live. The two are necessary complements that jointly determine happy living. Tragic is the life of a child who has access to color television but no place to play. Tragicomical is the life of a man who has to breathe suffocating smog while driving a shiny automobile. Producing consumer goods and building sufficient social services are costly; both require the use of tremendous amounts of resources. What has been happening in Japan is that so much energy has gone into the production of private goods and so little into building a good community environment. More accurately, the Japanese economy could grow so fast because it deliberately ignored the question of community environment in order to concentrate the nation's resources on industrial expansion.

If you tour the major cities of Japan, you will note that there are no "residential sections." There are clusters of better-looking houses here and there as well as areas where the majority of residents are poor. But, on the whole, everything is mixed up. In Japan the rich and the poor are neighbors. It is not uncommon for shacks and substandard houses to be located but a short distance from a big, expensive house surrounded by its tall fence. Tokyo, the capital, which houses 10 per cent of the total population, is a huge juxtaposition of all the imaginable objects of urban life. Mazelike roads run in all directions. Thousands of little stores are found everywhere. Small factories are sandwiched between private houses. Bars and all-night cafes cluster around college campuses. The wards into which the city of Tokyo is divided either lack zoning regulations or have nominal ones only.

One Japanese urbanologist recently remarked: ''I don't see why the masses haven't revolted. Life in Tokyo has become intolerable.'' The majority of those who live in Tokyo inwardly feel that traffic congestion, noise, smog, and numerous other public nuisances are already beyond human endurance. They have, as it were, been pushed to the very edge of the cliff. Yet their discontent does not explode in violence. A few years ago, the residents of Tokyo elected as their mayor a soft-spoken, mild-mannered Marxist professor of economics. This was a sign of their frustration. But they are not radicalized by their dissatisfaction, which remains latent, repressed, and lonely.

While Japan in aggregate has become a superindustrial state, her citizens remain atomized and fulfill their needs in a privatized manner. Their consciousness of the meaning of ''community'' in human existence has historically been tenuous. The rich who live in smog-filled Tokyo seek a solution by building beach houses miles away or cottages in the mountains to which they escape for weekends. The not so rich, whose small houses in noisy, crowded neighborhoods are hardly an ideal site for rest, choose to stay out late into the night after the day's work. Cities are filled with places of entertainment —bars, coffee shops, restaurants, movie houses, strip joints, pinball parlors. The late-hour recreation and long commuting hours leave little time for family life. To many Japanese salarymen, home is but a place to sleep. Husbands and wives seldom go out together. Members of the family tend to act separately. While father stays late in a bar with his colleagues, his son goes out to see a movie with his classmates. Family outings in Japan are far less frequent than in the United States. On Sunday, father prefers to sleep late to recover from the past week's hard work. In the subways during the weekdays, many salarymen uncontrollably fall asleep.

There is a lot of masochism in the Japanese character. The traditional ethics have always emphasized the importance of negating one's ego, of sacrificing one's petty, personal desires for the sake of a higher cause. Farmers' wives sometimes work to the point of a breakdown as a way of retaliating against their hostile in-laws. In schools, members of athletic teams are often forced to endure vigorous practices that resemble torture. The attempt to transcend human bounds is thrilling to many Japanese. If a man works himself to death for his company, people regard him as heroic, not foolish. Even today, many Japanese wives will tell you that they prefer a man dedicated to his work to one who cheats on his work and tries to be home as much as possible, playing the role of a good, sweet papa. The same masochism also accounts for the way the Japanese react, or rather do not react, to the mounting crises of their environment. They choose to escape from reality rather than confront and cope with that reality by organizing massive resistance. Instead of mustering community action, they try to perfect a method of worming into packed trains and getting out of them without losing their buttons.

Japan has long been a highly centralized state. Local autonomy has been systematically and deliberately discouraged for the sake of national unity. Given the small size of the country and its ethnic homogeneity, the concept of ''federation'' as a form of political organization has never gained popularity. During the Meiji era, Japan faced the urgent task of converting the country into a modern industrial state as quickly as possible, and for this objective it was vital for the central government to keep control over the entire resources of the nation; during subsequent decades till the end of World War II, the country was in continual need of fortifying its power position vis-à-vis the rest of the world. In short, local governments in Japan have been rather powerless organizations, functioning primarily as subordinate arms of the central government. They have existed mainly as effective instruments for mobilizing the country's resources toward a national goal—rather than as agents of community-oriented, regional, and environmental projects.

Japan's highly centralized administration was made possible by centuries of conditioning toward the values of sacrifice, obedience, and restraint. During the Edo period, all Japanese except the samurai were disarmed. The Meiji reform disarmed even the samurai. If one party is armed and not the other, the nature of the contest between the two is predictable. People know they are no match for the state. It is more practical and sensible to follow whatever the state intends. "Don't bother to fight too strong an enemy," they say.

Most cities in Japan grew out of castle towns in the feudal era. Those castle towns were built not as centers of trade but as local administrative headquarters of the Tokugawa regime. Local lords followed the routine of *sankin kotai* (alternate-year residence) in Edo, by which the lords and their vassals customarily left their wives and children in their home towns. Hence, while the samurai lived in castle towns, serving as functionaries of the regime, many of their families lived elsewhere. Japanese cities thus grew around a transient population —developed for and by those who held political power. Many castle towns later became large commercial centers where various kinds of trade, manufacturing, and crafts flourished. The ruling class catered to the needs of the merchants and manufacturers, as a community, only to the extent necessary to return favors for the financial resources these trading classes supplied to the regime.

City planning as a way of enhancing the welfare of the general public has received little attention in Japan, either before or after the reforms of the Meiji era. There have always been "more urgent" tasks to be accomplished, from the national standpoint. The inertia of this tradition is still in force in Japan today. Even to this day most Japanese have little awareness or understanding of "community" (in the American sense of the term). Residents of Tokyo are unhappy about the deterioration of their environment. Yet they do not relate the problem to their lack of community consciousness. Their unhappiness is mixed with stubborn complacency and a touch of fatalism. They are more attentive to the statistics of their gross national product and what foreigners have said about the New Tokaido Super Express than to concrete steps to improve their environment. The concrete steps they do take are in the form of *chinjo* (appeals). A group of people ask a local boss to go to the ward office for some gravel to fill mud holes or to fix a leaking sewage pipe. This is usually the extent of their community action.

A horizontal grouping of people with common interests does not suit Japanese society, where communal association tends to be arrayed vertically. There are no

Japanese equivalents of the League of Women Voters, city councils, citizens' associations in unincorporated districts, and the like, that are active participants in local politics in America. Civic organizations do not flourish on Japanese soil. Social intercourse among neighbors in Japan is much weaker than in the United States. Typically, houses are surrounded by high walls. To enter a house, one has to walk through a gate facing the street, then through a main door to the house. This physical setting creates a powerful psychological barrier against casual visits. The man of the house is gone all day, and his mind is so thoroughly occupied by company matters that he hesitates to waste his time and energy with neighbors who share no common interests. The custom of informally inviting neighbors for dinner is uncommon. Japanese companies form a system of quasi communities, providing all sorts of welfare programs and activities for employees and their families. To Japanese men a company is not merely a place to work and earn money. It is the organization to which they dedicate their entire lives. They seldom associate themselves with people other than their colleagues and old classmates, and their social existence is thoroughly enmeshed with the affairs of the company. Thus, it is not in their neighborhood but in the company that they find their community.

The hierarchical structure of Japanese society can be a powerful instrument for the mobilization of the nation's resources at a time of national emergency and the achievement of internal political order and stability. The paternalistic structure of Japanese corporations can be an effective tool for accelerating industrial production. These structures, however, are not capable of turning out optimal solutions to the problems of environment and community. Men and institutions are motivated by things of immediate concern. To the state, the question of environmental improvement appears too remote and local to arouse keen interest. The business of corporations is to make profits, and they lean toward selling more goods rather than paying higher taxes to help build a "better community" for the benefit of those who are not necessarily their employees. From the standpoint of individuals, the whole issue seems too huge to deal with. The striking underdevelopment of communities in Japan is a result of the fact that the country has not been equipped with the political and economic institutions that can serve as optimal means of solving community-related problems.

∗

Each country usually has several faces that are seemingly conflicting and inconsistent with one another. Depending upon one's criteria of perception, for example, the United States may be viewed as a forward-looking, dynamic country or as an extremely uptight, conservative society. The Japanese themselves hold two conflicting images of their country. One is that Japan, behind the façade of a modern industrial state, is still a closed society where personal connections count a lot, where all sorts of cliques are formed in business and government, where productivity is not the criterion for promotion, where people are status-conscious, with the superior protecting his inferior, who in turn considers loyalty to his boss as something of a virtue, and so on. Another image is that Japan is, and has been over the past hundred years, a dynamic, mobile, restless society where people cannot sit still too long and where things change rapidly. The ideology of success and achievement is not merely a postwar phenomenon. In prewar Japan, the expression "returning to one's hometown with a victory flag" was common. It was possible for a nameless fellow who was born and raised in a remote village to go to a city and succeed in life through education and hard work, then return, decked out, to the awe of the villagers, in an expensive modern suit and shiny shoes, to visit his peasant parents.

The rapidity with which the transformation from feudalism to industrialization was accomplished suggests that toward the end of the Edo period Japan was already becoming a fairly mobile society. Symbolic of this is the case of Shibusawa Eiichi, one of the greatest entrepreneurs of the early Meiji period, who began as an obscure farmer, became a samurai working for the Tokugawa regime, held a government position after the Meiji reform, and finally established himself as a successful financier and business executive. Ito Hirobumi, a great statesman of the same period, also was of peasant origin.

Throughout the prewar decades a national mood prevailed that made everyone feel guilty and ashamed unless he worked hard. This mood was a reflection of prewar ethics, which dictated that each Japanese has a duty to work hard for the sake of his parents, as a matter of filial piety, and for the sake of his country, as a matter of loyalty to the emperor. Filial piety and loyalty to the emperor were not incompatible. Japan was—the handbook of Japanese ethics held—one nation, one family, united under the divine descendant from heaven. To serve the emperor and his state was also to serve one's parents. It was unpardonable to work only for one's selfish gains. All this is feudalism . . . a philosophy more akin to a traditional society than to a technological-ly advanced modern state. Yet it was this traditional ethics that motivated Japanese workers before the war, sustained a high degree of mobility, and thus contrib-uted to the country's industrialization.

After the war the emperor lost his divinity, and it be-came fashionable to regard filial piety as too old-fashioned to be compatible with the expectations of the new era. In postwar Japan there was no emperor to serve, no house to honor. But this did not destroy the incentives of the Japanese. They continued to work as hard as ever because tangible rewards resulted from their efforts. Their standard of living kept rising. The nation's eco-nomic growth made it possible for them to acquire goods to an extent unthinkable before the war. Having those goods stirred a new appetite for more.

Japan's accelerated growth after the war presents a puzzling problem. According to Western textbooks on economics, mobility means an efficient allocation of resources since materials and manpower can be moved to where they are most needed. Therefore, the greater the mobility the more efficient the use of resources . . . which in turn leads to faster economic growth. The Japanese economy has been growing much faster than that of the United States, but the Japanese are not mobile in the way Americans are. In America, factory workers get hired and fired all the time; office workers and ex-ecutives freely change their jobs without compunction. In Japan, management will often keep workers whose services are no longer required, and white-collar em-ployees hesitate to move to another company unless the situation has become truly unbearable. This shows immo-bility, bad from the standpoint of resource allocation.

There are different sorts of labor mobility, however, and American labor is perhaps too mobile. Some people change their jobs so they can function more productively. Some others move, not because they have found a better job, but because the present one has become intolerable or has been eliminated. Many more just keep wandering from one job to another without any definite increase in their productivity.

In many instances, mobility has a negative impact on society because it incurs tremendous costs in recruiting, training, and retraining. These are costs that must be absorbed by someone. The Japanese have tried to minimize this sort of mobility through the lifetime employment and seniority-based compensation system. Though low mobility has entailed some loss of productivity in Japan, this has been more than offset by gains in productivity resulting from the group cohesion, high morale, and harmonious human relations maintained by the quasi-family system of Japanese enterprises.

Japan has been a hierarchical society, but the rigidity of social structure can be more apparent than real. Hers has been a pliant sort of hierarchy. In Europe a bastard born of a nobleman and a woman of lesser background would typically be taken in by the lower-class family. In traditional Japan it was not uncommon for children born under similar circumstances to be adopted by the upper-class family.

Marriage was another instance of a theoretically rigid institution which, in practice, worked for mobility. Arranged marriage was the norm in prewar Japan. (The number of love marriages has been increasing after the war, but the custom of arranged marriage still prevails.) According to the rationale for arranged marriages, falling in love, no matter how precious it might be as a human experience, is not a solid, wholesome foundation for marriage. Passion, like fashion, does not last very long. A man and a woman are to marry to sustain the family lineage and raise children. Marriage is not a mere personal affair; it bears multitudes of social implications and responsibilities. A successful marriage requires careful examination of social and economic compatibility. Inexperienced, immature sons and daughters are hardly in a position to evaluate the shades of the problem. They will be better off if their marriages are arranged by the parents, who know better.

Most of this, of course, is poppycock. In practice, arranged marriage has been a powerful instrument for promoting social mobility in Japan. The Japanese are supposed to be a spiritual people interested more in the cultivation of a sound, calm mind through flower arrangement, tea ceremony, and the writing of haiku poems than in the naked pursuit of material possessions. This supposition is a lot of nonsense as far as an arranged marriage is concerned. The parents scrutinize each other with utmost care—about property, inheritance, family backgrounds, education, the company where the son works, and his promotion prospects. Keen attention is paid to the material aspects of marriage, and somehow one does not hear much about what the marriage will really mean to the man and his bride, whether or not they will get along and be happy with each other, whether the man will be tender to his bride and sweet to his children. Whenever possible, the arranged marriage functions as an instrument of upward social mobility. The nouveau riche tries his best to marry his son to an upper-class girl. The parents of lesser background try any maneuver to marry their beautiful daughter into a family of higher status.

Perhaps the most important factor helping to sustain the viability and the flexibility of Japanese society is the system of public education. In the past, Japanese schools may have taught the wrong subjects for the wrong reasons. Since the Meiji era, however, they have served as elevators to success for latent talents throughout the country. Unlike universities in many other countries, those in Japan did not cater to the privileged class exclusively. Instead, they have created an elite in which the criterion for membership has been ability and excellence rather than blood or family background. The cost of education has largely been borne by the state, so that any person has been able to acquire the sort of education that he or his family alone could not possibly afford.

Since the Meiji reform, the system of public education has been extensive and multilayered. In Meiji Japan, a son of a peasant family who finished elementary school could go to a normal school to become a teacher in a local school, then move on to a higher normal school to receive credentials that entitled him to be a school principal. Thus, in one generation, a nameless farmer's son could rise to a position of leadership and prestige in the village community. The more ambitious could go to military preparatory school, then to a military academy to become army or navy officers. Bright sons were encouraged by parents, relatives, and friends to go to the prestigious national universities where the cost of education was modest. Admission to one of these national universities more or less automatically entitled the bright ones to a lifelong membership in the elite class. All that really counted was the fact they had all taken the same entrance examination and passed it. Sons of the rich and the poor attended the same classes and listened to the same lectures. After graduation, they went into various ministries of the national government and into leading business firms, and began their steady, assured ladder-climbing within each hierarchy.

Essentially the same pattern has prevailed in postwar Japan. The difference is that, in the absence of military and colonial establishments, the majority of graduates from the national universities have gone into private business. Since the 19th century, there has generally been a surplus of educated personnel relative to demand. Even today, many college graduates perform the sort of work that could be handled just as well by high school graduates. In many developing countries endowed with a superabundance of labor, business firms paradoxically suffer from a shortage of qualified personnel. In the overdeveloped countries such as the United States and Great Britain, where the labor supply has largely been drained out, firms must cope with demanding, choosy employees. In contrast to both, the Japanese firms have had access to an abundant supply of cheap, well-educated, disciplined, conditionable workers. Education costs for graduates of national universities and other public schools have been absorbed by the state (or, more accurately, by the taxpayers at large). For graduates of private universities, the extremely high cost of education has been borne by the parents. Thus, Japanese enterprises have been heavily subsidized by the state, taxpayers, and the parents of not-so-bright sons who could not pass the entrance examinations for the prestigious national universities.

In Japan, professors are underpaid and over-respected,

whereas in the United States they are under-respected as well as underpaid. In America "professor" is a joke; in Japan the word "teacher" carries a connotation of reverence and indebtedness. Japanese parents take for granted the importance of children's education. They know that Japan is a rigid society, but also a pliant one. The walls of the hierarchy are there, but, with education, they can be broken. They have heard numerous success stories: the family doctor comes from a petty merchant family; a mathematics professor is the son of a coal miner; a distant cousin passed the senior administrative officers' examination to become a career diplomat and is now stationed in London as second secretary in the Japanese embassy there. The Japanese are aware that despite the appearance of inflexibility Japan is actually a highly mobile society.

The number of students at all levels has been increasing explosively since the war. Rising incomes have only intensified demand for education. Classrooms have become more crowded than ever before, and passing the entrance examinations to the prestigious universities becomes harder and harder each year. Japanese children grow up under tremendous pressure to learn from their parents and society. Competition begins at the nursery school level. Ambitious parents try hard to send their children to "prestigious" nursery schools to bolster their chances of admission to "prestigious" kindergartens. After elementary school, a child has to take an entrance examination to enter junior high school and another examination to be admitted to senior high school. The worth of each senior high school is judged by the number of graduates who go from there to the University of Tokyo each year. The higher the rating of a school, the more difficult it is to get in. During the last two years of high school, the ambitious students study doggedly to prepare for the university entrance examination. (By this time, many of them have had mental breakdowns. The frequency of teenage suicides in Japan is the highest in the world.) The entrance examination for the University of Tokyo is incredibly difficult. A professor at the same university, after supervising the examination, remarked "I don't see how anyone could pass that kind of test." An assistant professor of chemistry at the university could not solve one problem in his field. A visiting American scholar who had an opportunity to see the test reported, "I would have flunked the English section."

Only a few exceptionally bright high school graduates pass the examination for the University of Tokyo on their first try. Many others, instead of giving up and choosing universities of lower prestige, become *ronin,* masterless samurai. There are numerous prep schools to accommodate these students, who may continue preparing for the entrance examination two to three years or longer after graduation from high school.

By the time students have finally managed to get into the prestigious universities, many of them are thoroughly exhausted—both mentally and emotionally. About 15 per cent of the students at the University of Tokyo are said to be in need of some sort of psychiatric care. But dropouts are few. Japanese universities are hard to get into but easy to stay in. Knowing the ordeal the students have survived, the university administrators feel obliged to graduate them. After graduation there is one more hurdle to be jumped. Graduating students must take a final employment examination to assume positions in government and business. From then on, competition in general is confined to the place of employment as the bright and ambitious continue to struggle up the promotional ladder in hopes of eventually reaching the senior executive positions.

11 ✦ From Onda to Honda

> *Article 1. Do not be preoccupied with small matters but aim at the management of large enterprises.*
>
> *Article 2. Once you start an enterprise be sure to succeed in it.*
>
> *Article 3. Do not engage in speculative enterprises.*
>
> *Article 4. Operate all enterprises with the national interest in mind.*
>
> *Article 5. Never forget the pure spirit of sincerity and public service.*
>
> *Article 6. Be hard-working and frugal, and thoughtful to others.*
>
> *Article 7. Utilize proper personnel.*
>
> *Article 8. Treat your employees well.*
>
> *Article 9. Be bold in starting an enterprise but meticulous in its prosecution.*
>
> —THE HOUSE RULES
> *Iwasaki, founder of Mitsubishi*

Impressed by the dynamism of Japanese corporations, many Westerners have wondered, "What is the secret of their managerial system?" The secret is found in an obscure little book, *Higurashi Suzuri,* written in the 18th century by Baba Masakata, a poet and a chronicler of what is today Nagano prefecture. It tells the story of Onda Moku (1717–1762), who saved his provincial government from financial and moral bankruptcy.

Most Japanese have never heard of *Higurashi Suzuri*. They need not read the book to learn the secret of Japanese group dynamics, for Onda's philosophy of human management is deeply imbedded in their minds. The 18th-century official's conception of human relations has been shared by generations of Japanese corporate leaders from Onda to Honda, Matsushita, Mitsui, and Mitsubishi. Onda's approach has been followed by practically all successful Japanese corporations, while the majority of Japanese companies whose management adopted a course of action antithetical to Onda's have failed. Yet Baba's work is not just a classic manual of Japanese management. We conclude our inquiry into Japan with the tale of Onda, in the spirit of an extended epilogue, for it distills the essence of the earlier chapters of this book and gives a symbolic illustration of many things Japanese.

*

The provincial government of Matsushiro was in a fiscal crisis. The high costs of reconstruction after floods and provincial battles were further inflated by the Tokugawa regime's demand for exorbitant sums of money to share the burden of rebuilding Edo, the capital, which had been extensively destroyed by a major fire. In desperation, the provincial government cut and delayed payment of its officials' salaries, required farmers to pay their taxes for two years in advance, and borrowed heavily from merchants even though it was unable to pay even the interest on their loans.

To cope with the grave situation, the government appointed Tamura Hanemon, a man noted for his no-nonsense approach to budgetary matters, to serve as controller. He immediately proceeded to minimize waste in the house of the provincial lord. In the kitchen he ordered an enclosing wall built right behind the man attending the furnace so that excessive burning of wood would generate too much heat for him to bear. He prohibited monks from visiting government offices to save on gratuitous contributions to the local temples. He prepared a list of officials whom he suspected of accepting bribes and asked them to make voluntary donations to the government or else risk disclosure of their shady activities. Wealthy merchants, too, were subjected to Tamura's tough campaign. He reminded them of their moral obligation to repay their spiritual debt to the lord by contributing generously to the authorities. "I want you to remember," he told them, "your wealth depends upon the benevolence of your lord."

Despite Tamura's single-minded endeavor, the provincial government's fiscal crisis deepened, further aggravated by the extensive property damage wrought by a major earthquake that struck the area. Tamura switched to an even more authoritarian approach. Farmers were told to pay 15 per cent higher land tax in exchange for abolition of unpopular periodic inspection tours by the officials. Those who refused to comply with the order were threatened with confiscation of tax-exempted possessions. To everyone's astonishment, Tamura suggested leniency toward thieves and gamblers if their illegal acts helped them to pay their taxes. One night, two thousand angry farmers, united in revolt against his policies, marched to his house while shouting their intent to execute him in the name of Heaven. He hurriedly hid himself in a nearby temple during the night, and on the following day he escaped to Edo disguised as a hermit.

The ousting of the tyrannical controller did not improve the provincial government's financial condition. Three years after the popular revolt, Sachihiro, the sixteen-year-old lord, appointed Onda Moku as his minister of finance. Onda was noted for his ability and impeccable integrity, but his appointment was nevertheless controversial and unprecedented, for at the age of thirty-nine he was the youngest of all seniority-conscious retainers. Sachihiro, to win approval for his selection, traveled to Edo, requested an assembly of all his relatives serving as senior officials in the central regime, explained his decision, and asked for their full support, which he soon obtained. Sachihiro then urged them to meet the higher officials of his provincial government and persuade them to accept his decision. The higher officials and Onda were summoned to the capital and heard a plea from the young lord's relatives. Within a feudal hierarchy, it was unthinkable for the local officials to reject a plea from the officials of the central regime. This was especially true since the officials of the central government also happened to be relatives of their lord—although not a few of them, especially elder retainers, were inwardly disturbed by their lord's decision, which grossly violated the convention of the day. Nevertheless, before the assembly of the lord's relatives, the provincial officials all bowed down and promised to cooperate fully with the young appointee.

Then Onda came forward and humbly submitted his

resignation: "I am deeply honored by the lord's appointing me to a position of awesome responsibility, and the senior officials' consenting to the lord's decision. With much hesitation, however, I beg you to accept my resignation because I am not capable of fulfilling my duties."

The lord's relatives replied: "We, in the capital, are well aware of the prolonged plight of Lord Sachihiro's province. Even if the condition fails to improve during your tenure, it will not necessarily prove your incompetence or lack of endeavor. We shall understand if you first serve your office to the best of your ability, then fail. But to resign without even trying is a sign of disloyalty. We want you to withdraw your resignation."

"I never allow myself to be disloyal to my lord," responded Onda. "In all humility, I then accept the responsibility."

Now that Onda's appointment had become official, the lord's relatives told him, "Take this occasion to make any wish you may have."

After thanking the senior relatives for their generous suggestion, Onda laid down one condition for assuming his task. "I cannot accomplish my task as long as there are those who overtly or covertly oppose my undertaking. I want all the retainers and other officials of the provincial government to make a written pledge to fully cooperate with my decisions. At the same time, I shall submit my solemn promise to accept any criticism of my action from everyone, above or below me, and harsh punishment for any wrongdoings or misjudgments on my part."

Everyone present agreed to comply with Onda's request.

After exchanging these oaths with other officials, Onda called all his family, vassals, and relatives in the province to a meeting. His words shocked everyone. "As you know, I have just returned from Edo, having been appointed the new minister of finance. Reluctantly I accepted the awesome task because my humble request to decline the offer was firmly rejected," he told those who gathered before him. "I want you to understand that whatever I do in this new role is going to determine the rise or fall of my entire career. As a preliminary step, I must ask all of you to sever your ties with me completely, and I want every one of you to give your consent to my action. I want to cut off all relations with my kin. I want to divorce my wife, and I ask her to return to her parents. I want to disown my children so they may go anywhere as they wish. I want all my vassals to leave me and look for new masters. As you go away, take anything you find and desire in this house."

As soon as Onda finished, the relatives protested this bewildering abnegation. "On what grounds do you wish to sever the ties with your own wife, children, and vassals? Have they done something wrong? Have they been disloyal to you?"

"No, they have done nothing wrong," Onda replied nonchalantly. "I want them to leave me because their presence, I fear, will disturb my work."

One of his relatives moved forward and said impatiently: "Your honor, have you lost your senses? We all appreciate the gravity of your task, but why does it cause you to sever relations with all those who have been faithful to you? After everyone leaves your house, how are you going to live? You cannot live alone, can you?"

"Oh, I'll manage," responded Onda, "though I may

later hire some new vassals. And let me assure you, I don't think I've gone mad. The only reason for your dismissal, I repeat, is that I don't wish to be disturbed by your presence."

Onda's wife protested in tears: "I shall accept the divorce with grace if you can explain to me what wrongs I have done. With no explanation, how can I return home and face my parents? And I want you to explain to our children why you are disowning them, and in what way their presence will disturb your work."

The relatives joined in: "Yes, we'll understand your decision if you can fully convince us how our presence will upset your new responsibility."

Onda finally revealed his true feelings: "Well, I did not elaborate on my intent, for I was afraid you would not understand it. Since you insist—and your insistence is reasonable—let me explain. You see I have pledged to myself never to lie or make statements that I cannot account for. But never to lie is much easier said than done. If anyone in my family, relatives or vassals, should lie or make irresponsible statements, people will say, 'Look, Onda took an oath of truthfulness but his relations do not follow his example. So I do not really trust him.' With such distrust prevailing among the people below me, I cannot possibly fulfill my duties. That's why I decided to sever my ties with all of you. Besides, I have also pledged to live only on rice and soup, forgoing even pickles, and to wear only cotton clothes after my present wardrobe wears out. But I thought my wife and others might wish to occasionally indulge in harmless lying, eat pickles and other fancy foods, and wear silk clothes. They may do so after leaving my house."

His wife asked him, "Do you mean to say you won't

divorce me if I promise to speak always truthfully, live on rice and soup alone, and wear only cotton?''

"Yes, that is correct."

"All right, then I'll make all those promises, so I beg you not to divorce me."

"You realize that after all the vassals and servants leave, you must carry water and cook rice for yourself."

"I understand. I've neither cooked rice nor carried water, but I promise to learn to do those things."

"Are you sure?"

"Yes, I give you my word."

"In that event, divorce is unnecessary. You may stay as my wife. But I want my children to leave the house. Since they are still young, I will of course provide them with ample allowances."

The children replied, "We promise to tell no lies, eat only rice and soup, and wear cotton clothes all the time. Please do not disown us."

"Are you absolutely sure you can honor all those promises?"

"Yes, we're absolutely sure."

"Then you may stay on as my children."

"Now," Onda turned to his vassals, "I want all of you to leave my house immediately."

The vassals responded, "Your honor, have mercy upon us. We will take an oath to make no false remarks, live on rice and soup alone, and wear only cotton, so please retain us. If you dismiss us, we shall never be able to find another master, for people will say, 'Those fellows were fired from the house of Onda because they could not even promise to be truthful and frugal. They must all be a useless bunch.' We shall be grateful for your benevolence if you keep us."

"If you are serious about those promises, I shall retain you. I would have had to hire new vassals anyway to maintain this house even if I dismissed you. Be assured that you will receive the same wages. Keep up with your diligent work."

"No, we don't want our wages—if you could provide us with food. When our present clothes wear out, we will ask to borrow your used ones."

"Your wages will be duly paid. I receive a stipend of one thousand *koku** for my job. After deducting your wages, the cost of rice and soup, and my wife's expenses, I plan to return the balance to the lord. You need wages to support your wives and children."

Looking grateful, the vassals agreed to comply with Onda's suggestion.

"Now then," Onda said, facing his relatives, "I trust you will cut off your relations with me?"

"No, no, what you ask of us is utterly impossible. We and our own families will make the same promises all the others have made."

"It is against my will to let your families conform to the new rules of my house on food and clothing. It will suffice for you just to promise to be always truthful. I have no right to interfere with what you eat or wear."

The relatives accordingly pledged unconditional honesty and went home relieved.

Shortly afterward, Onda called for an assembly of all the retainers and other officials of the provincial government to explain his new policy.

"I want you to understand that without your full cooperation I alone cannot possibly solve our fiscal

---

*One *koku* was the equivalent of about five bushels of rice.

crisis. Frugality is our fundamental principle, but I shall never try to economize on the expenditures necessary to sustain the prestige and dignity of our lord.'' While urging the officials to save on all nonessential public expenditures, Onda did not ask them to follow his and his family's example of living on rice and soup and wearing only cotton clothes.

Onda went on, ''I know during the crisis your salaries have been cut—in some years up to even 50 per cent. This economy measure will be terminated right now, and during my tenure you will always be paid the full amounts as stipulated by law. You must agree with me that my measure is extraordinary considering the continuing fiscal difficulty. I want all of you to fulfill your duties to the fullest extent possible. After you have done your work each day, however, I suggest that you enjoy your leisure as much as you can. Read literature, compose poems, indulge in calligraphy and tea ceremony, play or listen to music, or do whatever else gives you pleasure. Gamble, if you like, provided it's strictly for fun and not for illegal money-making. Work is important, but one cannot keep on working hard and well all year round without rest and recreation. Fiscal reconstruction of our government is our goal, but, given the nature of the problem, we are not going to accomplish our aim overnight. We must prepare ourselves for a long-run solution to the problem. Do not bother to initiate a drastic change toward stringent austerity. Such an action would cause more strain than solution.''

Some weeks later, having thought out the specific guidelines of his policy, he requested a grand assembly of all the representatives of farmers and merchants in the province, together with the government officials. He sat in front of the large gathering and thanked them for bearing the inconvenience of traveling from distant places to attend the meeting. After explaining the history of his appointment, he, a high official of the provincial government, said to the assembled commoners, "The problem we face is so enormous that I alone cannot possibly solve it. I requested that you come here today because I wanted to discuss the problem with you. You know as well as I how difficult our lord's financial condition has been, and I am thoroughly aware that you, too, have suffered for many years. My heart is tormented by the thought that you may perhaps have to suffer more during the tenure of such an incompetent official as myself. I shall first express my views, and later I wish to hear your opinions on the matter."

"First of all," Onda continued, "I have taken a solemn oath never to lie about anything, and other officials have sworn to do likewise. From now on, every statement I make will be always honored, I shall never change or modify my word . . . and I want you to remember this very carefully. I sincerely believe that I cannot accomplish my task in the absence of your full cooperation with, and understanding of, my policy, and the only way for me to have your cooperation and understanding is through heart-to-heart talks between us on the nature of the problem. I therefore want you to react to my plan as candidly as possible. If you agree and cooperate with me, I know we can together solve the problem; if you don't, I cannot fulfill my aim and will ask for your forgiveness by committing hara-kiri. In other words, how you react will determine my life or death. I realize, however, that you may find the present setting too delicate for you to express your true feelings on the matter, so it is perfectly all right with me if you just listen to me today, discuss these matters with other people in your towns and villages, and submit your views to me later. Now, on the oath I and other officials have made, will such a pledge in any way cause you inconvenience and embarrassment?"

"No, sir," emphatically replied the farmers and merchants. "To tell the truth, many of us have suffered greatly because of the officials' deceiving words. Nothing can give us greater joy than your assurance that the officials will in the future be always true to their word."

"I am so glad you agree to my first policy rule," said Onda. "Now the second rule. From now on, I shall never accept any present from you, regardless of the occasion. You will not be allowed to bring gifts, large or small, to my office. Or do you find this rule awkward and inflexible?" They all insisted they did not.

"In the future I want you to submit all your appeals and requests to me directly, and I in turn will transmit them to the proper officials. In this way you will no longer feel obliged to bring gifts to officials. Presenting gifts to officials for any other purposes will also be strictly prohibited." The assembled representatives expressed their appreciation.

"I am happy to have your agreement on my second rule as well."

Onda then disclosed his plans to dismiss 900 footmen from the job of tax collection and to free farmers from the obligation of donating their labor to the provincial government.

"I have been told," Onda said to the audience, "that of 1,000 footmen employed by the lord's house, only 100 have been assigned to guard duties, and the other 900 dispatched to collect taxes from the farmers each month. Is it true?"

"Yes, your honor, it is true."

"Let it be understood that in the future not a single footman will be sent to the villages for that purpose. Or will it cause you inconvenience if they suddenly stop coming?"

"No, sir. On the contrary, we welcome the change. Every time those footmen come to our homes, they not only collect taxes but also stay on from five to seven days, demanding free meals as well as gifts. In truth, they have been giving us a good deal of strain. We will be gratified by the termination of their visits."

"Now, I am a mortal human who may at any time fall ill or die; I shan't be serving as minister of finance forever. I anticipate staying in office for five years, and during this period you will be exempted from the duty of working for the provincial government without pay— though this rule does not apply to road repairs and other communal projects that accord with local convention. Or do you foresee any situation in which you will be troubled by this rule?"

"No, sir, we appreciate it, for in the past, that work for the provincial government took up so much of our time."

"I am deeply pleased," responded Onda, "that you have agreed to all the points I have raised thus far. Let me repeat once more . . . do I have your consent to my implementing those policy rules that I have spelled out?"

"Yes, indeed," answered the farmers and merchants.

Onda moved to the next point. "Are there any farmers who have had to pay taxes in advance?"

"Yes, there are . . . often for two years in advance."

"I don't quite see how it happened. Is there any advantage to making an advance tax payment?"

"Not at all. There is absolutely no advantage to it. Many of us had little choice but to pay taxes for next year or even for two years ahead to comply with the officials' orders."

"But the law only requires you to pay tax for the current year. If it is foolish enough to pay tax for next year, it is utterly stupid to pay tax for two years in advance." Onda became visibly irritated. In a loud, angry voice, he said, "Those farmers who have done so are incurable idiots, and those officials who illegally collected taxes in advance simply because the farmers did not resist are unpardonably cruel!"

Onda, resuming his soft, quiet tone of voice, asked the audience as though he were asking himself, "It is false reasoning, isn't it? We cannot really call those officials cruel and merciless, can we? They were not embezzling those advance taxes. Their knowledge of the plight of the lord compelled them to collect taxes in advance; their sense of loyalty drove them to commit an act which they knew would burden the farmers. At the same time, the farmers complied with the illegal demand because they sympathized with their lord and trusted their officials. Our lord is fortunate to have so many dedicated officials as well as honest, kindhearted farmers. What interests me, however, is that these desperate efforts do not seem to have alleviated the financial crisis of the government at all. At any rate, from now on, advance payment of taxes will be strictly prohibited." The farmers bowed deeply to express their appreciation.

Onda turned to the merchants in the audience.

"I understand some of you gave credit to the provincial government . . . is that correct?"

"Yes, your honor."

"Please tell me why you did so. Do you receive high interest, or is it profitable to you in some other way?"

"On the contrary, sir, we have lost from lending to the government, which neither pays interest nor returns the principal. We provided credit because the officials ordered us to do so."

"I don't see why you accepted such unfair deals. You should have had enough courage to refuse by stating that you had no money available for the purpose. If the central regime in Edo asks our lord for credit now, I will go to the capital and simply explain that we cannot favorably respond to the request. I don't imagine they would execute me for refusing to lend them money when there is none. Those officials are no better than you. It is immoral for them to demand money from you when they know they cannot return it."

"But it is false reasoning, isn't it?" Onda questioned again. "The truth is, our public funds have completely dried up. Our government cannot even pay its obligatory dues to the central regime. Those officials were compelled by their sense of duty to ask for your money, and they have failed to pay interest or return the principal, not because they are fraudulent, but because there is no money to be returned. I trust that you, the merchants, agreed to provide credit despite the risks because you wanted to help the authorities. Your lord is fortunate to have so many considerate and selfless merchants among his subjects. In the future, however, there will be a strict ban on private credit to the provincial government."

The merchants rejoiced to hear Onda's decision.

Onda turned to those farmers who had not paid their taxes. "Our tax rate is set in such a way that, after paying the tax, you are left with enough to support your families and enjoy yourselves. If you have cultivated your land diligently, planted seeds at the right time, fertilized the soil sufficiently, and harvested the crop as scheduled, there is absolutely no reason why you should not be able to fulfill your tax obligations. You must have shamelessly neglected your work, cheating the authorities and other farmers who, through hard work and dedication, have paid their taxes in advance. I cannot despise you more. You deserve severe punishment. I am also appalled by those officials who let the chiselers get away without contributing their share to the welfare of the province. The officials should have collected the taxes by any means in the name of the law and in fairness to the honest, hardworking farmers." Onda's body was trembling with anger.

"But it is a misguided explanation, isn't it?" After a pause, Onda's voice became gentle again. "I suppose the truth is that you have been struck by misfortune—a prolonged illness, an unexpected tragedy in the family, or whatever—and not a grain of rice was left to pay the tax after feeding your family. I sympathize with your plight. The officials waived your tax obligation, I believe, because they knew and appreciated your hardship. I am fortunate to have officials with such a sense of compassion. Now, I am going to give you grace on your tax liabilities, for it is senseless to insist on collecting where there is nothing to be collected. Our lord will absorb those liabilities as his loss, and you are no longer obliged to pay your tax due this year, so treat it as a gift from your gracious lord. However, I expect you to pay your tax without fail next year. If you don't, please remember I shall prosecute you in the criminal court."

"Yes, your honor, we solemnly swear to pay our tax in full in the future even if it requires us to sell our possessions."

"I am grateful," responded Onda to the farmers, "for your kind cooperation."

Onda once again faced the farmers who had paid their taxes in advance. "I have a favor to ask of you. I sincerely wish we could return all your taxes illegally collected in advance, but, as you know, our government is penniless at present, and my decision to ignore the unpaid taxes makes the problem even more difficult. I want you to be good-hearted enough to take them as your losses. Or do you find my request too unreasonable for you to accept?"

"No, not at all," said the farmers, "you promised us not to demand advance payment of taxes in the future. Please be assured we shall expect no refund of our tax payments."

"I have yet another favor to ask of you. I want you to discuss it with other villagers and submit your response to me later, for I am afraid it is too delicate to be settled immediately at this gathering. The favor is this—I would like you to pay this year's regular tax despite your loss of advance taxes. This is the only way I can balance our budget this year, and if I fail to do so I am prepared to commit hara-kiri. To find out how much actual burden my proposal will bring to you, my accountant and I did some calculations, independently of each other, and reached the same conclusion. According to our estimate, the total cost of bribes to the officials, providing free labor for nonessential projects of the provincial government, and entertaining the 900 footmen during their visits to the villages amounts to 70 per cent of the annual tax. These wasteful practices have been abolished, and their costs, hitherto unilaterally absorbed by the farmers, will be saved. In other words, from now on your tax burden will be considerably less than before, since you can fulfill your tax obligation each year by adding only 30 per cent of the total annual tax liabilities to the amount of those gratuitous expenditures you are no longer required to absorb. I want you to take my proposal to your villages and discuss it carefully with your people.''

"We appreciate your thoughtfulness," responded the farmers. "We are happy to present our opinion right at this moment, but, since you insist, we will first bring your good word to our people and submit our reaction subsequently."

"I have a favor to ask of you, too," Onda said to the group of merchants who had lent money to the provincial government. "I wish I could find a way to pay you back, but to do so at present is impossible. I must therefore ask you to forget about your credit for now. However, in life you never know when misfortune may strike you, and you may see your business ruined and your wealth dispersed. It may not happen in your lifetime but it may occur in the generations of your children or grandchildren. When it does happen, we shall return the principal of your loan—though we cannot promise to pay the interest. So I want you to regard your credit as a form of saving for rainy days, kept in trust by our lord. I do not believe your businesses will be ruined unless we pay your loans back immediately. Or do you consider my request too unreasonable?"

"No, not at all," answered the merchants. "We were willing to help the lord with our credit and did not really expect it to be returned. We are overwhelmed by your generous suggestion to save it for the benefit of our offspring.''

''I have come to my final request to all of you,'' said Onda. ''I want you to write down without your signature the wrongdoings of all the officials, including myself, that you have witnessed in the past, carefully seal the notes, and submit them to my office. The meeting is now adjourned.''

The farmers and merchants went home in high spirits. Many of the officials in the audience, who had been increasingly impressed by Onda's power of persuasion, suddenly turned pale at his final suggestion.

Upon reaching home, the village representatives called all the farmers to a meeting and related to them the details of the session with Onda. The farmers' reaction was immediate and unanimous. They said, ''Our new minister of finance must truly be a man of integrity and wisdom. We are no longer required to accommodate those arrogant footmen and leave our farms during the busy season to work for the provincial government, and how much relief that will give us! Let us return our thanks by doubling our annual tax contribution.'' They urged the representatives to convey their decision to Onda as quickly as possible. The representatives reminded them to write down all their complaints about the injustices of the officials—which they did with great enthusiasm and pleasure after years of suffering from the high-handed attitude of the previous administration and its officials.

Soon the representatives returned to the provincial capital to report to Onda on the villagers' decision.

"They are so grateful for your actions," the representatives told Onda, "that they are perfectly willing to help you by paying twice as much tax each year."

"I am deeply touched," replied Onda. "Thanks to their cooperation, I shall be saved from the pain of hara-kiri. I will convey their willingness to our lord, for I am sure he will be deeply pleased to hear it, but I must make it absolutely clear that the doubling of their tax contribution is not necessary. Paying the normal tax as stipulated by the law will suffice. But I want you to remind your people that daily work is absolutely essential for them and for all of us. Neglect of one's duty is a criminal offense, and the offender will not be tolerated. After they have done their day's work diligently, however, I want them to pursue their own pleasures. I shall approve even gambling if it is done with moderation and for amusement—though professional gambling is illegal under the national law and will be severely dealt with. One cannot keep on working productively without some relaxation. By the way, did you bring the sealed notes of complaint that I requested?"

After accepting the farmers' notes, Onda said to their representatives, "I am going to submit these notes to the lord without opening them. Today we should not spend any more time for our meeting. I ask you to return to your work, and please give my appreciation to your people."

After the village representatives had left his office, Onda went to see Lord Sachihiro. "I have good news for my lord," he said. "I am now confident that we can solve our fiscal crisis. All our debts have been canceled, and there will be enough tax revenue to balance our budget. Please rest assured that no one in the province expresses rancor against you on account of the measures I have taken. On the contrary, they are deeply grateful to you, as can be seen in their willingness to double their annual tax contributions. And here are the notes of complaint written by our farmers. I should like you to open and examine them. No one else has seen their contents before."

A few days later, the lord summoned Onda to his office. "You had better read these complaints for yourself," the lord said, giving Onda a bundle of the farmers' confidential testimonies.

After examining them, Onda said, "I was afraid that the situation might be this bad."

"I need your advice on how to prosecute those officials who have indulged in improper conduct."

"It is not necessary for my lord to prosecute them," replied Onda. "These people will practice good or bad deeds, depending on the circumstance. Their conduct is a reflection of the quality of their superiors. Some of them seem to have committed crimes that call for the death penalty, but we should not worry about it. It takes talent and intelligence to engage in a delicate act of illegality. We should make use of their talent for a good cause. I want you to commission them, never hinting at your anger with their crimes, to serve in my office as my colleagues and urge them to work conscientiously and diligently in support of my difficult task."

"Will you not be troubled by their presence?" The lord sounded a little apprehensive.

"No, not at all, my lord," replied Onda.

"Well, if it does not trouble you, I shall be happy to comply with your request," said the lord.

Lord Sachihiro called the bad officials to his office and appointed them to work with Onda. After humbly accepting their appointments, they gathered together and expressed their puzzlement. "The lord's decision is perplexing," they said to one another. "No doubt the lord as well as Mister Onda have learned, by now, all about our immoralities as reported by the farmers. How then do you explain our appointments? It must have been suggested by Mister Onda himself, and we now realize that he is truly an extraordinary person. If we were in his position, we would be charging those who have committed similar acts with high crimes, including those punishable by death. But he is not only forgiving us but is also asking us to work with him. We must repent and dedicate our absolute allegiance to his cause; otherwise, we will ruin our lives and dishonor our ancestors."

They agreed to visit Onda immediately to express their gratitude. They said to him, "A thousand thanks for giving us the opportunity to work in your office. We know that you know we have engaged in shameful acts in the past. We swear never again to repeat our sins, and we humbly beseech your wise guidance."

"I don't deserve your thanks," responded Onda. "I should have paid you a visit first, to express my appreciation for your willingness to work with me. I need all your help, since I alone can hardly accomplish the task. I beg you to make suggestions and call my attention to anything that you think is wrong with my policy."

From this moment on, people in the province no longer heard of officials committing bribery, embezzlement, fraud, or any other improper conduct.

Later, a provincial official serving his tenure in Edo

dispatched a request to Onda asking for 2,000 *ryo*,* which he said was needed to accomplish his project for the central regime. Onda consulted with two officials in his office who had previously served the same tenure in the capital. They advised Onda that they were acquainted with the nature of the project, and the sum of money requested was a bit too large. Onda reassured them, saying, "The central regime deals with many problems unfamiliar to provincial governments. I have no reason to believe that our man in Edo is unnecessarily inflating the figure, and we must guard against false economy." The two officials insisted that, were they sent to Edo, they would accomplish the same project for 1,200 *ryo*. Onda agreed to send them to the capital and gave them 2,000 *ryo*, nevertheless. "Spend as much as you must in order to fulfill your duty to perfection," he told them, "and come home with whatever is left." He wrote a note to the official in Edo, asking him to cooperate with the two officials bringing the money. The three worked closely and wisely on the project, which was executed to the central regime's satisfaction for 1,300 *ryo*, and the two returned home with a saving of 700 *ryo*. Onda petitioned the lord: "This surplus of 700 *ryo* would have left our treasury for good without the efforts of our three officials. Might I suggest that we give 100 *ryo* to each of the three as a reward and keep the remainder of 400 *ryo* as an unexpected surplus?" The lord happily consented to Onda's suggestion, and the three, moved by the generous rewards, strove even harder to fulfill their duties.

In response to Onda's rule of leniency toward gam-

*A *ryo* was a unit of coinage.

bling as a pastime, some professional gamblers in the
area began to abuse the rule by setting up gambling joints
and enticing innocent farmers and merchants to come
and lose their money, allegedly all for amusement. The
number of victims increased steadily, and some even
went bankrupt. Onda sent a notice throughout the province, asking all the losers to come forward without
hesitation to receive aid from the provincial government.
A large number of losers appeared from all corners of the
province. Onda asked them to identify the winners, and
they willingly supplied their names, believing that they
had done nothing wrong. Onda summoned all the winners to his office and asked them, "Is it true that you
gambled with so and so and collected money on such
and such date?"

Believing in their own innocence, they all replied,
"Yes, your honor, it is true."

"Then I want all of you immediately to return the
money you won to the losers."

Shocked by the demand, the winners pleaded, "That
will give us great strain, your honor. We beg you to reconsider your decision."

"Let me ask you a question," Onda said to the
trembling winners. "You know as well as I that professional gambling is a crime punishable under the national
law. If you did gamble for money, I must prosecute you
right away, . . . but I trust you gambled only for
amusement."

"Yes, of course, it was just for entertainment."

"Yes, I understand," Onda replied. "But it is unthinkable that people should lose a fortune and go bankrupt as a result of gambling for amusement. I expect you
to return all the money to the losers within a reasonable

amount of time, and if you fail to do so I'll interpret it to mean that you have engaged in illegal gambling. I will then take proper action in accordance with the law.''

"We will comply with your request immediately," the winners hurriedly replied, and they returned home badly shaken. The losers received all their money back, while the winners, having already spent some of the money collected through gambling, had to borrow to meet the obligation. Thereafter, nobody in the province gambled—for money or amusement.

*

Besides being a master of human management, Onda was a man of piety who prayed daily and often cordially received Buddhist priests at his home. His servants welcomed their visits because they were allowed to ignore Onda's austere dietary rules whenever the priests were entertained with a feast. Onda was also a great practitioner of the martial arts, which he strongly recommended to the young lord, Sachihiro, his own children, and all other children of samurai in his province as a way of achieving physical and spiritual fitness.

His administration dispelled the cloud of distrust and corruption that had hung over the province for so long a time. In less than five years, the fiscal crisis of the provincial government was over, and its budget even began to show a surplus. An atmosphere of mutual trust and cooperation prevailed throughout the community. When Onda died on January 1st, 1762, at the age of forty-six, all the people in the province mourned his death by removing the New Year's Day decorations from the fronts of their houses.

✦ Notes and Bibliography

The nature of this book and the diversity of topics it deals with make it inappropriate to provide readers with a complete and comprehensive bibliography. The book, however, embodies numerous ideas, facts, and interpretations that I borrowed from other authors, and I gratefully acknowledge my large debts to the efforts of others by citing below those sources that I have consulted—though the listing is by no means exhaustive. For the benefit of English-speaking readers, I shall also make suggestions for further reading.

While organizing my thoughts for the book, I relied heavily upon Eiichiro Ishida, *Ishida Eiichiro Zenshu*—Collected papers of Eiichiro Ishida, vols. 3 and 4 (Tokyo: Chikuma Shobo, 1970). The following works cover similar ground, and I found them useful in developing my own frame of reference: Yuji Aida, ed., *Nihonjin no Tankyu*—A study of the Japanese (Tokyo: Nihon Noritsu Kyokai, 1972); Masatoshi Sera, *Nihonjin no Kokoro*—The Japanese mind (Tokyo: Nihon Hoso Shuppan Kyokai, 1965); Tadao Umesao and Michitaro Tada, eds., *Nihon Bunka no Hyojo*—The face of Japanese culture (Tokyo: Kodansha, 1972); and Arata Yoda, ed., *Nihonjin no Seikaku*—The Japanese character (Tokyo: Asakura Shoten, 1970). For historical backgrounds, I derived much benefit from Saburo Ienaga, *Nihon Bunka Shi*—Japanese cultural history (Tokyo: Iwanami Shoten, 1959).

The other works I consulted for general references include:

Tatsusaburo Hayashiya et al., *Nihonjin no Chie*—Japanese wisdom (Tokyo: Chuo Koronsha, 1962); Kiyoyuki Higuchi, *Nihonjin no Chie no Kozo*—The structure of Japanese wisdom (Tokyo: Kodansha, 1972); Hidetoshi Kato, ed., *Nihon Bunka Ron*—On Japanese culture (Tokyo: Tokuma Shoten, 1966); Shuzo Kuki, *Iki no Kozo*—The structure of "iki" (Tokyo: Iwanami Shoten, 1930); Takeo Kuwabara, ed., *Nihon no Meicho*—Masterworks of modern Japan (Tokyo: Chuo Koronsha, 1962); Otoya Miyagi, *Nihonjin no Seikaku*—The Japanese personality (Tokyo: Asahi Shimbunsha, 1969); Yujiro Nakamura, *Nihon Bunka no Shoten to Moten*—Points and counterpoints of Japanese culture (Tokyo: Kawade Shobo, 1964); Tatehiko Oshima et al., *Nihon o Shiru Jiten*—A dictionary to learn Japan (Tokyo: Shakai Shiso-sha, 1971); George B. Sansom, *Sekaishi ni Okeru Nihon*—Japan in world history, trans. Genji Okubo (Tokyo: Iwanami Shoten, 1951); Masataka Takagi, *Nihonjin*—The Japanese (Tokyo: Kawade Shobo, 1955); Kunio Yanagida, ed., *Nihonjin*—The Japanese (Tokyo: Mainichi Shimbunsha, 1954); and Yasuhiko Yuzawa et al., *Nihon no Miraizo*—The future image of Japan (Tokyo: Hara Shobo, 1969).

Frois's remark quoted in the Prologue is from p. 239 of Michael Cooper, ed., *They Came to Japan: An Anthology of European Reports on Japan, 1543–1640* (Berkeley: University of California Press, 1965), which is a fascinating account of how Europeans viewed Japan in the 16th and 17th centuries; Shinoda's is from the *San Francisco Chronicle,* April 24, 1973.

For English-speaking readers, Edwin O. Reischauer, *Japan: The Story of a Nation* (New York: Alfred A. Knopf, 1970), is a highly readable, balanced historical introduction with a bibliographical guide. Richard Halloran, *Japan: Images and Realities* (New York: Alfred A. Knopf, 1970), takes up many similar topics—though from a different perspective. A Japanese intellectual's essay, available in English translation, is Nyozekan Hasegawa, *The Japanese Character,* trans. John Bester (Tokyo: Kodansha, 1966). Ruth Benedict, *The Chrysanthemum and the Sword: Patterns of Japanese Culture* (New York: World Publishing, 1967), originally published in 1946 and now outdated for understanding present-day Japanese social psychology, retains a certain timeless quality and is worth reading. Anyone seriously interested in Japanese cultural history will greatly benefit by opening George B. Sansom, *The Western World and Japan* (New York: Alfred A. Knopf, 1970). See also Jackson H. Bailey, ed., *Listening to Japan: A Japanese Anthology* (New York: Praeger, 1973); Edward Norbeck, *Changing Japan* (New York: Holt, Rinehart and Winston, 1965); and Bernard Silberman, ed., *Japanese Character and Culture* (Tucson: University of Arizona Press, 1962).

Japan Quarterly (published by Asahi Press) and *Japan Interpreter* (a quarterly published by Japan Center for International Exchange) frequently run good articles on cultural themes. The best source of bibliographical information is the annual *Bibliography*, published in September, by the *Journal of Asian Studies*.

CHAPTER 1

For the theme of Japanese coolness in rejecting and accepting foreign cultures, I relied heavily on Yoshio Masuda, *Junsui Bunka no Joken*—The conditions of pure culture (Tokyo: Kodansha, 1967). I also consulted Kunihiko Shimonaka, ed., *Nippon Zankoku Monogatari*—Cruel tales of old Japan, vol. 3 (Tokyo: Heibonsha, 1960), for religious persecutions during the period of isolation; Ryoichi Suzuki, *Oda Nobunaga* (Tokyo: Iwanami Shoten, 1967), for Nobunaga's life history; Otoya Miyagi, *Nihonjin towa Nanika*—Who are the Japanese? (Tokyo: Asahi Shimbunsha, 1972), for historical origins of Japanese social psychology; and Yoshitomo Ushijima, *Seiyo to Nihon no Ningen Keisei*—Human developments in Japan and the West (Tokyo: Kaneko Shobo, 1962), for changeability of Japanese beliefs. Sadao Matsuyoshi, *Taiko to Hyakusho*—Taiko and farmers (Tokyo: Iwanami Shoten, 1957), is a readable treatise on the life and philosophy of Toyotomi Hideyoshi.

The opening quotation of Valignano's words for Part One is from Cooper, *They Came to Japan*, p. 229; Soseki's are quoted from Takeo Kuwabara, ed., *Ichinichi Ichigen*—A word a day (Tokyo: Iwanami Shoten, 1971), p. 4.

For Japanese views of the Western world in the latter part of the Tokugawa period, see Donald Keene, *The Japanese Discovery of Europe, 1720–1830* (Stanford: Stanford University Press, 1969).

CHAPTER 2

For historical facts and illustrations, I relied on Mitsukuni Yoshida, *Nihon o Kizuita Kagaku*—Science that built Japan (Tokyo: Kodansha, 1966). Hiromi Arisawa et al., *Nihon Sangyo Hyakunen Shi*—A century of Japanese industry (Tokyo: Nihon Keizai Shimbunsha, 1967), gives many examples of how Japan absorbed Western technology in the late 19th century. For a social-historical explanation of Japanese curiosity, see Kazuko Tsurumi, *Kokishin to Nihonjin*—Curiosity and the Japanese (Tokyo: Kodansha, 1972).

Keene is quoted from Keene, *The Japanese Discovery of Europe*, p. 16.

CHAPTER 3

For developing the theme of this chapter, I consulted and adapted many ideas from Toyoyuki Sabata, *Nihon o Minaosu* —Reconsider Japan (Tokyo: Kodansha, 1964). I gained new insights into Japanese morality and conceptions of war from Ryotaro Shiba and Donald Keene, *Nihonjin to Nihon Bunka*— The Japanese and Japanese culture (Tokyo: Chuo Koronsha, 1972), especially chapters 1, 4, 5, and 7. Asahi Shimbunsha, ed., *Nihon to Amerika*—Japan and America (Tokyo: Asahi Shimbunsha, 1971), researched and written by the correspondents of the Asahi Newspaper Co., provides numerous episodes— military, diplomatic, political—about U.S.-Japan confrontations from the mid-19th century to the present. For the psychology of Japanese fanaticism, see Fusao Hayashi and Yukio

Mishima, *Taiwa: Nihonjin Ron*—A dialogue on the Japanese (Tokyo: Bancho Shobo, 1966). A description of pre–World War II public-school education in Japan is found in Shuichi Katsuta and Toshio Nakauchi, *Nihon no Gakko*—Japanese schools (Tokyo: Iwanami Shoten, 1964).

Benedict is quoted from Ruth Benedict, *The Chrysanthemum and the Sword*, p. 1; Carletti from Cooper, *They Came to Japan*, p. 42.

The book listed above as *Nihon to Amerika* is available in English as Asahi Shimbun staff, *The Pacific Rivals: A Japanese View of Japanese-American Relations* (Tokyo: Weatherhill/ Asahi, 1972).

CHAPTER 4

For the theme and legal cases, I consulted Yuji Aida, *Nihon no Fudo to Bunka*—Japan: its soil and culture (Tokyo: Kadokawa Shoten, 1972), and Takeyoshi Kawashima, *Nihonjin no Hoishiki*—Legal consciousness of the Japanese (Tokyo: Iwanami Shoten, 1967).

Emperor Meiji is quoted from Ryusaku Tsunoda, Wm. Theodore de Bary, and Donald Keene, comps., *Sources of Japanese Tradition* (New York: Columbia University Press, 1958), pp. 646–47; Carletti is quoted from Cooper, *They Came to Japan*, p. 153.

See Takeyoshi Kawashima, "The Status of the Individual in the Notion of Law, Right, and Social Order in Japan" and Hajime Nakamura, "Basic Features of the Legal, Political, and Economic Thought of Japan," both in Charles A. Moore, ed., *The Japanese Mind* (Honolulu: East-West Center Press, 1967). Kichisaburo Nakamura gives a concise legal history of the Meiji era in his *The Formation of Modern Japan* (Honolulu: East-West Center Press, 1964).

CHAPTER 5

In drawing a profile of the Japanese bureaucrat, I relied heavily on Hirotatsu Fujiwara, *Kanryo*—Bureaucrats (Tokyo:

Kodansha, 1964), and Hajime Shinohara, *Nihon no Seiji Fudo*—
Political culture in Japan (Tokyo: Iwanami Shoten, 1968).
The "system of nonresponsibility" is expounded in Masao
Maruyama, *Nihon no Shiso*—Japanese thought (Tokyo: Iwana-
mi Shoten, 1961).

Yanaga is quoted from Chitoshi Yanaga, *Japanese People and
Politics* (New York: John Wiley, 1956), pp. 27–28.

Available in English are: Marshall E. Dimock, *The Japanese
Technocracy* (New York: Walker/Weatherhill, 1968); Robert
A. Scalapino and Junnosuke Masumi, *Parties and Politics in
Contemporary Japan* (Berkeley: University of California Press,
1965); Nathaniel B. Thayer, *How the Conservatives Rule Japan*
(Princeton: Princeton University Press, 1969); and Chitoshi
Yanaga, *Big Business in Japanese Politics* (New Haven: Yale
University Press, 1968).

CHAPTER 6

Takeo Doi, *Amae no Kozo*—The structure of "amae" (Tokyo:
Kobundo, 1971), is the single most important source of ideas
for this chapter. The Japanese concept of "amae" is untransla-
table, and in its place I substituted the "psychology of dependence." There are numerous books published in Japan that deal
with the subject. Those that I consulted include: Satoshi Ikeda,
Wakamono o Kangaeru—Thoughts on youth (Tokyo: Daiyamondosha, 1970); Ryoen Minamoto, *Giri to Ninjo*—"Giri" and
"ninjo" (Tokyo: Chuo Koronsha, 1969); Kiyomi Nakano,
Genkeiteki Nihonjin—Original Japanese (Tokyo: Tokyo Bijutsu,
1969); Keiichi Sakuta, *Haji no Bunka Saiko*—Reconsidering the
culture of shame (Tokyo: Chikuma Shobo, 1967); Tadao Sato,
Hadaka no Nihonjin—The naked Japanese (Tokyo: Kobunsha,
1958); and Kemmei Yamamura, *Nihonjin to Haha*—Japanese
conception of "mother" (Tokyo: Toyokan Shuppansha, 1971).
Eijiro Inatomi, *Nihonjin to Nihon Bunka*—The Japanese and
Japanese culture (Tokyo: Risosha, 1963) gives a penetrating
discussion of the Japanese psychology of self-denial. I also
found useful Toshi Kimura, *Hito to Hito tono Aida*—Between

persons (Tokyo: Kobundo, 1972), and Tsuneo Muramatsu et al., *Nihonjin: Bunka to Personality no Jissho-teki Kenkyu*—The Japanese: empirical studies of their culture and personality (Tokyo: Ryokumei Shobo, 1962).

The opening quotation of Reischauer's remark for Part Two is from Reischauer, *Japan*, p. 3; Giron's from Cooper, *They Came to Japan*, p. 39; and Kawasaki's from Ichiro Kawasaki, *Japan Unmasked* (Tokyo: Tuttle, 1969), p. 26. Nakamura is quoted from Moore, *The Japanese Mind*, p. 148.

See Takeo Doi, "'Amae': A Key Concept for Understanding Japanese Personality Structure" in Robert J. Smith and Richard K. Beardsley, eds., *Japanese Culture* (Chicago: Aldine, 1962). Doi's book, *Amae no Kozo*, is available in English as *The Anatomy of Dependence*, trans. John Bester (Tokyo: Kodansha, 1973).

CHAPTER 7

For Japanese group-orientation, I consulted: Hiroyuki Araki, *Nihonjin no Kodo Yoshiki*—Behavior patterns of the Japanese (Tokyo: Kodansha, 1973); Takenori Kawashima, *Nihon Shakai no Kazokuteki Kosei*—Family-like structure of Japanese society (Tokyo: Nihon Hyoronsha, 1950); and Chie Nakane, *Tateshakai no Ningen Kankei*—Human relations in vertical society (Tokyo: Kodansha, 1967).

Kahn is quoted from Herman Kahn, *The Emerging Japanese Superstate* (Englewood Cliffs, N. J.: Prentice-Hall, 1970), p. 20; Yoneyama from Bailey, *Listening to Japan*, p. 108.

See Chie Nakane, *Japanese Society* (Berkeley: University of California Press, 1970).

CHAPTER 8

For the characteristics of the Japanese language, I relied on: Gen Itasaka, *Nihonjin no Ronri Kozo*—The structure of Japanese logic (Tokyo: Kodansha, 1971); Haruhiko Kindaichi, *Nihongo no Seiri to Shinri*—The physiology and psychology of the Japanese language (Tokyo: Shibundo, 1962); and Noboru

Ode, *Nihongo to Ronri*—The Japanese language and logic (Tokyo: Kodansha, 1965). For Japanese nihilism, see: Giken Honda, *Nihonjin no Mujo-kan*—Japanese nihilism (Tokyo: Nihon Hoso Shuppan Kyokai, 1968); Hiroshi Minami, *Nihonjin no Shinri*—Japanese psychology (Tokyo: Iwanami Shoten, 1953); and Munesuke Mita, *Gendai Nihon no Seishin Kozo*— The mental structure of modern Japan (Tokyo: Kobundo, 1965). Peculiarities of the Japanese language are discussed in chapters 3, 8, and 9 of Arata Yoda, ed., *Nihonjin no Seikaku*— Japanese personality (Tokyo: Asakura Shoten, 1970).

Xavier and Mexia are quoted from Cooper, *They Came to Japan,* p. 180 and p. 175, respectively.

CHAPTER 9

Many ideas embodied in this and the next chapters were drawn from Mikio Sumiya, ed., *Nihonjin no Keizai Kodo*—Japanese economic behavior, vols. 1 and 2 (Tokyo: Toyo Keizai Shimposha, 1969). For the theme of moil and parsimony, I consulted: Jiro Kamijima, *Kindai Nihon no Seishin Kozo*—The mental structure of modern Japan (Tokyo: Iwanami Shoten, 1961); Minoru Kida, *Nippon Buraku*—Japanese village (Tokyo: Iwanami Shoten, 1967); and Shunsuke Tsurumi and Yoshiro Hoshino, *Nihonjin no Ikikata*—The Japanese way of living (Tokyo: Kodansha, 1966). For a concise discussion of the factors in Japanese economic development, see Tamotsu Matsuura, *Nihon Keizai no Riron*—The logic of Japanese economy (Tokyo: Nihon Hoso Shuppan Kyokai, 1970).

Ninomiya's aphorism is quoted from Kuwabara, *Ichinichi Ichigen,* p. 174.

See *Economist* Correspondents, *Consider Japan* (London: Duckworth, 1963), and Ichiro Nakayama, *Industrialization of Japan* (Honolulu: East-West Center Press, 1964).

CHAPTER 10

For perspectives on Japanese family life, I consulted Kokichi Masuda, *Amerika no Kazoku, Nihon no Kazoku*—American family, Japanese family (Tokyo: Nihon Hoso Shuppan Kyokai, 1969).

Sakakibara is quoted from Bailey, *Listening to Japan,* pp. 138–39.

William W. Lockwood, ed., *The State and Economic Enterprise in Japan* (Princeton: Princeton University Press, 1965) has many papers on political and social aspects of Japanese economic development. For urban life in contemporary Japan, see R. P. Dore, *City Life in Japan* (Berkeley: University of California Press, 1967), and Ezra F. Vogel, *Japan's New Middle Class* (Berkeley: University of California Press, 1971).

CHAPTER 11

The story of Onda is based on the version that has been annotated and translated into modern Japanese by Kuniyoshi Urabe in his *Nihon Keiei no Shinzui: Kaisetsu "Higurashi Suzuri"* —Higurashi Suzuri: A study of the philosophy of Japanese management (Tokyo: Nihon Keiei Tosho, 1972). Books about the Japanese approach to human management are: Yoshimatsu Aonuma, *Nihon no Keieiso*—Japanese managers (Tokyo: Nihon Keizai Shimbunsha, 1965); Isaiah Ben-Dasan, *Nihonjin to Yudayajin*—Japanese and Jews (Tokyo: Yamamoto Shoten, 1970); and Sadaichi Kamiyoshi, *Nippon-teki Keiei*—Management, Japanese style (Tokyo: Daiyamondosha, 1965).

The House Rules of Iwasaki are taken from Robert Bellah, *Tokugawa Religion* (Glencoe, Ill.: Free Press, 1957), p. 187.

Available in English are: James C. Abegglen, *Management and Worker: The Japanese Solution* (Tokyo: Sophia University Press, 1973); T. F. M. Adams and Noritake Kobayashi, *The World of Japanese Business* (Tokyo: Kodansha, 1969); and M. Y. Yoshino, *Japan's Managerial System* (Cambridge, Mass.: M.I.T. Press, 1968). Ben-Dasan's book is available in English as *The Japanese and the Jews,* trans. Richard L. Gage (Tokyo: Weatherhill, 1972).

✦ Index

Adams, William, 40–41
agriculture: and ancestor
    worship, 95–96; com-
    pared with Europe, 99;
    and rice production, 98
Aida, Yasuaki, 80
Aira, Tomoyasu, 65–66
ambivalence toward for-
    eigners, 30–33, 199
American occupation, 22,
    27, 30, 114, 160; and bu-
    reaucrats, 161–64; concept
    of freedom brought by,
    191–92; effect on ruling
    classes of, 161
ancestor worship, 109; and
    agriculture, 95–96; and
    family, 95
Arai, Hakuseki, 43
Araki, Kohei, 54
Ashikaga, Yoshimitsu, 28
Ashikaga, Yoshimochi, 28
Ashikaga, Yoshinori, 28
Aston, William George, 235

Baba, Masakata, 288
Balz, Erwin, 21–22
Bank of Japan, 262

beriberi, and Imperial
    Armed Forces, 68–69
Biddle, James, 50–51
book publishing, 83–84
borrowing: of education,
    82–84; of foreign cultures,
    23–49, 50–85; of military
    science, 80–81; of science
    and technology, 52–55,
    101, 262 (*see also* calen-
    dar; mathematics; medi-
    cine; weights and mea-
    sures); of theories of man
    and society, 70–78, 102–
    3; of weaponry, 35–36,
    52, 63, 65
Buddhism, 38, 43, 97–98,
    103
bureaucrats, 144; and A-
    merican occupation, 161–
    64; as defenders of status
    quo, 170–71; and democ-
    racy, 154, 170–71, 175–
    76; as interpreters of law,
    169–70; loyalty of, 164–
    65; and Meiji govern-
    ment, 145; and nonre-
    sponsibility system, 157–